MW00990121

DAYS OF DARKNESS

DAYS OF DARKNESS

The Feuds of Eastern Kentucky

JOHN ED PEARCE

THE UNIVERSITY PRESS OF KENTUCKY

Copyright © 1994 by The University Press of Kentucky

Scholarly publisher for the Commonwealth,
serving Bellarmine College, Berea College, Centre
College of Kentucky, Eastern Kentucky University,
The Filson Club, Georgetown College, Kentucky
Historical Society, Kentucky State University,
Morehead State University, Murray State University,
Northern Kentucky University, Transylvania University,
University of Kentucky, University of Louisville,
and Western Kentucky University.

Editorial and Sales Offices: Lexington, Kentucky 40508-4008

Library of Congress Cataloging-in-Publication Data

Pearce, John Ed.
    Days of darkness : the feuds of Eastern Kentucky / John Ed Pearce.
        p.   cm.
    Includes bibliographical references and index.
    ISBN 0-8131-1874-3 (alk. paper)
    1. Vendetta—Kentucky—History. 2. Kentucky—Social conditions.
HV6452.K4P43   1994
976.9'104—dc20   94-2773

This book is printed on acid-free recycled paper meeting
the requirements of the American National Standard
for Permanence of Paper for Printed Library Materials. ♾ ⊕

Contents

Maps

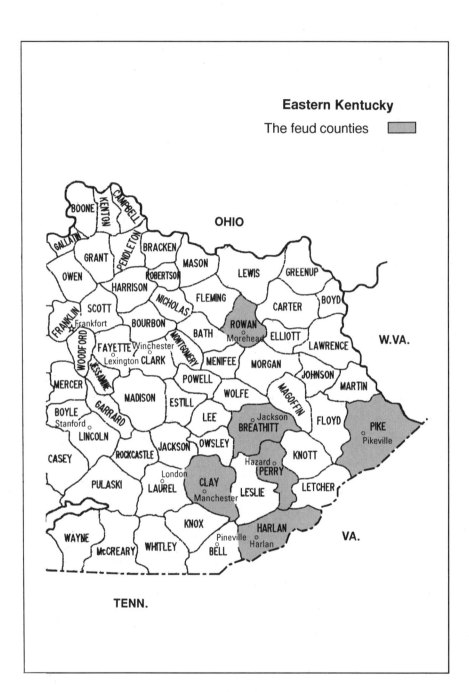

Eastern Kentucky

The feud counties

Map 1

What This Is All About

The feuds of Eastern Kentucky have always been the stuff of legend and folklore, in part because there is so little substantial evidence on which the writer can depend. Courthouse fires have destroyed many records relating to the feuds. Much of the feud violence never reached the courts, as the feudists, either distrusting the courts or dissatisfied with jury verdicts, preferred to settle matters themselves. In many cases all we have is word of mouth, handed down over the years like folk songs, with the facts bent to reflect the loyalties of the speaker. Probably for this reason, every tale, every account, every magazine article or newspaper story concerning a feud is invariably contrary to, in conflict with, or contradicted by another account. This applies as well to the recollections of the few surviving descendants of the feudists.

For that reason, I cannot claim that the accounts in this book are the truth, the whole truth, and nothing but the truth. They are as near to the truth as I can find. Generally speaking, the newspaper accounts of the time are almost always sensational and inaccurate. Magazine articles were worse. Courthouse records, when they are available, tend to be incomplete and confusing. Even some accounts of feuds written by reputable authors contain legend for which I can find no supporting evidence. One book states that the Clay County feuds erupted when Dr. Abner Baker called Daniel Bates's dog a cur. The French-Eversole War is said to have begun over a woman. They are good stories; it is always disappointing to find that they are not true.

In writing about the feuds, there is always a tendency to fall into stereotypes. The image of the bearded, one-gallus, barefoot mountaineer, sucking his corncob pipe, his jug of moonshine on his shoulder and his trusty rifle ready to deal death to his neighbors, has for more than a century made the mountain people objects of ridicule and contempt. The feuds undoubtedly fed this stereotype. But for the most part the feudists were ordinary Americans, surging across the Appalachian Mountains in the aftermath of the Revolutionary War, in which many of them had fought, trying in a harsh, raw land to establish an acceptable society in which to live and rear families.

As in most frontier regions, few Kentucky mountaineers were of aristocratic background. Most Cumberland settlers were of English or Scotch-Irish descent, farmers or lower middle-class workmen, hoping to better themselves in a rich, new land. Inevitably some were, as author Harry Caudill has described them, the sweepings of the streets of London and Liverpool, or poor people who had earned their passage to America as indentured servants, "temporary slaves." As might be expected, such people were a flinty, volatile mix. They had escaped the oppression of throne and aristocracy, had found a new way of life in a new land, and did not want anyone, including the law, to infringe upon rights they were willing to defend to the death. This made law enforcement difficult in an area where law was still vaguely defined, precariously established, and haphazardly enforced.

Furthermore, it was only natural that people with bitter memories of harsh English law and of government that favored the rich and high-born would seek regions remote from government's heavy hand. Just as western ranchers shot it out with Indians, farmers, and lawmen in order to remain free of fences and legal restrictions, so the mountaineer fought for what he considered justice and hard-won freedom.

It has become popular among writers to trace the feuds to the clan warfare of "their Scottish ancestors." An interesting theory—but there were, actually, few pure Scots among the feudists. Most were of Anglo-Saxon, Scotch-Irish ancestry, with some German, French, Portuguese, and Indians (Native Americans) thrown in. Those whose forebears had come from Scotland had married so widely that they were not apt to carry clear memories of old hatreds. The resentments they inherited were usually of crown and gaol and English nobility, not neighbors.

Most of these people had come westward from North Carolina or Virginia, often when family farmland was divided among too many sons. Some had, over a century or more, drifted down from New England or Pennsylvania, following the Ohio River down to rivers leading to the interior of Kentucky territory. Others struggled through the Pound, Hagan, and Cumberland Gaps. As Kentucky sage Edward Prichard said, the greatest difference between the settlers of Eastern Kentucky and the "bluebloods" of the Bluegrass was that the former stopped sooner.

It might be well to note here that the term "feud" is used rather loosely in reference to trouble in the hills. Because it is a convenient term for describing violence between families, it has come to be used to describe almost any form of violence, no matter how widespread or of what duration. Puristically, the term feud should be limited to inter-family or clan rivalries persisting over one or more generations and involving armed combat to the death. Both Webster and American Heritage dictionaries define the feud as a bitter *prolonged* hostility. People in the areas involved usually referred to their clashes as "wars" or "troubles," which may be more accurate labels. I have used the term feud because it is familiar to more people.

The way of life along the mountain frontier offered fertile soil for the violence that led to the feuds. A man living at the head of a remote hollow had little hope of getting the sheriff in time to save his cabin from bushwhackers. He had to depend on his rifle, just as he had become accustomed to doing through the decades of exploration, settlement, and war. He also had to depend on his reputation as a man ready and able to use that rifle.

On the frontier—whether Kentucky or Texas—toughness, independence, and reliable friends became matters of life and death. Mountain settlers had a rough code that said, in effect: You are my friend or kinsman. Who strikes you, strikes me. If you are in trouble, I will stand by you despite danger. And when I am in trouble I will feel safe calling on you. If you fall afoul of the law, I will not testify against you. If you are a law officer you will not arrest me but send me word to come into court, thus respecting my dignity as a man and attesting my trustworthiness.

Another view of mountain justice may be gleaned from the following instructions given to the grand jury by a Letcher County circuit judge in 1904. Said the judge:

If a civil citizen kills another citizen and it is clear in self-defense, don't indict him. If a civil citizen kills an outlaw, don't indict him, no matter whether he killed in self-defense or not. If one outlaw kills another outlaw, indict him without questioning the motive for killing. In such a case it would be well to sentence the outlaw for life and so get rid of him as well as his victim. If a civil citizen takes a bag of provisions on his back and pursues an outlaw all week, and then kills him as he would wild game, don't indict him. If you want to do anything, give him a better gun and more ammunition so that he can get the next outlaw more easily. If you do indict such a man, be sure that I will file the indictment away as soon as I reach it.

As you can see, it well became a man not to gain a reputation as an outlaw.

It is not true that mountain people had no use for courts, but many regarded courts as the instruments of limited justice. When brought to trial the mountaineer knew he would probably be tried before a jury of men who would have done as he had done under the same circumstances. And with intermarriage inevitable in remote areas, he knew also that many of the jurymen might well be kin. But the man bringing him into court knew this also and figured that he would have a better chance of justice if he handled the matter himself. In failing to depend on the law of courts, he weakened it so that it was less able to protect him when he needed protection.

And protection was often needed. For example, Governor Simon B. Buckner on September 8, 1889, received from A.J. Robards, a doctor in Breathitt County, the following, which gives an idea of the state of affairs in the hills:

Sir, this morning i take a plesher of writin to you to in form you of the conduc of our men in Breathitt, perry and Knot and Lecher. Sir, good men can't pass up and down our county rodes with out beain shot at from the bresh and it is from the French and Eversole and Johns facts and it is not on a count of political a fares. When one gits soe he can hire a man to kill his neighbor he is redy to doe it see how Rose was murdered and Buck Combs Cornet and others and the partys are running at large with their guns shooting cursen and drinkin and good sciticins are a feared to pass there for we pray to you that some step may be tacen to put this down and there ant noe use of ordern our officers in this part to stop it as they only push it on.

As i was on my way home from seeing a sick man onley yesterdy a man from the bresh shot at me and come near killen me and I will haft to leave home on less som step is taken and i did not noe of a man in the world that had out a ginst me thoe i think it was done threw a mistake for some one elce. So please excuse me for my long leter i am yours fraternally Dr. A.J. Robards, MD of Medicin.

Whatever the causes of the feuds, they are elusive. Still, anyone who writes of the feuds is expected to reveal some thread that runs through them, some circumstance, some trait of character that is common to feuds or feudists. I doubt that I can. Historians tend to tie the feuds to the Civil War, and there is a certain validity in their thesis. Men coming home from the war, having fought against each other, suffered defeat and loss, or survived painful battle, undoubtedly nursed grudges. Further, those few who had not known before the war how to use guns had learned, and many had brought their guns home with them, creating an explosive opportunity.

But take the feuds one by one: In Pike County, nearly all of the Hatfields and McCoys had been Confederates. In Harlan, most of the Howards had been Unionists; the Turners, or most of them, had been

Confederates, but several Turner allies had been for the Union. In Clay County, as in Breathitt, nearly everyone had fought for the Union. In the French-Eversole and Martin-Tolliver fights, Civil War status seems to have had little or no influence, as both Rebels and Yankees fought on both sides.

The feuds have been blamed also on geographic and cultural isolation, remoteness from urban centers, and the degree of difficulty of transportation and communication. These were not, I would guess, major factors in the Rowan County affair, since Morehead enjoyed relatively convenient rail and road access to Lexington, Louisville, and Cincinnati. Remoteness had a far greater effect, I would judge, on Harlan, Pike, and Perry Counties, and a somewhat lesser effect on Breathitt and Clay.

The Kentucky feudist has for too long, I feel, been depicted as ignorant and totally lacking in culture, a brush too broad for all the cases. At one end of the spectrum, the Hatfields and McCoys were uneducated; at the other, Fulton French and Joe Eversole were attorneys. The Whites and Garrards of Clay County were college graduates. Jim Howard was quite literate. Many of the Bakers—such as Gardner and Thena—had relatively little formal education but were well read. Most of the major figures in the Breathitt County War were educated—lawyers or businessmen. Boone Logan of the Rowan County War was a fine lawyer and later a remarkably successful businessman. The Turners and Howards of Harlan County had the schooling common to the day, the equivalent of high school. Bad Tom Baker was uneducated but believed deeply in formal education and worked hard for it in Clay County.

There is no common denominator here, and no common thread.

Were these feuds clashes of different social and cultural classes? Seldom. Not often was a feeling of social superiority or the resentment felt by inferiors the spark that ignited a war. The Hatfields and McCoys were both common mountain yeomen, though the McCoys, as historian Altina Waller says, may have envied the greater landholdings and potential wealth of the Hatfields. The Turners of Harlan County seem to have felt superior to the Howards, though both families were of comparable background, and the Howards no doubt resented the Turners' attitude. This may have been a factor. In Clay County, the Whites and Garrards were equally wealthy and prominent, well known and respected statewide. Their differences were not social. Neither were the differences between the Howards and Bakers, though Jim Howard apparently felt more urbane, polished, and educated than the Bakers, who were a rough lot. Fulton French felt an economic superiority to the Eversoles, and Joe Eversole felt a definite moral superiority to French. But in general it would be inadvisable to place much blame on social or cultural differences between the warring factions.

Now we get down to more tangible factors—money and politics. Except in the fight between the Bakers and Howards in Clay County, and perhaps the Hatfields and McCoys in Pike, financial rivalry was nearly always a factor. Competition over salt sparked the rivalry between the Whites and the Garrards. Craig Tolliver wanted to control the whiskey and hotel business in Morehead and saw the Logans as threats. Wilson Lewis of Harlan is thought to have wanted to control the whiskey business and saw the Howards as obstacles. George Turner wanted to control the mercantile business, and he too ran into competition from the large Howard family. The French-Eversole war was, as Allen Watts says, "a business fight." French was squeezing the small landowner on behalf of the big land companies; Joe Eversole was trying to stop him, with the help of Josiah Combs. Jim Hargis, along with Ed Callahan, wanted not only to run but to own Breathitt County.

Aside from Perry Cline's political ambitions, political, partisan competition had little role in the Hatfield-McCoy fight. The families lived in different states. Politics was a major factor in Rowan, Harlan, Clay, and Breathitt Counties, a minor factor in Perry.

So, once again, it is risky to impute to any one of these factors total or major blame for the feuds. None of them constitutes a thread that runs throughout the feud fabric.

Is it feasible, then, to assess blame? Altina Waller blames the feuds on tensions arising between people who were trying to adjust to the changes that accompanied industrialization and the coming of railroads and mining to the mountains. This may have been true of the Hatfield-McCoy trouble, which she examines in unmatched detail. But the same conditions do not apply in other cases. What specifically caused the Hatfield-McCoy fight? Well, whiskey, for one thing. Circumstances. Times that were bringing changes only faintly understood.

Changing times were a major source of the trouble that led to the French-Eversole war—the coming of big land companies that led to exploitation of coal and timber and the resulting threat to the mountain way of life. Then, too, there were differences in moral standards, differences in principles.

The Turner-Howard feud was fueled by Civil War hangovers and resentments, by Turner arrogance, Howard pride, Lewis chicanery.

This feud, I believe, may have sprung from conflicts of personality and character more than any of the others save that of Perry County. Mrs. George Turner was symbolic when she declared that Harlan would be ruled by Turners or Howards, but not both.

One gets the feeling that the Baker-Howard feud in Clay County could have been avoided many times had it not been for peculiar times and circumstances. Then there were the financial rivalries, the hangings of Abner and later William Baker, both of which contained the poisonous seeds of injustice. Abner was crazy and should not have been hanged. William was innocent, apparently protecting his wife. The involvement of Garrards and Whites on opposing sides of these cases cast a dangerous pall over the county. Add to this the violence of the times, the bitterness of politics in Clay, and the abuse of politics to handicap and deny justice to the losing opponent. Whiskey was an exacerbating factor.

The Martin-Tolliver mess in Rowan County was simply a political and financial fight complicated by whiskey. In Breathitt County politics, money, brutal arrogance on Hargis's part, and the emotional holdover from the Strong-Little Wars contributed to disaster. And again, whiskey played a terrible role.

A common thread? Whiskey, perhaps. Pride in some cases, politics in most.

Did heroes and villains emerge from the feuds? The answer depends, of course, on one's definition. If there were heroes in the Hatfield-McCoy feud, they were probably the McCoy boys—Bud and Jim, who kept their senses in times of violence and prevented worse violence, and Calvin, who sacrificed his life to save his sisters and parents. It is hard to find anything admirable about the Hatfields, although Wall deserved better than he got. Devil Anse, Jim Vance, Johnse, and most of the other Hatfields were little more than thugs. I cannot find grounds for admiring Devil Anse, who not only engineered the two instances of brutal murder but lacked the backbone to commit them himself and sent his underlings out to do the slaughtering.

Craig Tolliver was an interesting villain, and I wish I could have learned more about him. Boone Logan has been accorded the hero's laurel in the Rowan County fight, but he was not one without flaws; he chose killing when he might have forced a surrender of the Tollivers. He didn't stick around to help clean up the blood, and he let his co-warriors face the trials. I think Fred Brown was near to correct when he said, "There were no heroes here, no villains, just people." But you have to admit that there were some pretty bad people.

In the Turner-Howard feud, there were villains enough to go around, especially among the Turners, including Wilson Lewis and Mrs. Turner, she a bundle of hate. Wilse Howard was a violent man, but he had reasons to be. So did Will Jennings. Fult French was a villain. Joe Eversole and his wife Susan were heroes. That's about it.

The Clay County War? Take your pick. I suppose you have to list George and Jesse Barrett, Frank McDaniel, and James and Bad Tom Baker among the bad ones, although Bad Tom had mitigating characteristics. Lucy and George Goforth, Gardner and Thena Baker, and, above all, T.T. Garrard had streaks of nobility. Big Jim Howard will always remain an enigma. So will Chad Hall, if he indeed did the things he said he did.

In Breathitt County, Jim Hargis, Ed Callahan, Curtis Jett, Tim Smith, John Aikman, Hen Kilburn, Bill Strong, and Jerry Little were killers or hired the killers. Beach Hargis was a nut. J.B. Marcum, the Cockrells, and Dr. D.B. Cox were victims. It's hard to find heroes.

Now, is there a characteristic, a trait of personality common to these people? Greed? A lust for money or power? A willingness to avoid or violate the law for advantage? A willingness to sacrifice for family or friends? Loyalty? A sense of fair play? Pride? Faith? About the only common trait I can see is a certain loyalty to family and friends, often a sense of pride.

All of this leaves only one constant—the times—and that is uncertain as a causative factor. Time and circumstance, as the preacher said, affect them all: postwar violence, the growth of Democratic Party dominance, the slow growth of formal religion in an area where people had tended to equate organized religion with the power and oppression of the state, the hurtful effect of poverty on formal education, and the generally debilitating effect of the advent of industrial colonialism in the heavy hands of mining and timber companies. Then there was the growing resistance to whiskey as an acceptable social custom. And the melting away of the frontier—its remoteness, its attitudes, its customs, its opportunity for personal privacy and independence, the need for self-dependence.

We must keep in mind that most of the feuds were of brief duration. The outside world pressed in, conditions changed, and so did the people. The feuds reflect the Kentucky mountaineer only in the sense that rapid growth and a tendency toward brash manners reflect the adolescent. But as with the man who makes a fool of himself in youth, the mountain feudist's violent reputation has tended to linger.

HARLAN COUNTY
The Turners Meet the Howards

Choose Your Outlaw

Devil Jim Turner didn't get his nickname by accident. Once, while hiding from the law, he got hungry, slipped up on a herd of dairy cows, knocked one unconscious, cut a hunk of meat off the cow's hindquarter, ate it perhaps raw, and ran the cow, bleeding, limping, and bellowing, back with the others. Jim terrorized members of his own family as well as neighbors. After an argument with an aunt, he knocked her down and raped her.

Jim was not the only free spirit in the clan. The Turners were often ready to resort to gunplay to get their way. Along with the Howards, Cawoods, Brittains, and Halls, the Turners were among the early settlers of Harlan County, coming from Lee County, Virginia, shortly after the turn of the century, before Harlan was carved out of Lincoln County. Well to do by frontier standards, they brought slaves with them, bought some of the better land on the Clover Fork of the Cumberland River, and later built a home known as the Turner Mansion in Mount Pleasant, the first name of the county seat. (There was already a Mount Pleasant in Kentucky, so the village was later renamed Harlan Courthouse when the county was formed in 1819 and finally simply Harlan.)

William Turner established a large farm on Clover Fork and opened a general store in Harlan. His son, William II, was born in 1812 and married Elizabeth Brittain. They had one son, George Brittain Turner, who grew to be six feet, three inches tall, and weighed 350 pounds. William and his second wife Susannah also had James, Sarah, and Lucy. James married Elizabeth Clay in 1833, and they had nine children; their sons William and James (Devil Jim) seem to have had a vicious streak and caused trouble. Some people considered the Turners community leaders who helped less fortunate families get a start. C.A. Ballou, author of *A Cumberland Vendetta*, called them "demons of greed and ambition."

The Turners were causing trouble long before their fight with the Howards began. A storm blew down one of the Turners' fences in the spring of 1852, and the cattle of J.T. Ward, a neighbor, wandered into the Turners' pasture. The Turner boys, William and Devil Jim, solved the matter by shooting the cows. Ward, saying that he was afraid to press for damages, left the county. John Skidmore opened a hotel and a general store, but when his store began to rival that owned by the Turners, he was threatened with death. He closed the store, sold his hotel, and moved to Indiana. Campbell Hurst, who owned a prosperous hardware business, was elected county court clerk, defeating the Turners' choice. Hurst was shortly afterward killed by a man named Jones, a Turner relative. Jones was not indicted.

The Howards had no such rowdy reputation when they began to clash with the Turners in the years following the Civil War. Ben Howard, a veteran of the Revolution, had come through Cumberland Gap from Virginia around 1800, settling near Cumberland Ford (now Pineville). The Howards seem to have been regarded as peaceful citizens when they moved up the Cumberland River and settled in what became Harlan County. Samuel and Chloe Howard were probably the first permanent settlers, building a home there in 1796. When Harlan County was created in 1819 the county court bought twelve acres of land from John and Susannah Howard and Samuel and Chloe Howard for five dollars. The land, located where the Martins Fork, Poor Fork, and Clover Fork join to form the Cumberland River, became the county seat. The first records list as owners of town lots Joseph Cawood, Berry Cawood, Adron Howard, Andrew Howard, John Howard (seven lots), Benjamin Harris, Alfred Hall, Wix Howard, John Jones (two lots), Abner Lewis, and Edward Napier. No Turners are listed, indicating that they were living outside the town, but they had a great deal of property on county tax rolls. Sam Howard built the first courthouse and jail shortly after the county was formed, and in 1833 added public stocks and a whipping post near the jail. The Turners by that time had bought much of the good acreage in town. William Turner also owned a tavern and two stores, and for several years he was one of the few county residents taxed for owning a silver watch.

In 1853, when he was sixteen, Devil Jim Turner married Sarah Jones, but marriage didn't settle him down. He and his older brother William, John and Hezekiah Clem, and Joseph Nolan formed a dangerous gang. In 1854 Hezekiah Clem and Nolan allegedly killed John Clay and robbed him of ninety-five dollars. David Lyttle, their attorney, got them acquitted, and Nolan decided to go straight, but Clem became known as a gunslinger, and Jim fell in with him. By 1860 Jim was in trouble with his cousins, the Middletons, and Narcissa Middleton accused him of trying to kill her husband William.

When the Civil War erupted, Jim enlisted in a Union outfit, but he deserted when his term was half over and, according to Narcissa Middleton, "gathered up a guerrilla company, he being the captain, and kept up a regular system of murder, robbery and horse stealing throughout the war, southern men being the principal sufferers." Incidentally, Confederate William Jr. and Unionist Devil Jim often rode together, one robbing southern sympathizers, the other Unionists, both getting fairly rich. The sign on the lawn of the Harlan County courthouse today states that it was burned by Rebel troops in retaliation for the burning of the courthouse in Lee County, Virginia, but some local historians maintain that Devil Jim and his outlaws did it. Wood Lyttle, in his memoirs, says that Devil Jim "burned it in broad daylight."

At the end of the war, William Middleton was killed, allegedly by Devil Jim and his men, on his way home. In 1869, William's widow, Narcissa, testified that Jim, his brother William and Francis Pace killed David Middleton, William's brother. Before they could be tried in Clay Circuit Court, Campbell Hurst, who was scheduled to testify against them, was stabbed and killed on the main street of Harlan in what Narcissa Middleton swore was a set-up to keep him from testifying. On December 5, 1874, Jim, William, and Francis Pace were convicted and sentenced to life in prison. William died in prison in 1877. Francis Pace was pardoned in 1891 and vanished. Devil Jim got out on parole and went with his son Hiram to Washington, where he suffered a stroke, fell into the fireplace, and died of burns. (Tom Walters says that Devil Jim was shot by Wood Lyttle. In any event, he died.)

The Howards, like their cousins in Clay County, had been Whigs and fought for the Union and had come home to take up the job of making a living. They spread out around the county, some on Martins Fork, some on the Cumberland River south of Harlan. Hiram and Alice Howard ran a grocery store on the southwest side of Harlan and made whiskey. In 1869 a Hiram B. Howard sold his store to William Blanton, Jr., but whether this Hiram was the father of Wilson, and also owned a store and sold whiskey, is not known.

In 1884 George Turner built a handsome home, usually referred to as the Turner Mansion, not far from the courthouse. The Howards looked upon the Turners as nouveau riche. Wix Howard opened a store in Harlan, but he claimed the Turners were threatening his customers and quit the business. This was not the only instance of friction. The Howards, with their friends the Gilberts, had angered the Turners as early as 1855 when they insisted that Devil Jim be arrested and tried for theft, assault, and rape. He was, and sent to prison. Shortly after the trial, Will Turner met Bill Gilbert on the street and killed him, reportedly raising his pistol and shouting, "Dead center, by God, Sir!" He was arrested but freed on bond and never tried.

But the Turners had poked a hornet's nest.

The Turners Meet the Howards

The Howards had been a large, peaceful family, mostly storekeepers and farmers, whereas the Turners had often been the source of friction and outright crime. Yet when historians write of the feud, many tend to refer to the Howards as "outlaws." This may be due to the hostility between the Howards and County Judge Wilson Lewis, who was suspected of conspiring against the Howards to control the whiskey business in Harlan County.

The Turners were naturally indignant when the Howards helped to send a Turner to prison. But several years elapsed between the time Devil Jim and Francis Pace were convicted and the time the feud began. As usual, the origins of the clash are murky. John Egerton, in *Generations*, reports that the Ledford family left Harlan because of feud violence that they said started when a Day, allied with the Howards, and a Cawood, a Turner ally, clashed. But the crucial conflict may have resulted from a poker game in which Wix Howard and Little Bob Turner got into a dispute over the pot and each accused the other of cheating. (Wix said that Turner, half drunk, was taking a nap when another player, as a joke, set his hair on fire. Turner accused Wix and threatened to kill him.) The next day they met on the street, and Little Bob shot Wix in the arm. Raising his shotgun with one arm, Wix fired, and the load of buckshot blasted a hole the size of a baseball in Little Bob's chest. He died that evening in the Turner Mansion. Wix was arrested, tried, and acquitted on grounds of self-defense. Curiously, it was the last time Wix was involved with the Turners. Somehow the torch passed to his cousin and friend, Wilson Howard, who proved to be a real wildcat and turned the friction into a feud.

Though Wilson (Wils or Wilse) had been in no trouble with the law, he was regarded as a tough, dangerous man. This may have stemmed from an experience he had when he was only fifteen. In an argument with one of the Cawood boys, Wilse was jumped by a half-dozen older boys, including Cawoods, Baileys, and Turners, and while two of the Cawoods held him, the others gave him a bad beating that he never forgot. He began carrying a gun.

A few weeks after Wix killed Little Bob, Little George Turner and one of the Bailey boys went down to the Howard store, where Hiram and Alice Howard also made and sold whiskey. They ordered Alice, who was alone in the store at the time, to stop selling whiskey to George Sr., who was known to drink more than he could hold. Alice told them that if they didn't want George to drink, they should tell him not to buy it.

Little George apparently spoke roughly to Mrs. Howard. That was a mistake. Tall, slender Alice Howard had been a Jennings, a family known as tough, proud people. Hezekiah Jennings, Alice's father, was in the thick of the Howards' feud with the Turners. Alice's brother Will and her son Wilse formed a team that more than held up the Howard end of the violence.

It is significant that the running battle between these two families apparently started over whiskey, and one must wonder how much Judge Wilson Lewis had to do with lighting the fire. Lewis himself, in a letter to the *Louisville Courier-Journal* of September 23, 1889, declared that the death of Little Bob Turner at the hand of Wix Howard had for all purposes ended the real family feud. From then on, he said, it was really a matter of the "Turners joining an effort by law enforcement officers to control the whisky traffic" personified by Wilse Howard, who resisted efforts of the law-abiding people to bring the evil booze under control. His own statements strengthen the belief that Lewis was the one who kept the feud going and provoked Wilse Howard into retaliation.

Most of the Howards seem to have been reluctant about entering the armed conflict; indeed, most of the large family never took part in the feud. Wilse was an exception, and it is probably significant that the ties between Alice and her slender, dark-haired son were especially strong; Wilse had a lot of Jennings blood in him. When he heard of the encounter between his mother and the Turners, he took the news sourly.

The following week, on the road to Hagan, Virginia, Wilse ran into Will Turner, reputedly the toughest of the Turners, and a man named Bob Maupin. Insults were followed by gunfire, but no one was hurt. Wilse went home and reported the skirmish, and the Howards took precautions against a possible attack. Sure enough, that night the Howard home was attacked by a group led by Will Turner. In the dark, little was accomplished, but Will Turner was wounded. He left a few days later, saying he was going out West to recuperate. Will Jennings, Alice's brother, had moved to Indiana, but with trouble looming, Wilse and his mother sent for him, and he was soon seen riding with what became known as the Wilse Howard gang.

In the late summer of 1887, Will Turner came home and George Turner wrote Captain Ben Howard a most remarkable letter, one that again raises questions about which side was outside the law. "The bulldog of the Turners has returned," he wrote, "with all of his teeth intact." He then challenged the Howards to meet the Turners "in open battle at Harlan Courthouse [He may have meant the town rather than the building, but the Howards took it to mean the building] and decide by the arbitraiment of blade and bullet who has the better right to rule the county."

The Howards had cause for worry. Wilson Lewis, who was kin to the Turner and Cawood families, had been elected county judge and was said to be determined to kill off the Howards and take over the whiskey business. Moses Turner had been elected sheriff. While Will was out West recuperating, a man named Huff had tried to negotiate a truce between the two clans but had received little encouragement from the Turners. "I'd rather have my boys brought home on blankets," said Mrs. George Turner. "My boys will never lay down their arms." But Huff persisted, James Howard and Hezekiah Jennings came into Harlan and met with the Turners, and a truce of sorts was accepted. But Little George and Carlo "Bony" Turner were not parties to the agreement, and Wilse warned that they could not be trusted to keep the peace. He was right. As the Howards rode home from the meeting, someone—Wilse claimed that it was Little George—fired at them from a brushy cliff. No one was hurt, but Wilse swore he would clean out the Turners, truce or no. The shooting soon resumed.

So when the Howards received George Turner's challenge, Ben Howard sent out word to family members, and a council of war was held at the log "fort" on the river. (Relatively few of the Howards attended, indicating that most of the family wanted to be left out of the feud.) James Howard, Wilse's older brother, sent word back to George Turner that the Howards would meet them on the appointed day in Harlan. Berry Howard, who had been jailer and sheriff, warned that Lewis would deputize a crowd of gunfighters and occupy the courthouse, forcing the Howards to attack from the street. James had not specified at what time they would arrive, however, and on Monday morning the Howards gathered before dawn, rode into Harlan and quietly took up positions; Berry, Hiram, and James Howard and Hezekiah Jennings were in the courthouse; Wilse, Alex, and Elijah Howard were across the street. It is possible that Chad Hall and Bud Spurlock were with them.

The Turners must have intended the battle to be a showdown to impress the large crowd expected to watch. It didn't turn out that way; in fact, it was something of an anticlimax. Shortly after breakfast time, a dozen or so of the Turners, unaware that the Howards were waiting for them, walked casually out of the Turner Mansion toward the courthouse. They had almost reached it when someone spotted the Howards in second-floor windows and gave the alarm.

Everyone started shooting. Will Turner, the returned bulldog, showed his courage, if not his common sense, by attempting to rush the front door of the courthouse. He was hit before he reached it, got up and retreated, firing as he went, but was hit agian. He got up and, with the help of others, staggered up the street to the Turner home, where his mother came out and helped him onto the front porch. He had been hit in the stomach and was screaming with pain. "Stop that!" his mother snapped. "Die like a man, like your brother [Little Bob] did!" Will stopped screaming and died.

The firing went on for a few more minutes. Four men were hit, none seriously, and no one else was killed. After Will was shot, the Turners fell back to the mansion, spectators peered from around corners, and the Howards came out of the courthouse, sat for a few minutes smoking and talking, then mounted their horses and rode home.

Judge Lewis, instead of trying to arrange a truce, began writing letters to the newspapers and the governor, condemning the Howards for their "attack" on the courthouse and the killing of Will, and asking for troops to save the county from outlaws. Finally Mrs. Hezekiah Jennings, Will's mother, called on Mrs. Turner and asked her to help end the trouble. Will went with her to show that the effort was sincere, but again Mrs. Turner refused. Walking to the front porch, she pointed to the spot where Will had fallen, dying from Howard bullets. "You can't wipe out that blood," she said. "Either the Turners will rule or the Howards, but not both." Strong words from the matriarch of the clan that, according to Judge Lewis's letters to the governor, wanted only peace.

For a few weeks there was an uneasy calm, but it couldn't last. Wilse heard that Little George Turner was following him, so he began to follow Little George. It was only a matter of time until they found each other, near Sulphur Springs, on August 4, 1889. As usual, there were several versions of the encounter. According to J.K Bailey, in one of the endless stream of letters to the governor, "This morning George B. Turner, Jr., was travelin on foot up Catrons Creek some five miles from this place [Harlan] when Wilson Howard the murderer and fugitive from justice overtook him and shot him dead. Howard the murderer had been informed this morning that young Turner had passed up the road . . . he set out in pursuit . . . meeting one Fields riding a mule, Howard demanded the mule, which Fields reluctant surrendered. On this mule Howard was able to overtake young Turner at a spring."

Whatever the role of the mule, Wilse came upon George drinking from a spring and shot him. George rolled behind a large rock and shot Wilse. They emptied their guns at each other until Wilse noticed that George had stopped shooting. He himself was badly wounded in the thigh, but he had hit George four times, the last shot almost taking off the top of his head. Limping down to the road, Wilse stopped a preacher, took his horse (or perhaps a mule?), and rode to a cave where Bud Spurlock was hiding, and stayed there until his wound healed. Either Fields, who allegedly had been relieved of his mule, or the preacher, who had been robbed of his horse, walked into town and reported that Wilse had killed Little George. This did not seem to worry Wilse much, since it was obvious that he had shot George in a fair fight.

Any idea of a truce died with Little George, and September 1889 became the month of not-so-belles lettres. Everyone who could lay pen to paper began begging Governor Simon Buckner to send troops to Harlan County. John Bailey wrote a flowery, if not entirely grammatical, letter deploring the murder of Little George Turner. On September 6, attorney David Lyttle wrote to say that court could not safely be held as long as the Howards and Turners had the county divided between them, but emphasized that he was taking no sides, and blamed both for the trouble. On the same day Commonwealth's Attorney A.N. Clark seconded the call for troops, blaming the Howards. On September 7, attorney John Dishman wrote, saying that law officials were afraid to try to arrest Wilse, and that only troops could save the day. Between times, Lewis was firing off letters to both the newspapers and the governor. Then Judge Robert Boyd wrote, telling the governor that, in his opinion, both Turners and Howards were to blame for the trouble, that the county was fairly evenly divided between the two camps, but that he was not afraid to hold court, regardless of what Wilson Lewis said. But, he added, jurors and witnesses might feel safer if troops were around, and Governor Buckner agreed to send them in. Earlier in the summer, both sides had sent long petitions to the governor, one claiming hell would erupt if troops were not sent in, the other declaring that Lewis was behind the trouble and no troops were needed. One petition said that Lewis was "a weak, ignorant, vacilating man who has been bribed," apparently by the Turners.

At any rate, on September 7, 1889, Buckner ordered the troops in but notified the people of Harlan that they were coming only to protect the court, not to intervene in the Howard-Turner trouble or relieve the elected officials of their duty to enforce the law and keep the peace. This did not please Judge Lewis, who continued to beg the governor to have the troops clean out the Howards. Court was held, apparently without interruption.

But no sooner had the troops departed than, on the morning of October 11, 1889, John Cawood was shot and killed from ambush near his home a few miles east of Harlan, and Hezekiah Hall, who was walking with him, was also killed. A few miles up the road Hiram Cawood was shot a minute later and died the next day. Soon after that Stephen Cawood was fired at, a mile below John Cawood's farm, but escaped, rode into town and reported the killings, adding that he had seen Wilse Howard and Will Jennings in the neighborhood "with twenty outlaws."

No one was arrested for the murders, but Wilson Lewis finally had a bloody shirt to wave. He redoubled his letter writing and implored Buckner to send back the troops. "After the murder of Cawood and Hall," he wrote, "the remaining Cawoods and others fled to Harlan Courthouse for protection. Wilson Howard and Will Jennings organized a band of 25 armed desperadoes, left their stronghold on Martin's Fork, took possession of the home of E.M. Howard on Poor Fork and sent word to the good citizens of Harlan that they would do well to leave town, since the Howards were going to burn it down." Apparently all Wilse had to do was threaten to burn the town and Lewis went into a major panic.

Buckner flatly refused, and he told Lewis that he had the power to drive the Howards out if the people wanted it done. He empowered Lewis to raise a posse comitatus of a hundred men if he felt unable to enforce the law with his usual forces. Lewis issued to Sheriff Moses Turner warrants for the arrest of Wilse Howard and Will Jennings for the Cawood murders, and sent out a call for a hundred men. (Harlan genealogist Holly Fee says Lewis raised sixty men; E.B. Allen, of Rockcastle County, says he raised only nine. A later letter from Wilse to the governor indicates that Allen was about right. If so, Lewis was foolhardy to attack the Howards in their stronghold with so few men.)

With whatever numbers, Lewis and his posse rode out to assault the Howards. Lewis called on the Howards to surrender. They declined, and a gunfight broke out that lasted for some minutes. The posse rode back to town, where Lewis fortified the courthouse in case of attack, and in yet another letter to the governor wrote: "We proceeded upon them in their stronghold; they refusing to surrender, were fired upon by our posse, we wounding eight, all making their escape with Howard and Jennings but three of the most serious wounded. Howard and Jennings are now organizing over 100 desperadoes to get revenge."

The letter doesn't make sense. If Wilse and Will had been unable to take three of their wounded men with them, why were the three not captured and jailed by Lewis? And if the Howards had been defeated and forced to "escape" so hurriedly that they could not rescue their wounded, why did Lewis rush back to town and fortify the courthouse against a feared attack? Other accounts say that out of Lewis's posse of nine, six were killed or wounded. A reliable account by Kentucky State Historian James Klotter says that the Lewis posse suffered three killed and three wounded. Wilse mentioned no losses, though in a later letter he mentioned that Bird Spurlock, a young boy, was injured when "they fired on us."

Lewis renewed his plea for troops to capture the outlaws, and this time he added a request for the appointment of a new judge to take the place of Judge Boyd, asking for someone "who will be impartial and enforce the law"—in other words, someone who would convict Howards. This time the governor replied in tones that seem a little testy. Governors, he pointed out, had no authority to replace judges at will, and he added that Lewis had plenty of men "if the citizens really wanted to clean out law violators in your county."

Whether or not he learned of the governor's cool response to Lewis, Wilse felt, with considerable justification, that they were up against a stacked deck.

"I'm tired of this," he told Will. "If we don't kill them, they're going to kill us. If we do kill them, we'll get sent to the pen. Lewis can always kill us and say he is enforcing the law. I say maybe we ought to leave for a while and let things simmer down."

"Leave for where?" asked Will.

"Go out West," said Wilse. "I've always wanted to see that country."

"That's an idea," Will agreed, and the next day they announced that they were going to take a trip. When the Turners heard that they were leaving, some of them went down to Hiram Howard's to invite them to go along with Wilse and Will, but only Wilse's mother Alice was at home, and she met them with a rifle and told them to get off her property. (This part of the story sounds a lot like the earlier account of how the Turners incited Wilse's rage by telling Alice to quit selling whiskey to George, and "talking rough to her.") When they left, Alice saddled a horse and rode through the rainy night to Ben Howard's, where Wilse and Will were spending the night. When Wilse heard of the Turner warning, he went into a rage. He and Hezekiah Jennings rode into Harlan (Will did not go, for some reason) and at dawn the two of them attacked the Turner home, where sixteen members of the faction were having breakfast. That, at least, is the legend; it seems unlikely that they would have attacked the house alone, though Lewis later complained that Wilse "lay in ambush and killed Alexander Bailey." Wilse testified at his final trial that he had killed John, not Alexander, Bailey and had done so by mistake; Will was sent to prison for killing John, though he had killed neither one.

The day after the attack, Wilse, Will, and two Hall boys (who were probably with them in the attack on the Turner home) started out for the home of Judge Middleton to surrender for the killing of either John or Alexander Bailey, neither of whom was dead. But before they could reach the Middleton home they were fired on from ambush. They ducked behind a log and returned the fire, when suddenly—and stupidly—Pearl Bailey stood up to get a better shot at them. Instead, he got a bullet in his head, killing him. So the four rode on toward Middleton's, this time to confess also to killing Pearl Bailey, who was actually dead. But the Hall brothers lost their nerve and refused to surrender, so Wilse rode up the path to the house alone. As he neared the house, the door opened and Little George Turner stepped out. Wilse thought he had a gun and fired at him, but he missed and hit John Bailey, who was standing beside George. This time he actually killed a Bailey, though he did not know at the time that he had killed John. Ironically, Will was in prison for killing John when Wilse confessed to his killing. Wilse was tried and acquitted of the murder of Pearl Bailey on the grounds of self-defense.

Few of the Harlan gunmen stayed in prison long, as Will and Wilse well knew. Indeed, few gunmen of any county did. One possible reason why feuding and other violence flourished in Kentucky around the turn of the century was the practice of pardoning killers. Beginning in 1889, 131 killers were pardoned in a decade. Governor John Y. Brown pardoned 51, W.O. Bradley, 58, and J.C.W. Beckham, 11. The average killer served only seven and half years.

At any rate, Wilse and Will figured it was a good time to see the West. They rode down to Pineville and caught a train heading in that general direction. They had a good time, traveling from St. Louis to Kansas, Colorado, and on to New Mexico. They apparently had a gunfight in Kansas in which seven Indians were killed, but they paid little attention to it, though Wilse did mention spending some time in what he described as a "sorry type" of jail. They had a more pleasurable time in some choice whorehouses. But then Wilse got into real trouble and was arrested and jailed for killing a deaf-mute in Missouri. He jumped bail and headed for home, arriving in March 1890. But, unknown to him, a detective named Imboden was on his trail. Imboden later got in touch with George Turner, who promised to help him run Wilse to ground. Wilse's time was running out.

Still, he felt great relief at being home. He had hardly been home a week when he received word from Judge Lewis that it would be better if he stayed out of Harlan Town. That irked Wilse, who sent back word that he had just moved freely through fifteen states and as many big towns, and figured he would exercise similar freedom of movement in his home county. Furthermore, he added, if anyone interfered, he might just burn down the town. Lewis and the Turners, alarmed, armed for battle. Raising another posse, Lewis rode out to capture the Howards. The posse surrounded the Howard home and tried to set fire to it. A gunfight ensued. Lewis reported that a dozen Howards were in the house; Wilse later claimed that only he, Bud Spurlock, and John Howard were there. But Wilse charged out of the house, and he and John drove off the attackers, driving three of them into the river. George Hall was killed. Bob Craig shot Bud Spurlock but saw Wilse approaching and ran.

"I jumped on my horse and took a short path to cut him off," Wilse wrote later, "but he went through the woods and I did not catch up with him until he was crossing a field. I yelled to him to stop; he dropped his gun and fell down, but when he got to his feet he pulled a pistol. I told him to throw down his pistol but when he would not I killed him. I shot at him four times, but I was on my horse running and did not hit him but two or three times."

Two of Lewis's men were killed, five wounded. The posses limped back to Harlan. (Some historians think this attack has been confused with the previous one and say that only one attack on the Howard home actually occurred. The results were quite similar, though Wilse's role, and the number killed, are different.)

Now Governor Buckner received another letter, and an intriguing one, this from Wilse and Will Jennings, interesting not only for its contents but for its grammar and rather literary tone, in contrast to the scribblings of Lewis and others, and because it indicates that Wilse was feeling a measure of desperation. Parts of it follow.

My Dear Sir:

We see from some of the Louisville papers that you have been asked to send troops up here in the mountains to capture us, and that the papers are full of slush about us being desperadoes, outlaws and thieves, murderers, cutthroats and God knows what else. In justice to ourselves and to the thousands of friends in Harlan and the surrounding counties, we cannot afford to let such outrageous falsehoods go unnoticed.

We will not pretend to give you a detailed account of the feud in this county . . . but it began as far back as the war. There was a crowd of people in this town who wanted to be supreme rulers . . . and when any stranger would come to town . . . they did not like, they would try to run him off or have him killed, and did send many innocent men to their eternal home. [We were] selected by some unknown power to resist their attacks and became involved in the feud . . . and must bear the hardships we now bear, and must sneak around at night "like a galley slave, scourged to his dungeon."

We are as anxious to give up and stand trial as men can be, but that would be like committing suicide, as old Judge Lewis and his crowd of bush-whackers of the "Law and Order" party say that if they get us in jail they intend to burn the jail and we know they will do it. We will give bail in the amount of $75,000 and . . . can get ¾ of the people in Harlan County to go on our bond. If we did give bond we would have to stay hid and would have somebody to fight all the time . . . they would try to kill us just as hard then as now. . . . One man can arrest both of us if we are guaranteed protection, but we will never give up to Judge Lewis and his bushwhackers . . . this is the kind of Law and Order Party the devil has presiding in Hell.

No one has ever asked us to surrender, and no attempt was ever made to arrest us, but on occasion they have come and fired on us, as they did this time, and then we would fight, and usually whip the hell out of them. Judge Lewis and his crowd slipped up to about 20 yards of where we were and fired on us, hitting one innocent boy by the name of Bird Spurlock, and then fled. Wilson Howard was the only one that fought them, and he whipped the entire ten bushwhackers [This would indicate that Lewis had a posse of only nine men, as E.B. Allen stated]. If there had been one man in the party with the least bit of bravery or manhood he could have killed Howard, as he stood out open and sent the lead sailing into them as they ran like the cowardly curs they are.

With reference to the people in this section, they are quite law-abiding people, are never molesting anyone. As there is a just God . . . they will have to answer for the unjust assault made on these people, whose only fault is they let us stay amongst them.

As to the charges they lay to us in Missouri, we desire to say that if your excellency will pardon us for the indictments in Harlan County against us we assure you that we will come as fast as the first train can carry us. Judging from the papers, you may imagine that we have 40 or fifty men with us. This is not so. We are alone, living as best we can. About three weeks ago Mr. Sam Kash, of Clay County, the deputy collector for this district, was up here on business and . . . he saw the majority of people in this county and . . . if you refer to him to tell you the sentiment of the people on this feud trouble. In closing we beg your excellency to consider and inquire well into this matter, and you will soon find where the blame lies.

Yours to command,
Will Jennings,
Wilson R. Howard

The Trap that Didn't Spring

Wilson Lewis should have felt fairly secure. The Turners owned much of Harlan Town, the county seat. Lewis was county judge, Mose Turner was sheriff. Furthermore, Lewis knew, though Wilse Howard did not, that the detective Imboden, who was trailing Wilse for the murder of the deaf-mute in Missouri, was closing in. Yet all Wilse Howard had to do was send word that he was going to burn down the town and Lewis fired off another letter to Governor Buckner, pleading for the protection of troops. Apparently Buckner finally got tired of the routine and on March 17, 1890, sent a company of militia under Captain Gaither of Harrodsburg and, to show his concern, sent General Sam Hill to report on the situation.

Lewis was delighted, but his joy was short-lived. General Hill interviewed as many people as he could persuade to talk and sent word to Wilse and Hezekiah Jennings that he wanted to see them. (Why he asked to meet with Hezekiah Jennings instead of Will is hard to understand. Perhaps it was because Hezekiah was older and had no charges against him.) At any rate, they met, "twelve miles out in the mountains," according to the *Courier-Journal* story from "Harlan Courthouse," which also reported the escape of three moonshiners and one murderer from the jail. "The jail," added the report, "is not as secure as it might be."

General Hill told Wilse that he had not come to Harlan to assess guilt but to find ways to bring about peace. He said he had read Lewis's letters to the newspapers and to the governor but had also talked to a lot of people in Harlan, many of whom had spoken well of the Howards. He was convinced, he said, that there was blame on both sides, and he urged Wilse to get the Howards and their allies to lay down their arms.

"General," Wilse said coldly, "if I put down my guns before Lewis and his bunch do, I'll be dead by night. I guess we're all sick of this; if you get the other side to put down their guns, we'll put down ours. But we want Lewis to enforce the law the same for all, not one kind for us, another for the Turners. If he'll do that, we'll keep the peace. Not till then. I'd rather be in prison for killing them than in the graveyard for them killing me."

General Hill agreed to talk with Lewis and later told Wilse that the Turners had assured him they would use their influence to see that everyone, Lewis included, kept the peace. Wilse promised him that the Howards would not be the first to break the truce, and the militia turned south for the trip down the valley to Pineville, where they caught the train for Frankfort.

Several weeks later, Wilse and Will hatched a plot that they thought would put an end to the Lewis threat. Will rode through the county and brought about twenty Howard sympathizers to Bud Spurlock's cave, where Wilse explained his plan to station them in an ambush on either side of the road through the narrow gap to Hagan, Virginia. Wilse then wrote a letter to Wilson Lewis, which he signed with the name of the county judge of Rogersville, Tennessee. According to the letter, the judge had in his jail two men, one claiming to be Wilson Howard of Harlan, Kentucky, whom he was holding awaiting identification. Lewis, wildly excited, quickly raised a posse and prepared to go to Rogersville and bring home their prize.

But old George Turner was not fooled. "We don't know who wrote this," he said. "Wilse Howard could have done it himself. You ride out there through Hagan Gap and they could cut you down like cornstalks." He advised Lewis instead to send a rider on a fast horse to Rogersville, but by way of Pineville, to the south, avoiding Hagan Gap. As he suspected, the county judge at Rogersville had no knowledge of the purported prisoners, the rider rode back with the revelation, and the Howard trap was never sprung.

Will and Wilse sensed that their luck was running out. Wilse rode into Harlan that night and told his mother goodbye, and once more he and Will headed West. This time, for some reason, they went separate ways. Will went to Missouri, where he was arrested, sent home, and imprisoned for killing John Bailey. Wilse, who was wanted in Missouri for killing the deaf-mute, said that he had always wanted to see California, and now he fulfilled his dream.

But apparently Wilse was running out of money, for in California he was arrested in June 1893 for robbing a Wells Fargo stagecoach and was tried and sent to prison. He was traveling under the name of Brown when arrested, and it is possible that he got himself imprisoned as Brown as a way of dropping out of sight and avoiding trial for the deaf-mute murder. It is also possible that by this time he had been warned that Imboden was on his trail. If that was his strategy, it didn't work. Someone in prison spotted him from a Wanted poster, Imboden came to the prison and identified him, and Wilse was taken back to Missouri to stand trial for killing the deaf-mute, a man named McMichaels.

As he surrendered to the sheriff who took him back to Missouri, he said, "I am Wilse Howard, of Kentucky, the man you are looking for." On the stand he recited without emotion the names of the men he had killed during the feud—Bob Craig, Will Turner, George Turner, George Hall, and John Bailey. He made no mention of the killings of the Cawoods and Hezekiah Hall, and to the end he maintained his innocence of the killing of the deaf-mute.

Throughout his trial and conviction, Wilse remained composed. Alice Howard and Rebecca, Wilse's sister, made the trip to St. Louis to be with him during his trial. Like Wilse, they received the jury's verdict of guilty, and the sentence of death by hanging, with a dignity mentioned in the St. Louis newspapers.

At his trial, the courtroom was packed and St. Louis papers carried detailed stories about the famous Kentucky mountain feudist. Wilse was surrounded by reporters, who took down every word he spoke as if it were of huge importance. Wherever the train stopped on his last journey, crowds thronged the platform, hoping for a view of the desperado, a title that amused Wilse but angered his mother and Rebecca.

Both women showed their usual composure until the last morning, when Wilse was taken, heavily shackled, to the train. The accompanying sheriff permitted Alice and Rebecca a final few minutes with their son and brother, and it was then that Alice finally broke down, sobbing and clinging to Wilse as he tried to console her. The sheriff eventually had to pull her away. Rebecca tried to smile, embraced Wilse, and patted him affectionately on the back. "I won't say good-bye, brother. I'll see you soon in a better world."

On the train taking him to Lebanon, Missouri, where he was to be hanged, Wilse met Imboden for the first time, looked at him coldly, but then relented and shook hands, saying he bore him no ill will. In his jail cell he showed his cellmates a knife he had hidden under his belt with which to stab Imboden, but he said that at the last moment he felt no desire to kill him.

On his last evening, Wilse sipped a glass of port to steady his nerves but told a reporter, "Let me tell you something: I am not going to die game. I don't believe in this business of bravado. But I will die like a man, and an innocent man. So, now, goodbye."

On the gallows on the morning of August 4, 1894, Wilse, asked if he had anything to say, said, "Only that I hope to meet you all in heaven."

Back in Harlan, the hatreds that had fueled the feud eventually cooled if they never actually burned out. Life returned to something approaching normal. The Howards were eager to forget the feud. In the 1910 Harlan *Business Directory*, four doctors were listed in the town—a Howard, a Cawood, a Martin, and G. Pearl Bailey. Listed as teachers in the public school were a Howard, a Turner, and two Cawoods. A Hall and two Howards were listed as engineers, and there were two Turners, three Howards, and a Hall among the lawyers. A haircut could be had from John Hall or from Daniel or Elijah Howard. In 1915 Dr. W.P. Cawood and Dr. E.M. Howard built a two-story building on the corner of Second and Mound Streets now known as the Smith-Howard Building.

A century after the Turner-Howard feud ended, few of the old resentments remained. Life had taken its course. Turners, Howards, Halls, and Lewises had intermarried. Except for genealogist Holly Fee, it is hard to find anyone who remembers who Devil Jim Turner was. Or Wilse Howard, for that matter.

Not that the feud did not exact a price. Like the other Eastern Kentucky feuds, it left an image, a reputation for violence, and the nickname "Bloody Harlan" that today is undeserved. In fact, it is a very hospitable town to visit.

BREATHITT COUNTY
A Talent for Violence

Almost a Romantic Journey

In the summer of 1780, while the Revolutionary War still raged along the American seaboard, a group of young Virginians walked and rode down the Shenandoah Valley, through southwest Virginia and the Pound Gap in the Cumberland Mountains into the wilderness of Kentucky. Though they were very serious in their search for a new life beyond the mountains, free of the strife between the restless colonists and the British crown, their journey had about it almost the air of a lark. They were very young—none was over twenty—and there was something youthful and romantic about their idealistic journey. Some had recently taken formal marriage vows, some had simply decided to set off together toward a new life in the mysterious, fabled territory of Kentucky.

Most were of the good English yeoman stock common on the frontier, with few possessions besides the skill of their hands, a few tools, and a blessed ignorance of the toils that lay ahead. Their surnames would be among those living in the mountains two centuries later: Nathan and Virginia (Neace) Noble; William and Enoch (strange name for a girl) Noble; Austin and Melinda (Allen) Neace; Henry Neace. Most were close kin. Others with them or following close behind bore other names still familiar in and around the region where they settled: Haddix, Combs, Hurst, Bach, Turner, Strong, Watts, Reynolds.

They were not the first white people to view what became Breathitt County. John Finley had crossed the Kentucky River near what is now Jackson in 1752. Christopher Gist, the Virginia surveyor, soldier, and scholar who later served as a guide for the young George Washington, came about the same time, probably in 1751. Washington himself may have come through the Pound Gap, though the indications are that they stopped north and east of that point.

Through the gap and what are now Letcher and Perry Counties they trudged, finally deciding, late in the summer, to settle along Lost Creek, Quicksand, and Frozen Creek. A group of them made a home that first winter in a rock house, a shallow cave actually, above Lost Creek, walling off the front with logs, building a fireplace—a remarkably dry, warm home until the men could get some cabins built. There, in November of 1780, young Virginia Noble gave birth to a baby girl. The baby died.

It was a rough land into which they had come, and one must wonder now why they stopped among the sharp, steep hills and narrow valleys of the central Cumberlands instead of going a little farther west into the rich and gentle Bluegrass region. From the first they faced the handicap of isolation. Until 1840, when a road was completed from the village of Jackson to War Creek, all merchandise had to be brought up the Kentucky River from a landing at Clay's Ferry, near Lexington. Not until 1890 did the Kentucky Union Railroad extend its line from the Red River to Elkatawa, and in 1891 to Jackson, the county seat. As late as 1930 there was one black-topped road in the county.

From its founding in 1807, Breathitt County grew slowly. In 1809 it contained 8,705 people, in 1900, 14,320. It was not an easy place in which to make a living. The rich river bottomland was good for farming but flood prone, and settlers were soon clearing timber from the hills to create farmland and pastures. On the steep slopes grew more than a hundred species of trees, but the land made cutting difficult, and the logs had to be floated down the swift, swirling waters of the Kentucky River at flood tide to sawmills fifty miles away. When the big lumber companies such as Mowbray-Robinson finally arrived in 1908, they were warmly welcomed for the payrolls and purchases they brought, but they were not an unmixed blessing. They stripped the hills, leaving them prone to erosion that silted the creeks and added to river flooding.

When and why the fighting began that gave this scenic mountain land the unwanted nickname "Bloody Breathitt" is hard to pinpoint. But apparently it began with the Civil War. During that disastrous conflict, army officers, Union and Confederate, were often obliged to live off the land and sent foraging parties out into the countryside to round up whatever food they could find. According to law, they were supposed to pay or give promissory notes for what they took. In practice, they seldom did, taking what they could find and making foraging parties the dread of the mountain citizens, regardless of their sympathies. Such men were referred to as bushwhackers—they whacked the bushes to drive out livestock, cattle, sheep, pigs, chickens—which they then appropriated. Soon the name would be applied also to those who lay in the bushes and ambushed and robbed passers-by.

It was assumed, of course, that the foragers would take the livestock and farm produce back to the troops. Again, it didn't always
work out that way. Frequently the leaders, especially leaders of the
Home Guard (regular or irregular troops who were supposed to protect citizens of a stipulated area from enemy troops or robbers) simply
rounded up the stock and divided it among themselves, with top dog
getting the biggest bone. That is apparently what took place among
the Union army units of the Home Guard representing Breathitt and
neighboring counties. Captain William Strong, of Company K of the
Fourteenth Regiment, had a falling out with Lieutenant Wiley Amis of
Company I over such a divison of spoils. Wiley Amis and his men had
been scouting the northern half of Breathitt, while Captain Strong,
with other Amises and Wilson Callahan, were robbing the Lost Creek
Section. According to his men, Captain Strong took more than his
share, the Amises and Wilson Callahan protested, and the incident led
to the Strong-Amis feud, which lasted well into the 1870s. It fairly well
ended when John Amis, the leader of the family, was killed in 1873 and
the other Amises, or most of them, moved out of the county. But before
it ended, it involved the Littles, another large family, when a gunfight
broke out in the Breathitt courtroom in which Bob Little, a nephew of
Captain Strong, was killed and five others wounded. In that same year
a fire destroyed much of the courthouse in Jackson, the county seat,
including most of the county records. There are few things more convenient than a good courthouse fire.

Like many feud leaders, Captain Bill Strong was a curious combi-
nation of altruist and tyrant. Having served in the Union army, he
apparently took the Union cause seriously and became known in the
hill country as the protector of the newly freed slaves. On the other
hand, he was a brutal enemy. After the war, when a man ran against
him or his choice for office, Strong was apt to take it as a personal
affront. If the offending party did not withdraw, he frequently wound
up dead. Bill Strong wanted the law enforced to accommodate Bill
Strong; he wanted his followers left alone, taxes on his land kept low,
and land disputes settled in his favor.

But the worst aspect of his rule was his tendency to act as com-
manding officer long after the war was over. He is said to have held
courts-martial and condemned to death those who challenged his
control. These courts-martial, it was reported, were held at night
with only a few trusted men present. There was no need for the accused to be on hand. Captain Bill would review the sins of the offender, ponder the case and, in most cases, sentence the offender to
death. Usually one of his trusted lieutenants was given the job of kill-

ing the condemned man at a convenient moment. No hurry. Sometimes it was months before the blow fell. But it fell, invariably. One day the doomed man would be riding along, going to work or to the store, probably not knowing he was doomed, when a shot would ring out from ambush.

Wilson Callahan, John Amis and two of his cousins, possibly others, went the way of the court-martial. The Amises fought back and are said to have claimed more than two dozen of the Strong forces. But Strong's executions had an inexorable air about them, as if by fate decreed, and one by one Captain Bill whittled away the enemy. Soon, few men wanted to challenge him. But in the mid-seventies a series of violent incidents marked the beginning of the end for the captain.

The events of 1874 involved not only Bill Strong but the Littles, the Jetts, and the Cockrells (sometimes spelled Cockrill), large and determined families. In the early summer of 1874 Jerry Little, not the most popular man in the hills, started a rumor, probably motivated by jealousy, charging one of James Cockrell's daughters with pregnancy or lack of chastity. A slur against the virtue of a female in the family could not be tolerated, and the Cockrells set out to avenge her honor. Two of Little's allies were shot, one killed. But at about the same time, Jerry Little shot and killed Curtis Jett Jr. in a bar near the Jackson courthouse. In return, Hiram Jett, Curtis's brother, shot but failed to kill Jerry Little. The fight persuaded the Jetts to join the Cockrells against the Littles.

Captain Bill Strong couldn't keep out of it. While the Littles and Jetts were banging away at each other, David Flinchum shot and killed a Negro. Ordinarily this would have caused hardly a comment, but now Bill Strong had made himself the special protector of the Negro population. The Flinchums joined the Cockrells for protection, so Strong joined the Littles against the Cockrells, and the lines were drawn. But at that point Captain Strong threw the whole county into confusion and brought in state troops for the first time by staging a coup d'état. Marshaling about two dozen of his old wartime followers, Strong rode into Jackson and took over the courthouse without firing a shot. He just walked in, told people in the offices to leave, and took over.

Feeling it advisable not to resist, the county officials in their offices at the time filed out and held a meeting at the home of Jim Cockrell, and decided to send a message to the governor complaining that there had been an insurrection and that Strong had illegally captured the courthouse. Governor Preston H. Leslie was astounded; he had had trouble out of the mountain courthouses before, and requests for troops to allow courts to function, but he had never before faced a coup d'état, the blatant capture of a county government. He sent in sixty soldiers on September 16, 1874. Some of Strong's messengers heard that the troops were on the way and warned the captain. A few hours before the militia arrived, Strong and his men very casually left the courthouse and rode out of Jackson.

The tension in Jackson, however, and the constant shooting between the Jetts and Littles worried the captain in charge of the troops, and before the episode ended five companies had arrived and encamped in the town. They remained through December 1874, protecting the court so that it could function.

The Little-Jett feud was ended, however, not by troops but Breathitt sheriff John Linville Hagins. A gunfight broke out between the two sides on Quicksand Creek. Logan Cockrell was killed and Jerry Little was wounded. Cornered, Little jumped into the creek and hid under some brush until dark, when he dragged himself out of the water and crawled home. Finally, Sheriff Hagins, a twenty-six-year-old who had friends on both sides of the feud and refused to be drawn into it, decided that the Little-Jett conflict had gone on long enough. Riding to the home of Hiram Jett, he said, "I've come to arrest you, Hiram, and would like for you to come peaceably." Jett's response indicates that he may well have been tired of the fighting but felt he had a tiger by the tail and was afraid to let go. "I will if Little will," he replied. So Hagins went to the Little home and made the same statement to Jerry Little, who made the same response; he would come peaceably if Jett would. Thus the leaders of both factions were brought in without a shot being fired, and the court took bond for their appearance at the next term of court, at which time they were tried. To everyone's apparent satisfaction, no one was sent to prison for the casual shootings and killings of the previous months, but the leaders were fined. That seemed proper.

A strange sidelight: Hiram Jett was tired of the hostility. A gentleman and prosperous merchant, he did not want the reputation of a gunfighter, but he knew that the image would follow him as long as he lived in Breathitt County. So shortly after the trials he sold his home and moved to Madison County, where he lived until his death in 1887. Two years after his death his widow married ex-sheriff John Linville Hagins. It proved to be a happy marriage. Blessed are the peacemakers.

Calm did not reign for long, however. In the summer of 1878 there was a heated contest for the office of county judge. Among the candidates were Judge D.K. Butler, who had held the office before, attorney John Wesley Burnett, and E.C. Strong, a cousin of Captain Bill Strong. E.C. was supported by the Littles. On June 3 a Democratic convention was held in Jackson. It was an ill-tempered gathering, marked by frequent gunfire, at which nothing was accomplished, since a majority could not decide on a candidate. Soon afterward, Judge Butler withdrew, and friends urged Burnett to do the same to avoid conflict with the Strongs. He refused, though E.C. Strong was gathering support, including that of Big John Aikman. But Aikman was Captain Strong's bitterest enemy, and the captain, caught between dislike for his old enemies—the Littles and John Aikman—and loyalty to his cousin E.C., deserted E.C. and supported Burnett, who had the backing of what law-and-order element there was.

To general surprise, Burnett won, but by a thin margin—eight votes. The Littles and Aikman swore that Burnett would not live to take office. Burnett feared they would fulfill their prophecy and with three friends rode to Frankfort, where he persuaded the governor to award him the commission of office without customary procedural delays. The Littles grumbled and made sullen threats but did little else.

But Big John Aikman was not content to talk. Three weeks after the election he collected a dozen or so supporters of E.C. Strong and rode into Jackson with the aim of killing Burnett. But someone talked—whiskey was probably involved, it usually was—and before the Aikman forces reached Jackson more than thirty Burnett partisans rallied at the courthouse. The attack never came off, but several times during the following week gunmen attacked the Marcum boardinghouse where Burnett stayed, leaving a few bullet holes but injuring no one.

Then a nasty event occurred that ignited the Little-Burnett fire again. A few weeks after he took office, Burnett heard that the wife of Jason Little, Jerry Little's uncle, had died under strange circumstances and had been buried hurriedly under Jason's home. Judge Burnett ordered the body disinterred. This caused a furor. The Littles swore they would kill anyone who tried to dig up the body, but Burnett was not to be bullied. He appointed a coroner's jury, deputized a cordon of guards, and directed them to the Little home, where they dug up the body. The coroner's jury found (1) that Mrs. Little had been pregnant at the time of her death, and (2) that her body had suffered gunshot wounds that had been stuffed with beeswax to disguise them. Jason was charged with her murder and lodged in the Jackson jail, but Burnett ordered him transferred to the jail in Lexington, fearing that as long as he was in Jackson, efforts would be made to storm the jail and free him or hang him.

What happened next demonstrated how shaky was the hold of

law in Breathitt County. During the second week of November 1878, Deputy Sheriff Charles Little, a cousin of Jason, obtained from Circuit Judge John Randall of Perry County an order directing the jailer in Lexington to release Jason to Deputy Charles Little. Charles then gathered some deputies, and they rode to the railroad station in Montgomery County to catch the train to Lexington. Sheriff Hagins, hearing of this, gathered a group of his own and set out for the same train station. When he arrived, Deputy Little and his band were waiting on the platform.

A tense moment. Sheriff Hagins ordered Deputy Little to disperse his men and return to Jackson. Little said that he had a court order to return Jason to Jackson and that he had no choice but to obey the order. About that time the train for Lexington arrived. They all stood, glaring at each other and wondering whether to reach for their pistols. Finally both parties boarded the train and rode to Lexington in tense silence.

In Lexington they went in search of the jailer and found him at home, and both demanded the release of the prisoner. The jailer, choosing to obey the rules of rank, released Jason to Sheriff Hagins. Deputy Little fumed, calculated his chances in a shoot-out, and decided to wait until they were back home and among friends to attempt to rescue Jason. Again they all boarded the train, got off in Montgomery County, mounted their horses, and rode toward Jackson. Deputy Little, with no prisoner to bother with, raced ahead, planning an ambush. Sheriff Hagins, knowing that was what Little would probably do, took a long, roundabout way back to Jackson, hoping to get behind the would-be ambushers and place Jason in the questionable security of the Breathitt jail.

Court was due to begin on Monday, November 25. On November 24 opposing feudists began arriving in Jackson in force. On Monday morning Captain Bill Strong and his followers arrived and took up quarters in a log building down the street from the courthouse. In Strong's group were his reputed top killer, "Hen" Kilburn, Steve McIntosh, former slave "Nigger Dick" Strong, mulattoes William and Daniel Freeman, and perhaps a dozen others. The Littles were backed by the Allens and Gambles and the famed gunman Big John Aikman.

During the noon recess of the court, Aikman and his men rode into town and hitched their horses on the public square. Bill Strong and his men were lounging just down the street, and for a while there was a tense silence. Then Daniel Freeman, one of the mulattoes with Strong, walked up to Aikman and, in a show of more courage than sense, asked him what he wanted.

With a mean smile, Aikman slowly drew his pistol.

"I don't know that I was wanting anything particular," he said, "but I'll take a dead nigger." Freeman turned to run, and Aikman shot him in the back. William Freeman had been a few steps behind his brother, and when he rushed forward to help him, Aikman shot him, too. This set off a general gunfight. Strong's forces withdrew to the log cabin, where they had left their rifles. Aikman, Justice of the Peace Whick Allen, and their men took over the courthouse, making it their headquarters. The streets were immediately deserted as noncombatants fled from town or to their homes.

Throughout the afternoon the two sides kept up a desultory and ineffective fire. Eventually Daniel Freeman, who had been left lying in the street, was rescued and taken to the Haddix home a few miles south of Jackson. A doctor was called, but the bullet had entered Freeman's back and come out on his right side, and he died. William Freeman, though wounded in the thigh and back, recovered.

When it grew dark, Aikman and the Little forces left the courthouse and gathered at the home of Alfred Little on the Kentucky River. They were there when Deputy Charles Little and his posse returned from Lexington bearing the bad news that they had not been able to rescue Jason and that Hagins would be returning with him at any time.

Dawn broke on a tense town. Aikman's force contained a number of Jason Little's relatives and friends. Bill Strong's band contained as many who wanted Jason hanged. There were rumors that some of Aikman's men had ridden out to lay an ambush for Hagins and rescue his prisoner. Circuit Judge Randall ordered Deputy Sheriff James Back to gather a posse of fifteen men and go out to reinforce the approaching sheriff. Judge Burnett, despite the warnings of friends, took over leadership of this posse. They rode out of town and met Hagins's force about five miles from Jackson.

Aikman, seeing the odds shift with the reinforcement of Hagins's forces, got on his horse and headed home. After he left, Squire Allen took command of the Little forces, who numbered about fifty men, and they took up stations to greet Sheriff Hagins and his posse. The battle never took place. Hagins and his men rode quietly into town by a side road and were approaching the courthouse before the Little forces realized they had returned. Jason Little was placed in the jail, and the posse members, thinking the danger had passed, started for home.

But as Judge Burnett and Sheriff Hagins started down the street to the nearby boardinghouse, two men stood in the street shouting insults at them. They ignored the remarks and kept walking, but suddenly someone shouted, "Watch out!" and Burnett turned and was shot, allegedly by Alfred Gamble. A man with Gamble, allegedly Alfred Little, a nephew of Jason, tried to shoot Hagins, but his pistol misfired. Burnett ran a few steps and collapsed. Hagins carried him into the home of George Sewell, where he died.

While this was going on, a group under Squire Allen rushed the jail and tried to break down the door. Tom Little, a cousin of Jason, pushed his way to the front of the mob and begged the men not to take the law into their own hands. Someone shot and killed him. The shot and the sight of him sprawled in front of the jail door cooled the mob, and they retreated.

Captain Bill Strong and his men took up positions in their log fort, Allen and the Little forces withdrew to the courthouse, and Sheriff Hagins and his guard took over the hotel across the street from the jail. Sporadic firing continued for several hours, but no one seemed to be sure who was shooting at whom, or for what particular reason. The Littles had brought into town a barrel of applejack that had reinforced the courage of the jail attackers, but as night drew on the barrel grew empty and thoughts sobered. By Wednesday morning the Little forces had disappeared. Sheriff Hagins took over the courthouse, from which he had a clear view of the jail. Captain Strong and his men left for their homes on the North Fork.

But peace did not immediately descend on Jackson. With Sheriff Hagins and his men holed up in the courthouse and Deputy Charles Little and his men riding around town, no one seemed sure who represented the law. To make matters worse, Judge Randall, disgusted—and probably frightened—suddenly rode out of town for Hazard at daybreak without giving notice. By midmorning a mob roamed the streets, drunk and dangerous, firing into the air, some of them again shouting their intentions to storm the jail and take Jason Little. Nothing came of it. Sheriff Hagins tried to establish some order, and eventually the drunks sobered up and went home. By December 7, when Lieutenant Thompson of the state militia visited Jackson, he could report to Governor James B. McCreary that everything was quiet, that "the excitement was nothing like so great as reported, and did not extend to the people generally."

The lieutenant could be excused for being deceived by the apparent calm. He was not familiar with the county or its conflicts and had no way to detect the currents of hostility beneath the surface calm. Unfortunately, his report made the governor inclined to minimize the Breathitt conflict, and it was not until Judge Randall warned that he would not convene a special term of court without the protection of troops that the governor took things seriously. On December 12, for the second time in five years, troops were ordered into Breathitt County. Even then Judge Randall did not feel secure in Jackson. He reentered the town quietly by night and showed up in court next morning flanked by soldiers.

With the help of troopers, Hagins and his men rounded up more than thirty men who had taken part in the violence. Twenty of them were taken to jail in Louisville and kept there until the following June, when they were brought back to Jackson under military guard and tried.

Jason Little was tried and found guilty but managed to get a sentence of life in prison and, after serving a little more than five years in the penitentiary, was pardoned and came home. Others took to the hills. Some came back and surrendered when things cooled off. Big John Aikman went over into Letcher County, where he was reported to be a hired gunman in the Wright-Jones feud. But Governor McCreary, irritated by the cavalier attitude of the Breathitt feudists toward the law, sent troops after him, found him hiding at the home of a half-brother, and brought him back for trial. He was sentenced to twenty years in the penitentiary but served only a little over a year before he was pardoned. He came home to Breathitt and got mixed up in the Marcum-Hargis War, the worst of the Breathitt blood-lettings.

The Little-Burnett feud was pretty well over. How many people had been killed is hard to calculate. Counting casualties in the Strong-Noble fights and the Strong-Amis feud, as many as seventy-five may have fallen. It was later estimated that more than a hundred were killed by the turn of the century, but such figures are estimates.

And little had been accomplished. At the election of a county judge to succeed the fallen Burnett, James Lindon was elected. Since Lindon was new to Breathitt County and had no long-standing ties to any faction, everyone assumed that he was an ally of his wife's brother, James B. Marcum, who would later become a main figure in Breathitt's worst feud. Charles Little, deputy sheriff and cousin of Jason, was elected sheriff to succeed Hagins. Any progress toward reform achieved in the Burnett-Hagins years was forgotten.

Above, Mt. Pleasant, later renamed Harlan, looks placid enough in this photo, but it was the site of the Turner-Howard feud, which kept things stirred up for years. All Wilse Howard had to do was threaten to burn it down and the whole town went into a panic. *Below,* Harlan County Courthouse around 1880. At least one good gunfight of the Turner-Howard feud took place here. Both from R. C. Ballard Thruston Collection, The Filson Club Historical Society.

Above left, a drawing of Wilson (Wilse) Howard, leader of the Howard family in its feud with the Turners, and usually considered the villain of the feud—though several others were equally qualified. *Above right,* Mrs. George Turner, who might have stopped the feud but apparently had no desire to do so. Both from the *Courier-Journal,* Louisville. Berry Howard *(left)* saw his kinsmen involved in both the Turner-Howard feud in Harlan County and the bloody Clay County War, though he was active in neither. He was acquitted of the assassination of Governor William Goebel. From Caleb Powers, *My Story.*

Above, Jonathan K. Bailey and his happy family, shown in Mt. Pleasant around 1884. The Baileys were generally allied with the Turners. Will Jennings, a leader of the Howards, went to prison for killing John Bailey, though Wilse Howard probably did it while shooting at a Turner. *Below*, the "Turner Mansion" in Harlan, home of the George Turner family, in 1884. Two of the Turner sons bled and died on the front porch. Both from R. C. Ballard Thruston Collection, The Filson Club Historical Society.

Curtis Jett, the infamous and reckless gunman convicted in the 1903 killing of J. B. Marcum in the Marcum-Hargis-Callahan feud in Breathitt County. He was just as mean as he looks in this retouched newspaper photo. After prison, he became a preacher of sorts, like a lot of the old gunmen. From the *Courier-Journal*, Louisville.

J. B. Marcum, a power in Republican politics and one of the most prominent attorneys in Eastern Kentucky. He tried to end the feud and save his own life with an appeal through the press, but failed. From the *Courier-Journal*, Louisville.

A sketch of Judge James Hargis of Breathitt County, from the *Kansas City Star*, January 25, 1931. Hargis, a wealthy merchant, a power in state Democratic politics, and leader of the Hargis-Callahan forces in their feud with the Marcum faction, helped make William Goebel governor and survived the feud, only to be killed by his son, Beach. Courtesy of *Kentucky Explorer Magazine*.

Devil Anse Hatfield (seated, second from left) surrounded by his lovely and lovable family, some carrying domestic implements, about 1897. Among Anse's descendants was a governor of West Virginia. Courtesy of the West Virginia State Archives.

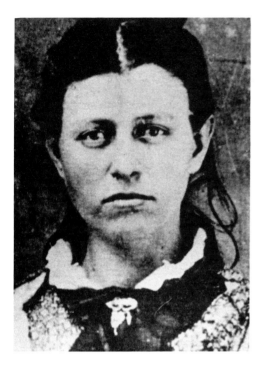

Left, Rose Anna (Rosanna, Roseann) McCoy, the bogus Juliet of the bogus Romeo and Juliet fable concocted by the press in its off-target reporting of the Hatfield-McCoy feud. Her life was about as happy as she looks. Courtesy of the West Virginia State Archives. *Right*, Johnse Hatfield, one of Devil Anse's sons, who took part in the burning of the McCoy home and the killing of Alifair and Calvin McCoy. He courted Rose Anna but later left her and married her cousin Nancy, who gave him a reputation for being henpecked. Courtesy of Leonard McCoy and Jimmy Wolford.

Randolph (Randall, Old Rannel) McCoy, head of the McCoys and a survivor of the feud with the Hatfields. Courtesy of Leonard McCoy and Jimmy Wolford.

Frank Phillips, deputy sheriff and freelance gunman who single-handedly went into West Virginia, captured a jailful of Hatfields, and almost caused a war between Kentucky and West Virginia. He later took up with the wife of Johnse Hatfield and eventually married her. Courtesy of West Virginia State Archives.

Devil Anse and his wife, Levicy (sometimes spelled Levisa or Louisa), taken in their later years, long after the feud ended. Courtesy of the West Virginia and Regional History Collection, West Virginia University Libraries.

A street scene on Court Day in Hazard, seat of Perry County and center of the vicious French-Eversole feud that almost wiped out the town. Courtesy of The Filson Club Historical Society.

If there were good guys in the French-Eversole war, they were Joe C. Eversole *(left)* and his father-in-law, Josiah Combs. Eversole, a Hazard merchant, opposed Fulton French and the big land companies he represented. For his trouble he was killed. Courtesy of Martha Quigley.

Fulton French, attorney, merchant, and agent for eastern coal and land companies. His heartless dealings with mountain residents embittered Joe Eversole and sparked the feud between them. From the *Courier-Journal*, Louisville, courtesy of Martha Quigley.

"Bad Tom" Smith, a gunman hired by French, the confessed killer of Joe Eversole, in a sketch from the *Cincinnati Enquirer*, 1894. Smith's hanging in Breathitt County in June 1895 drew throngs. Courtesy of *Kentucky Explorer Magazine*.

Craig Tolliver, an elected lawman who at times showed little concern for the niceties of the law. A leader of the Tolliver forces in Rowan County, Craig was killed in a shootout on the streets of Morehead in 1887. From *Days of Anger, Days of Tears,* courtesy of Juanita Blair and Fred Brown.

Daniel Boone Logan, young Morehead attorney who put an end to the Martin-Tolliver feud by leading a small army that wiped out most of the Tollivers. He later became a prominent businessman in Bell County. Courtesy of Pauline Asher Logan.

Above, the American Hotel and Saloon, Morehead. Legend has it that when Craig Tolliver expressed a desire to own the hotel, the owner sold it to him for $250 and left town. Tolliver may be the fourth man from the left wearing, strangely, a white hat. From *Frank Leslie's Illustrated Weekly*, courtesy of Morehead State University Special Collections. *Below*, the state militia pitched their tents on the lawn of the Rowan County Courthouse in Morehead in 1886 in another futile effort by Governor Procter Knott to restore order. From *Frank Leslie's Illustrated Weekly*, courtesy of Juanita Blair and Fred Brown.

Above, the Morehead Normal School, which grew to be Morehead State University. A son of feudist Z. T. Young helped obtain state funds for the fledgling school. Courtesy of Morehead State University Special Collections.

Above, the state militia on guard in Morehead. When the militia left, the feud resumed. From *Frank Leslie's Illustrated Weekly.* Courtesy of Morehead State University Special Collections.

Above, with the South Fork of the Kentucky River in flood, a Clay County logger steers his log raft toward a downstream sawmill. It was over such logs that the trouble between the Bakers and the Howards erupted, resulting in the ambush killing of the Howards and the eventual murder of Thomas "Bad Tom" Baker. Courtesy of the Matlack Collection, Photographic Archives, University of Louisville. *Below*, Tom Baker's home on Crane Creek near Jess Hollow as it looks today. Soon after the Baker-Howard fight on the log raft, someone (possibly Jim Howard) shot at Bad Tom as he sat on his porch. The bullet missed him and lodged in the door frame. Photo by Stanely DeZarn.

Above, the Clay County Courthouse in Manchester, with the tents of the state militia on its lawn in 1899. The troops were there to guard Tom Baker, who was being tried for the murder of Wilson Howard and Burch Stores. Courtesy of Stanley DeZarn. *Left,* Tom Baker, photographed on the afternoon of June 10, 1899, moments before he was shot and killed by a sniper. Much of the fury of the Baker-Howard feud died with him. Photo from the *Courier-Journal,* Louisville.

James Ballenger "Big Jim" Howard, a tall, quiet Clay County tax assessor and leader of the Howard clan in its feud with the Bakers. His life was blighted and his reputation stained by two murders, one of which he probably did not commit. From Caleb Powers, *My Story.*

Henry E. Youtsey, an emotional and eccentric state employee who was tried and imprisoned, along with Jim Howard and Caleb Powers, for conspiracy to assassinate Governor William Goebel. Governor Augustus Willson, who later pardoned Powers and Howard, said he considered Youtsey the guilty party. From Caleb Powers, *My Story.*

The remains of the home of Ballard Howard on Crane Creek, built around 1845, where his sons, including Jim, were born. Originally log, it is now covered with boards. After Bal was shot from ambush by the Bakers, he was brought back home to recuperate. Courtesy of Stanley DeZarn.

The Reverend John Jay Dickey, a lovable, selfless Methodist minister who founded the first newspaper in Breathitt County and the first school, now Lees College. He went from Breathitt to Clay County, hoping—and failing—to bring peace through religion. Courtesy of Richard Weiss, Archivist, Kentucky Wesleyan College.

Della and Esther Davidson, students at Clay County's Oneida Institute, whose father and brother were killed in the Clay War. Courtesy of the Matlack Collection, Photographic Archives, University of Louisville.

Captain Strong's Last Ride

Big John Aikman was home from the penitentiary in little more than a year, having been given the pardon that seemed routine at the time. Obtaining pardons for men in prison was one of the strongest weapons of state legislators and officials; relatives did not forget at election time the official who had gotten their husband or brother pardoned, and governors were inclined to go along, especially with members of their own parties. As a result, a life sentence was often little more than an extended vacation away from home.

Captain Bill Strong was still in command of his forces on the North Fork. But as Breathitt County entered the 1880s, peace of a sort reigned, partly because new clan leaders were emerging and a realignment of forces was taking place. The roots of the feud between the Callahan and Deaton families, usually called the Callahan-Strong feud, grew out of the old Civil War rivalry between Captain Bill Strong and Wilson Callahan. Captain Bill, according to legend, had condemned Wilson Callahan to death at one of his courts-martial. Ed Callahan, leader of the Callahan forces, was Wilson's grandson. The aging Captain Strong, who as he grew older was known almost affectionately as "Uncle Bill," was allied with James Deaton in opposition to the Callahans. It would prove to be Captain Bill's last ride.

Ed Callahan was a tall, heavy-featured man, a shrewd businessman and a ruthless competitor. He had inherited considerable land on the Middle Fork of the Kentucky River containing rich stands of timber and good farmland. Though his family had fought for the Union during the Civil War, Callahan became influential in the Democratic Party in Breathitt. More important, perhaps, he had managed to become the captain or leader of the Ku Klux Klan, and under his leadership the Klan grew to more than a thousand members. Some historians insist that these mountain groups were not klaverns of the real Ku Klux Klan, which had prescribed uniforms or robes, rules, and hierarchy, but can more accurately be termed Regulators, ad hoc informal armies, like the one in Rowan County, that usually operated under a loose leadership in the absence of accepted legal order. But by whatever designation, it exerted a strong influence throughout the county. It also helped Ed Callahan accumulate, for his time, considerable wealth. As he approached thirty, he was a man to be reckoned with. Young men volunteered eagerly to serve him. On election days, or when the Democrats were holding a convention, he would often ride into Jackson leading a force of four or five hundred men.

On the other side of the ledger was James Deaton, Callahan's rival in business and politics. He also had the support of a small army, most of them enemies of the Callahans and/or former followers of Captain Strong, and on convention days Deaton, like Callahan, rode at the head of several hundred men. Deaton was arrogant and boastful and several times made fun of the younger Callahan when they met at political functions.

Like the Callahans, the Deatons were a large and powerful family, but not all the Deatons were allied with James Deaton against Ed Callahan, partly because they regarded Captain Strong, Deaton's chief ally, as their primary enemy and didn't want anything to do with anyone, even a Deaton, who was in league with him. James Deaton was not very fond of Strong, either, and while he accepted his support, he didn't invite it and did not often consult with Strong.

Callahan and Deaton were always on the verge of conflict, partly because they owned adjoining land from which they both cut valuable timber which they rafted or floated from the same sandbar on the Kentucky. Usually a logger would fell his trees, cut them into uniform lengths, and burn or notch his brand into the butt end of each; he would then tie his logs, usually a hundred, into a raft. The raft would be put together on a bar or a flat place along the riverbank where it would be floated when the river rose with spring floods and carried downstream to the sawmill. Sometimes one logger would buy logs from another; he would then "dehorn" or cut off the brand of the original logger, put on his own brand, and incorporate the log into his raft. This could lead to friction because log thieves were common along the river. They would snag logs, dehorn them, put on their own brand, and sell them as their own. Both Ed Callahan and James Deaton had accused the other of dehorning logs, and both were rumored to have gone out on moonless nights and cut the lines holding the other's rafts. Both stationed guards at their rafting sites, and their clashes were the basis for a stream of lawsuits.

The Callahan-Deaton rivalry burst into open battle one day when Ed Callahan happened to go by the sandbar where both his men and a Deaton crew were rafting logs. Spotting a peavy or canthook, a tool used for turning logs, Callahan walked over, picked it up, and announced that it was his, in effect accusing the Deaton crew of stealing it. Deaton, standing nearby, flew into a rage and, according to the Callahan forces, reached for his rifle. As soon as he touched it, a dozen shots rang out and Deaton fell, dead on the spot.

In court, the Deaton men swore that Callahan had fired the first shot. The Callahan men swore the opposite and said that they had fired only to save Callahan's life. Strangely enough, Bob Deaton, a cousin of the dead man but a Callahan employee, admitted that he had fired the fatal shot. The jury was fed a mass of totally conflicting testimony.

Captain Strong had employed his nephew James B. Marcum, one of the best known and most highly respected attorneys in Kentucky, to prosecute the Callahans, and in the following years this fact turned out to be more important than the outcome of the trial, marking as it did the beginning of the hostility between Marcum and the Callahans.

As the trial progressed, it began to appear that Marcum was getting the better of the argument and that Callahan would not get off scot free. But one night while the trial was in session, a friendly guard let Callahan out of jail, and he proceeded to the boardinghouse where the jury members were housed. The husband of the woman who ran the boardinghouse was a member of the jury, and Callahan persuaded her (reportedly with a hundred dollars) to let him speak directly to the jury members. The majority of the jury were Ku Kluxers and for acquittal at any rate, but Callahan took no chances. Within an hour he was back in jail and sleeping soundly. The verdict of not guilty is said to have cost him less than $500.

But then someone, probably Captain Strong, overreached. It was rumored that Hen Kilburn, Strong's chief gunman, had been waiting for months for a chance to kill William Tharp, a prominent farmer said to have been condemned to death by Strong's court. Hen's chance came when he heard that Tharp was riding into Jackson alone. He stationed himself and his rifle, "The Death of Many," in bushes above the trail and killed Tharp. He soon discovered his error. Tharp was not only a respected citizen but an honored member of the Klan, and within hours Kilburn was arrested and thrown into jail. The same day Ed Callahan sent out word for every member of the Klan and every Callahan follower to report at ten o'clock that night "around the courthouse."

Shortly after dark the riders began arriving, and by ten o'clock a ring of hundreds of men encircled the courthouse and jail. Citizens of Jackson kept to their homes, and guards were posted at the door of practically every house in town.

With Callahan and a few close friends giving the orders, a committee was named to call on Bill Combs, the jailer, and demand the keys to the jail. Combs refused, but since he was a popular and re-spected man, he was not harmed and was allowed to keep the keys, but was escorted from the jail. Members of the mob then took axes and chopped down the jail door, seized Kilburn, and dragged him, struggling and cursing, toward the noose dangling above the front door of the courthouse. A black man, jailed with Kilburn but guilty of nothing more than having taken food to him while he was in hiding, was dragged out, too. Kilburn had been wounded by an axe blow and was bleeding profusely. The black man screamed and begged. But no word was spoken as the two of them were pulled up. Orders were given—and posted on the courthouse door—that the bodies were to be left hanging until after eight o'clock the next morning. The sight of them dangling there was a fearful message to Captain Strong as well as the people of Jackson.

Ed Callahan was now the most powerful individual in Breathitt County. Old Captain Strong seemed not only to realize the fact but to accept it. Increasingly he withdrew from active participation in the political life and conflicts of the county. He was called Uncle Bill by most of his neighbors and apparently assumed that the old enmities had been forgotten. He was wrong. One morning he had to go to the store, saddled up his old mule, put his little grandson on behind him, and made a leisurely ride through the familiar countryside.

At the store, the old captain bought a few things, sat for a while talking, and then began the trip home. He could not know, as he passed up Lick Branch, that Big John Aikman and two of his hench-men were lying in a dense clump of woods above the trail. Big John, released from prison, had vowed for a time that he had found religion and forsworn his violent ways, but in the end the call of the gun was too much. As Captain Strong rode slowly by, Aikman's rifle barked. The first volley killed the old Union bushwhacker. The second burst killed his mule. His grandson fell to the ground, screaming, as Aik-man and his men rushed from hiding and riddled the aged captain with a dozen bullets. They did not harm the boy, who ran home with the dread news.

The death of Captain Bill Strong marked an end to the feuds grow-ing out of the Civil War, though most of the feuds were not directly attributable to the war, as some historians have charged; practically all of the feudists had fought on the same side. But the bloodiest feud, one that shattered the image and the social fabric of Breathitt County, while it had no connection to the causes or outcome of the Civil War, sprang directly from the Strong-Callahan-Deaton conflicts.

The Last and Bloodiest Feud

The worst feud to tear Breathitt County apart has come to be known as the Hargis-Cockrell feud, though it might as easily be called the Hargis-Cockrell-Marcum-Callahan War. It started, not surprisingly, over an election. And it involved friends and close relatives. Scratch a feud and you'll find tragedy and heartbreak.

As has happened many times in Breathitt County, the first signs of this trouble appeared in 1898 at a school board election. James B. Marcum, a prominent Republican attorney, accused James Hargis, a former school superintendent, of trying to vote a minor. Tempers flared and, as usual, pistols were drawn—everyone seemed to carry a pistol—but friends prevented any shooting. Marcum and Hargis had been friends, but after this the relationship became hostile.

But the real trouble began with the elections of 1902. Hargis was Democratic candidate for county judge and Ed Callahan was candidate for sheriff, but some Democrats were so dissatisfied that they bolted and joined Republicans in a Fusionist ticket. Hargis and Callahan won, but by eighteen votes, and the Fusionists immediately moved to contest the election, charging vote-buying and intimidation, practices not unheard-of in Breathitt.

James Marcum and O.H. Pollard had been friends for many years and together formed one of the most prestigious law firms in Eastern Kentucky. But they fell out over the elections, and the partnership was dissolved. Pollard favored—and represented—the Democrats; Marcum represented the Republicans or Fusionists.

The political alignment of Breathitt County at the turn of the century reflected the shifting political currents of the region in the postwar era. Breathitt had been strongly pro-Union during the Civil War, as was most of Eastern Kentucky, and after the war some of the leaders, especially in the Strong camp, became Republican. But by the time the Hargis-Cockrell conflict erupted the county usually voted Democratic. Judge David Redwine of Jackson presided over the Democratic convention of 1899 that selected the controversial William

Goebel as Democratic candidate for governor, and in the voting for governor in 1899 Breathitt voted for Goebel.

The reason for this Democratic strength is not clear. A clue may be found in the popularity of the Regulator groups often claiming to be part of the Ku Klux Klan. Their rise reflected a dislike of federal postwar policies, a dislike that in part accounted for the pro-southern sympathies so prevalent in Kentucky following the war. Many slave-holding Kentuckians had remained loyal to the Union in the war and felt betrayed when Lincoln freed their slaves without compensating them for their loss. Others resented what they considered the high-handed methods of Union commanders who, in the months follow-ing the war, occupied Kentucky and treated its citizens as though the state had been in rebellion. And many simply hated blacks for their role in causing the disastrous war and for what whites considered their insolent or "uppity" conduct after emancipation. Thus many former Union soldiers became members of the Ku Klux Klan, harass-ing not only blacks but people friendly with federal officials.

It is strange that Marcum let political differences split his law firm. He had practiced in Breathitt for seventeen years and had represented the largest corporations doing business in Eastern Kentucky, including the Lexington and Eastern Railroad. He was a trustee of Kentucky State College (later the University of Kentucky) and a U.S. commis-sioner. His partner, O.H. Pollard, was almost equally prominent.

Relations between the two men remained polite, if chilly, until depositions concerning the election contest were taken in Marcum's office. Hargis and Callahan were there, as well as Pollard. Marcum was cross-examining a witness when Pollard objected to the line of questioning and the two former partners almost came to blows. Hargis and Callahan drew pistols, and Marcum ordered everyone to leave his office. Police Judge T.P. Cardwell subsequently issued war-rants for the arrest of the principals. Marcum appeared in court, con-fessed that he had drawn a pistol, and paid a fine of twenty dollars, but Hargis, for years a political enemy of Cardwell, refused to be tried by him. Tom Cockrell, at the time town marshal of Jackson, was sent to arrest Hargis and bring him into court. Cockrell took his brother Jim with him.

When Tom Cockrell informed Hargis that he was under arrest and asked him to come with him, Hargis started to draw his pistol. Cock-rell beat him to the draw, but Sheriff Ed Callahan, standing nearby, pulled his pistol and covered Cockrell. At the same time Jim Cockrell pulled his pistol and covered Callahan. Hargis and Callahan, seeing that they were outgunned, two pistols to one, surrendered. But Marcum had sent word to Cardwell that he did not want to prosecute Hargis and asked that his case be dismissed. This was done, and everyone hoped that friendly relations might be reestablished.

That was not to be. Several months later Marcum and Callahan had an argument over a school election. The trouble was settled amicably, but Marcum then charged Callahan with the murder of Marcum's uncle, and Callahan accused Marcum of assassinating his father. Something seemed to be happening to Marcum, embittering him. His actions at times seemed to invite trouble.

Then violence erupted. Town Marshal Tom Cockrell and Ben Hargis, a brother of James, met in a "blind tiger" (an illegal saloon—Breathitt had voted dry in 1871) and got into an argument. One thing led to another, both men drew pistols, and Ben Hargis was killed. Judge James Hargis and his brother, State Senator Alex Hargis, insisted on prosecuting Tom Cockrell for murder.

Dr. D.B. Cox, the leading physician of Breathitt, was the legal guardian of the orphaned Cockrell children, including Tom, who, though still under twenty-one, was town marshal. Dr. Cox had married a sister of Police Judge Cardwell and was a close friend of James Marcum, who agreed to defend Tom Cockrell without fee. Indeed, the Hargis-Cockrell feud, like the earlier conflicts, pitted relatives against each other. Senator Alex Hargis was married to a sister of J.B. Marcum. (Breathitt historian E.L. Noble says she was Marcum's niece.) Curtis Jett's father was a brother of Tom and Jim Cockrell's mother. Curtis Jett's mother (he became a major figure in the violence) was a half-sister of James and Alex Hargis. And so on. It is hard to see how these people managed an amicable home life, being constantly at war with their in-laws.

Jerry Cardwell, a cousin of Police Judge T.P. Cardwell and a member of the Cockrell faction, was a railroad detective. It was not his primary duty to keep order on passenger trains, that being the task of the conductor, but on this particular occasion he was riding in the passenger coach toward Jackson when John "Tige" Hargis, who had been drinking, became disorderly, cursing and waving a pistol. The conductor complained to Cardwell, who tried to quiet Hargis and, when Hargis kept threatening to shoot, tried to arrest him. Hargis resisted. Both fired. Cardwell was wounded, Hargis was killed. The Hargis family, charging that Cardwell had picked the fight and killed John without provocation, took him to court, and he was sentenced to two years in prison. Upon appeal, however, he was pardoned by Governor W.O. Bradley, left Breathitt, and went to live in Wolfe County. Two weeks after Tige was killed, Elbert Hargis, a half-brother of Judge

James Hargis, was shot from ambush and killed in the yard of his home in Jackson while making sorghum molasses. No one was ever arrested for the murder. The Hargises were understandably alarmed and angry. Ben, John, and Elbert had been killed, and no one was in prison for their deaths.

A few days later Dr. Cox received a message around eight o'clock at night asking him to attend a sick woman living near Jackson. He left, telling his wife that he would return shortly, but as he reached the corner across from the courthouse and opposite the stable of Judge Hargis, he was shot and killed. His murderer then ran up and fired another shot into the body. It was reported that the shot came from Judge Hargis's stable. Members of the Cockrell faction charged, of course, that Dr. Cox had been killed because of his interest in the defense of Tom Cockrell, and in court it was charged that Judge Hargis and Ed Callahan were watching from the second floor of Hargis's home when the fatal shot was fired. They said they didn't know anything about it. Never heard any shot.

Jim Cockrell, who had been busy gathering evidence for the trial of his brother Tom, succeeded Tom as Jackson town marshal. It was not an easy time to be marshal. He hadn't been in office long before he ran into Curtis Jett one night in the dining room of the Arlington Hotel. Words led to pistols. Neither man was hurt, though the dining room was battered. Then, at noon on June 28, Marshal Jim Cockrell was killed by a shot fired from a window on the second floor of the court-house. Judge James Hargis and Sheriff Ed Callahan were standing on the second floor of Hargis's store and saw Cockrell fall. Though law officers, they did nothing to assist him.

It was widely rumored that Curtis Jett, at the time a deputy of Sheriff Ed Callahan, did the killing and that he remained in the court-house until that night, when friends brought a horse to the side door and helped him ride off, undetected. Jett was a dangerous, hot-tempered young man who apparently took part—and a very bloody part—in the feud for the excitement of it. He was the son of Hiram Jett, who had left Breathitt for Madison County after making peace with the Littles, and the grandson of Curtis Jett Sr., a prominent merchant who took no part in the troubles.

Attorneys for Tom Cockrell, charged with killing Ben Hargis, asked Judge David Redwine to vacate the bench in the Cockrell case, since he was known to be a close political friend of Judge Hargis. Redwine stepped down, and Judge Ira Julian, of Frankfort, appointed in his place, granted a defense request for a change of venue. The case was transferred to Campton, in Wolfe County. But Judge Hargis and his brother Alex, who had brought the suit against Cockrell, refused to go to Campton. They protested that if they had to travel the road from Jackson to Campton their enemies would ambush them along the way, that they would never reach Campton alive. Judge Julian had no choice but to dismiss the case.

They probably were not exaggerating the danger. In a letter to the *Lexington Herald*, J.B. Marcum declared that over thirty men had been killed in Breathitt since Hargis took office as county judge, "and Lord knows how many wounded." In a similar letter written on May 25, 1903, Mrs. Marcum stated that there had been "thirty eight homicides in Breathitt County during the administration of Judge James Hargis."

The most notable among these was J.B. Marcum himself, who was shot down in the Breathitt County Courthouse on May 4, 1903. The shooting could hardly have been a total surprise. Ever since Marcum became attorney for the plaintiffs in the suit contesting the county elections, there had been reported threats against his life. On November 14, 1902, he said, in a written statement:

I heard the rumor that Dr. Cox and I were to be assassinated; he and I discussed these rumors and concluded that they were groundless. I went to Washington D.C. and stayed a month. While I was there Dr. Cox was assassinated. I was attorney for Mose Feltner. On the night of May 30th he came to my house in Jackson and stated that he had entered into an agreement with certain officials to kill me. He said that their plan was for him to entice me to my office that night, and for him to waylay me and kill me. He said that the county officials had guaranteed him immunity from punishment [for the earlier killing of a man named Fields], and he led them to believe he would kill me to secure their protection, all the time warning me of plans to kill me. He could visit me without arousing suspicion as he was my client and supposed to pretend friendship for me.

For weeks Marcum had been afraid to go outside his home, and in an affidavit he filed with the circuit court he declared that he was "marked for death." He was. Even after some of the bitterness of the election contest wore off, Marcum seldom went to his offices without taking his small grandson with him, thinking that would-be assassins would not chance hitting the child. (Again, some say that Marcum took his baby son, not grandson, with him for protection.)

But on the morning of May 4 he went alone to the courthouse to file some papers in the election case. After filing, he walked from the clerk's office to the front door, where he stood talking to his friend Captain Benjamin Ewen. Suddenly there was a shot from the hallway behind them, and Marcum slumped forward. "Oh, Lordy," he moaned, "I'm shot. They've killed me!" Ewen turned and saw Curtis Jett raise his pistol and fire another shot through Marcum's head. Marcum fell forward, brushing Ewen, who ran from the doorway to avoid being shot. He testified that a few minutes later he saw Jett and Tom White near the side door of the courthouse and heard Jett "express satisfaction with his aim."

Marcum's body lay in the doorway for some time (some witnesses later said it lay there an hour, others said it was only fifteen minutes), since his friends were afraid to approach the body and the local officers were paying no attention. At the time Marcum was shot, Judge James Hargis and Sheriff Ed Callahan were sitting in rocking chairs in the front door of Hargis's store, across from the courthouse, from where they had a clear view of the courthouse doorway where Marcum fell and of the hallway where the killer fired the shot. They looked on with some interest but without deserting their rocking chairs. It was generally assumed that they were not taken entirely by surprise.

Three weeks later, on May 21, 1903, Curtis Jett and Tom White were indicted for the murder of Marcum. White was a drifter who had come to Jackson a few days previously to get a job, he said, but he had applied only to Elbert Hargis. Also accused, but on the lesser charge of conspiracy to murder, were Mose Feltner, John Smith, and John Abner. But it was the case against Jett that drew national attention.

Tom Wallace, then a reporter for the *Louisville Times*, described the joys of covering the trial before it was transferred to Harrison County:

When we—the militia and reporters—arrived, not one light was burning inside any Jackson residence. Householders ate their evening meal while it was still light and sat in the dark till it was time to feel the way to bed. It was feared that the roystering young men who fired pistols in the streets at night might shoot at any residence light and kill someone sitting near it. Jackson sidewalks were made of plank. After dark people feared to walk on the sidewalks lest the rattling of a loose plank cause someone to shoot in the direction of the sound. The custom was to walk in the street where footfalls in the dust—streets were not paved—would be soundless. There was danger that two persons walking in the dark might collide. I know one man who carried a lantern swung about six feet from his shoulder on a pole. His hope was that if anyone should shoot at the lantern he would not be hit. On one occasion a warm controversy between a lawyer for the defense and the prosecutor was mistaken by the courthouse audience for a quarrel which might develop violence. Immediately the courtroom bristled with pistols drawn from under-arm holsters.

It would seem to have been a fairly open-and-shut case, but it created a sensation, even when transferred to Harrison County and the court of Judge J.J. Osborne. For two hired guns, Jett and White were defended by a remarkable group of attorneys, including Judge B.F. French (a notorious survivor of the French-Eversole feud in neighboring Perry County), John O'Neal of Covington, Captain Ben Golden of Barbourville, prominent Republican James Black, J.T. Blanton, and the firm of Rafferty and King.

Their efforts could not overcome the overwhelming evidence against the accused. Captain Ewen testified that he had seen Tom White pass him and Marcum in the courthouse doorway, staring at Marcum to make him turn so that he could be shot in the back. He also testified that after Marcum was shot, he (Ewen) turned and saw Jett holding a pistol in both hands and saw him take two steps forward and fire another shot through Marcum's head, and that later he saw Jett come out the side door of the courthouse.

Other witnesses testified that Jett had been seen with White before the killing and that, after the two shots were fired, White was seen to motion to Jett in the side courthouse door, and that the two of them left hurriedly. It took the jury only a short while to bring in a guilty verdict. Both Jett and White were sentenced to prison for life.

Tried with them were Mose Feltner, John Abner, and John Smith. Feltner testified that he, Abner, and Smith had been hired by James Hargis, Ed Callahan, and Fult French to kill Marcum but had failed to do so. Abner and Smith supported his testimony. Charges against Smith were dismissed following his confession. He later became the bitter enemy of Ed Callahan and was suspected of an attempt to kill him. The others were acquitted.

Curtis Jett was only twenty-four at the time. Tall, red-haired, and blue-eyed, he had, according to reporter Tom Wallace, a mean, hard-eyed look, thin lips, and a short chin. He was a cousin of the Cockrell brothers but had been suspected of killing Tom Cockrell. Jett had an unenviable reputation. He had been in jail a half dozen times for shooting and disorderly conduct, twice accused of rape, and twice tried for shooting and wounding. In prison he proved to be an obstreperous prisoner until, according to his own testimony, he heard the call of heaven, accepted Jesus Christ as his savior, and "got religion." He later became a preacher of sorts.

Judge James Hargis and Ed Callahan were indicted for complicity in the murder of J.B. Marcum but, after five trials, were acquitted. Interviewed by Tom Wallace, Hargis swore that he had nothing to do with any assassination and said that he did not approve of it "except when a man is so mean he deserves to die."

"But who would be the judge?" asked Wallace.

"Who," replied Hargis, "but them as knows him best?" That proved to be an ominous statement.

Though Hargis and Callahan escaped prison, Mrs. Marcum, widow of the slain J.B. Marcum, sued them for being instrumental in the death of her husband and was awarded eight thousand dollars by the court. They paid. If there was justice concealed in all this, it was well concealed.

The famed Hargis-Cockrell feud was, for all practical purposes, over. Two nights after Captain Ben Ewen testified against Curtis Jett, his home was burned. People in central Kentucky, led by the *Louisville Courier-Journal*, took up a purse to help him rebuild. He was also booked for a series of lectures in and around Cincinnati on the Breathitt violence, but drew smaller audiences than had been expected.

Judge Hargis at one point declared that he was sick of the violence that had marked his life and announced that he was preparing to sell his properties in Breathitt County and move to Lexington. Speaking for himself and his brother Alex, he told the *Lexington Herald*: "We began our business twenty years ago poor men, and we have accumulated wealth and position by dint of our industry. We own thousands of acres of land in this county, and lands and stores in other places. We never had any difficulty in our lives and we had no motive to assassinate Marcum or Cockrell or anyone else. Marcum was as intense a Republican as his uncle, Bill Strong, and he was willing to go to any extremity to further the interest of his party."

Ben Ewen announced that if the Hargises did move, he might go back to Breathitt to live. But before Hargis could move—if he had ever seriously contemplated moving—he ran into trouble at home.

Hargis's son, Beach, was known as a bad drinker, erratic and probably unbalanced. According to *Kentucky Reports* (Vol. 135), Beach, on or about February 16, 1908, came into the Hargis store and asked a clerk to give him a pistol. The clerk refused but pointed out that there was a pistol in the drawer of his father's desk. Beach took it and left but turned up the next morning with a badly swollen face, telling the barber into whose shop he stormed that "the old man hit me." This would not have been startling news. His father reportedly had beat him regularly as a boy, and even after he was grown would whip him with a rope or a pistol, and once beat his head on the floor.

Beach drank a bottle of Brown's Bitters, went to the drugstore of his brother-in-law, Dr. Hogg, and waved the pistol about, pointing it at several customers. He then went to his father's store and took a seat in a chair near the door. His father, seeing him, said to another man in the room, "He has gotten to be a perfect vagabond, and he is destroying my business, and if Dr. Hogg lets him stay there he will ruin his business."

After saying this, Judge Hargis walked toward Beach, who got out of the chair, walked behind a spool cabinet, and, as his father approached, shot him. Hargis shouted and grabbed him, and as they struggled Beach shot him four more times. By the time onlookers reached them, Hargis had Beach down, and had the pistol. "He has shot me all to pieces," he said. He was right. He died a few minutes later.

Beach was indicted, tried, and sentenced to life in prison, though defended by a prestigious array of attorneys led by former Governor W.O. Bradley, Judge D.B. Redwine, J.J.C. Bach, Sam H. Kash, and Thomas L. Cope. After a few years he was paroled and returned to Jackson.

One score was left, and it was not settled for some time. Some had not forgotten the murders of Marcum and the Cockrells. John Smith, for one, had become an avowed enemy of Ed Callahan, and Callahan knew it. He took steps to protect himself from ambush, but on May 3, 1910, as he was standing in his store at Crockettsville, he was shot by someone standing on a bank opposite the building. He survived the wound and built a stockade around his home and store so that he could go from his house to his store without exposing himself to gunfire. But on May 3, 1912, he was shot while crossing the front room of his store by someone hidden in the same spot from which he had been shot exactly two years earlier. This time he did not survive.

There were other minor disturbances in Jackson in 1941, but the feuds had run their course, leaving in their wake a heritage of violence and the nickname "Bloody Breathitt," which lingered long after any justification for it remained.

PIKE, PERRY, AND ROWAN COUNTIES
Mayhem Everywhere

No Romeo, No Juliet, No Heroes

Of all the feuds that tore the mountains of Eastern Kentucky during the nineteenth century, the Hatfield-McCoy feud was surely the strangest. It didn't amount to much—a dozen people killed over a period of eight or ten years—but mainly because of sensational coverage by press and magazine writers, it was blown out of all proportion. Today, thanks to folklore and legend, it is still thought of as a mountain bloodbath, a time of terror in the hills, or as the story of Romeo and Juliet in the mountains. It was none of these.

Actually, were it not for the legend and for the political problems that accompanied and helped prolong the feud, it would not be worth recounting, but it has been taken very seriously by historians and sociologists. Probably the best straightforward account of the feud is *The Hatfields and the McCoys*, written in 1978 by Otis K. Rice of West Virginia Institute of Technology. The most unusual—and thorough—survey of the feud is *Feud: Hatfields, McCoys and Economic Change in Appalachia, 1860-1900*, by Altina Waller of the State University of New York. Her work is more a study of the economic transition of the remote valley where the feud occurred than of the feud itself, but perhaps that puts the feud into a more logical context. If it hadn't happened when and where it happened, probably few people would have paid much attention. As it was, the killing associated with the feud was almost over before the press began its sensational coverage, which was usually full of error. And the latter half of what is called the Hatfield-McCoy feud was actually a battle between other men trying to use the feud to further their political and economic ambitions.

Waller's view of the feudists is more charitable than most, depicting both Hatfields and McCoys as solid mountain folk caught in economic and social changes brought about by the advent of industrialism in the form of railroads and mining. She sees Randolph (Ranel or Randal) McCoy as a moping failure who resented Anderson ("Devil

Anse") Hatfield for his greater entrepreneurial success more than for the Hatfields' murder of his family. Tolbert McCoy stabbed Ellison Hatfield because of his feelings of inferiority, not because he was a mean drunk. And so on.

Waller may be right. Certainly hers is the most painstaking study of the feud. But the layman, lacking psychological or sociological expertise, might be forgiven for seeing the feudists as two groups of basically backward, mean-tempered people, by no stretch of the imagination mountain aristocracy. It is true that descendants of Devil Anse Hatfield, like the offspring of many of our frontier thugs and robber barons, rose to positions of prominence, as did some McCoys. But, again, it is hard to see Anse himself as much more than an illiterate, selfish killer and a rather cowardly one at that, a frontier Godfather who sent his minions out to kill off his enemies, and who let them go to prison and the gallows for it while he sat back and profited from the killings.

How did it start in the first place? Was it because of a hog, as some have claimed? Emotional holdovers from the Civil War? A romance shattered by family hatred? Was it a clash of modernism with mountain tradition? As Kentucky historian James C. Klotter has written, it is unlikely that there was one single cause. "In their time," he says, "the Hatfields and McCoys fought for justice as they envisioned it." And Otis Rice probably puts it succinctly when he says in his study of the trouble between the two families, "The conflict grew out of an accumulation of honest grievances and imagined wrongs" rather than a specific incident.

Whatever its causes, the bad blood between the families burst into open violence on August 7, 1882, at the Blackberry Creek precinct polling place in Pike County, Kentucky. Though they lived across the Tug Fork of the Big Sandy River, in Logan (now Mingo) County, West Virginia, the Hatfields ordinarily came over for the day, since election day was a social as well as a political occasion. The women cooked a lot of food, the men brought a lot of whiskey, and there was a great deal of visiting and talking, and flirting among the young.

The Tug was more a geographic than a social boundary. Many Hatfields lived on the Kentucky side of the river, some McCoys or their relatives lived on the West Virginia side. There was quite a bit of social interplay between the two families; McCoy boys referred to Valentine ("Wall") Hatfield as "Uncle Wall," and two of the men who later helped beat her almost to death and burned her home called Sarah McCoy "Aunt Sally." A Hatfield was sheriff of Pike County,

Kentucky, and several were magistrates when the feud was in full cry. Trouble-making Johnse Hatfield married Nancy McCoy. And so on. But little frictions build into major conflicts. Time and circumstance.

On this particular election day, August 7, 1882, Tolbert McCoy, with a good load of whiskey aboard, chose the occasion to demand that Elias ("Bad Lias") Hatfield pay him the $1.75 that Tolbert claimed Lias owed him. Lias replied angrily that he had paid the debt months before. Tolbert called him a liar. Deacon Anse Hatfield (not to be confused with Devil Anse) was able to calm the two, but just then Ellison Hatfield awoke from a liquor-induced nap and called Tolbert names. Tolbert turned his wrath on Ellison. Pulling a knife, he hacked away at Ellison's stomach, while Tolbert's brothers, nineteen-year old Pharmer and fifteen-year old Randolph Jr., rushed to help him. Ellison tried to wrestle the knife away from Tolbert, but the two younger McCoys also began cutting at him. When Deacon Anse again tried to separate the battlers, Ellison grabbed a large rock. Pharmer pulled a pistol and shot Ellison in the back. Elias wrested the pistol from Pharmer and tried to shoot him, but the McCoys at that point turned and ran into the woods.

They were overtaken and placed in the custody of Pike County Justices of the Peace Joe and Tolbert Hatfield and Constable Matthew Hatfield. Figuring that the West Virginia Hatfields would soon try to avenge the shooting of Ellison, Deacon Anse urged that the McCoys be taken to the Pikeville jail at once, where they would be safe. They agreed. They never got there.

This was not the first disagreement between the two clans. Some scholars have tried to trace the feud to the Civil War, but the fact is that the majority of both Hatfields and McCoys fought for the South, though members of both clans, including Devil Anse, leader of the West Virginia clan, deserted and came home well before the war ended. Upon his return home, Devil Anse formed a unit of the Home Guards known as the Logan Wildcats, in whose ranks were several McCoys, including for a while clan leader Randal McCoy. These Home Guards were little more than bushwhackers, foraging to support their ranks and stealing livestock for which they were supposed to pay. Seven years after the war, Asa McCoy was still trying to settle a suit against various Hatfields for four of his hogs they had taken. Various members of the McCoy clan were charged with stealing everything from horses to bee gums and raw leather.

The first real trouble, however, resulted from the death of Harmon McCoy, younger brother of Randal. Unlike most of his family and neighbors, Harmon joined the Union Army. He stayed only a year and came home after being hospitalized with a broken leg. He was not given a big welcome. In fact, he was warned that the Logan Wildcats, all ex-Confederates, would be calling on him. This alarmed him, and he hid out in a cave, where the Wildcats caught and killed him. Devil Anse and his lieutenant, Jim Vance, were the wildcats most often mentioned as the trigger men. No one was ever brought to trial for the killing, and it is doubtful if most of the McCoys cared much. But the incident created some tension between the families.

Mountain families at the time let their hogs run loose in the woods; it was cheaper and easier than keeping them penned and having to feed them. They marked their hogs with ear marks or clips so they could identify them when the hogs were rounded up for fall hog-killing. In the autumn of 1878 Floyd Hatfield rounded up his hogs and drove them to his home at Stringtown, on the Kentucky side of the Tug Fork. It was there that Randal McCoy, stopping casually on his way into Stringtown, saw a hog that he thought bore his markings, and said so, in effect accusing Hatfield of stealing his hog. This was a serious insult in the hills, and Floyd took offense, denying it heatedly. Randal, a contentious sort, went immediately to the Deacon Anse Hatfield, a justice of the peace, and brought suit against Floyd.

The trial, held in Deacon Anse's home, brought out the folks from all around. Both Hatfields and McCoys arrived in force, all heavily armed. Deacon Anse saw the danger in a decision that was bound to leave one side unhappy, and in an effort to calm the waters named a jury of six Hatfields and six McCoys, possibly hoping for a hung jury. Among the witnesses was Bill Staton, a nephew of Randal McCoy whose sister had married Ellison Hatfield, younger brother of Devil Anse. Though Staton had ties to both sides, the McCoys were outraged when he testified that he had seen Floyd Hatfield notch the hog's ear. But their anger really boiled over when the jury voted in favor of Floyd Hatfield and it was revealed that Selkirk McCoy, a juryman who was Randal's cousin, said he could find no reason to dispute Staton's word and thus had to vote for Floyd Hatfield. From then on, Selkirk was considered a traitor.

So was Bill Staton, and the McCoys made open threats that they would even the score with him. This was a typical reaction and a root cause of lawlessness in the mountains; people would take their grievances to court, but they would not accept a court ruling that went against them and would turn to direct revenge instead. When, a few weeks later, Sam and Paris McCoy ran into Staton while hunting, shooting began. When it ended, Paris was badly wounded, Staton was dead. Ellison Hatfield swore out a warrant for the arrest of Paris and Sam, and eventually Sam was arraigned in Logan County, West Virginia before Justice of the Peace Wall Hatfield, a brother of Devil Anse. Though he was tried before a jury picked by Hatfields, Sam was acquitted on the grounds of self-defense. The McCoys were surprised but were still indignant because Sam had been arrested by West Virginia authorities, and they were not mollified by reports that Devil Anse had passed the word to the jury to go easy. The McCoys, especially Randal, seemed always to be looking for a chance to be indignant.

So the fires of hostility were smoldering when the two families met at the Blackberry Creek precinct polling place in the spring election of 1880. The West Virginia Hatfields were in good attendance, since they were kin to many of the candidates and other assorted residents, as were the McCoys. Among the visiting Hatfields were Devil Anse, his son Cap, and Johnse, the youngest son, who was not too bright and had a talent for trouble. Described by Otis Rice as "a small-boned rounder of eighteen, dressed fit to kill in yellow shoes, a mail-order suit and a celluloid collar," Johnse was "ruddy, ham-handed, sandy-haired, with blue eyes that set the mountain belles a-flutter. He was a great fellow for putting on the dog." Johnse had already run afoul of the law several times for moonshining, bootlegging, and fighting.

Shortly after Johnse arrived, Tolbert McCoy rode up with his sister Rose Anna riding behind him. Johnse had already met Rose Anna, a pretty, dark-haired, melancholy girl of twenty, but on this occasion she seemed to strike his eye. Johnse struck hers, too, and while the others were eating and drinking, Johnse and Rose Anna sneaked off to the bushes. There they stayed until it was dusk and the visitors had left for home. Afraid to go home, knowing what her father would say, Rose Anna let Johnse persuade her to go home with him. The Hatfields were surprised to see her, as can be imagined, but gave her a decent welcome. Devil Anse, however, put his foot down when Johnse proposed to marry Rose Anna, which probably did not disappoint Johnse too much, since he was already courting Mary Stafford and Nancy McCoy, both cousins of Rose Anna.

Randal tried to get Rose Anna to return home and sent her sisters, Alifair, Josephine, and Adelaide, to try to persuade her, but Rose Anna was smitten and did not leave the Hatfield home until she became convinced Johnse was not going to marry her. When she did leave, she did not go home but to the home of her Aunt Betty at Stringtown, where she was warmly and affectionately welcomed. She may have been pregnant.

That might have ended it, but Johnse, though he would shortly marry Rose Anna's cousin Nancy, kept hanging around near Aunt Betty's house, and poor, love-sick Rose Anna kept slipping out to see him. On one such occasion, they were surprised by old Randal and Pharmer and Jim McCoy, the latter a law officer, who grabbed Johnse and announced that they were taking him to Pikeville to answer indictments for moonshining and other capers. This might have improved matters, but muddle-headed Rose Anna, afraid that her menfolks would kill Johnse, borrowed a horse and rode off toward the Hatfields. Hearing the news, Devil Anse gathered a dozen men, including his top gunman, Jim Vance, took a shortcut, surprised the McCoys, and rescued Johnse. Fortunately, thanks in part to Jim McCoy's courage and cool head, no one was killed, but another brand had been flung on the fire.

Some accounts say that Rose Anna was pregnant at the time and that she later gave birth to a daughter who died in infancy. The *Louisville Courier-Journal* stated that Rose Anna had a boy named Melvin. Another version held that Rose Anna contracted measles and miscarried. At any rate, the following years were not happy for her. Her father never forgave her for warning the Hatfields. And in 1881 Johnse married Nancy McCoy, daughter of the slain Harmon. He lived to regret it. Nancy was as tough as Johnse was weak, and it was soon gossip that he was the worst hen-pecked man along the Tug Fork.

So there was already bad blood between the families when they met on the fateful election day on August 7, 1882, and it is puzzling why Devil Anse and his crew chose to attend. Perhaps he underestimated the resentment of the McCoys, perhaps he felt strong enough to ignore it, or perhaps he had simply been too busy to give it much thought. He was a large landowner over on the West Virginia side of the Tug Valley, and the approach of railroads into the region posed both promise and threat.

But when the McCoy boys cut and shot Ellison Hatfield, Devil Anse again became the concerned leader of his clan. A litter was put together on which Ellison was carried back across the Tug to the home of a Hatfield ally. The three McCoy boys were placed under arrest and started for the county jail at Pikeville. The justices of the peace guarding the McCoys were in no hurry and with their captives spent the night at the home of John Hatfield on Blackberry Creek. The next morning they again set out for Pikeville. They had not gone far before they were overtaken by Devil Anse and a large party of Hatfield men, who simply took the McCoys away from the justices and Old Randal, who was accompanying them. Randal rode toward Pikeville to get help.

Devil Anse and his crew took the McCoy boys across the Tug to West Virginia. With night coming on and a hard rain falling, they spent the night in an abandoned log schoolhouse. They had been there ony a few minutes when Sarah McCoy, Randal's wife and mother of the captives, and her daughter-in-law Mary, Tolbert's wife, arrived and begged to be allowed to see their boys. Wall Hatfield was opposed to the idea, but Devil Anse finally gave permission, and the two women were allowed to stay with the men for some time. Sarah was almost hysterical, crying and pleading for mercy, when someone rode up and announced that Randal McCoy was organizing a rescue party on the other side of the Tug (there was no truth to the rumor), and the women were forced to leave. Sarah came back the next morning but was not allowed to see her sons.

On the afternoon of Wednesday, August 9, 1882, Ellison Hatfield died from his wounds. When the news reached the Hatfields, Devil Anse and his followers tied the McCoy boys together and marched them down to the Tug, where they were taken across in a boat to the Kentucky side. There in a small hollow they were tied to pawpaw bushes while still tied together. Then the Hatfields stood back a few yards and shot the boys to pieces, Devil Anse leading the firing squad.

Not far away Jim McCoy heard the shooting and suspected what was happening. That night he went down to the Tug and found the bodies. One of Tolbert's hands was over his head, as if to ward off the shots, but his skull was blown almost in two. Pharmer's body was riddled. Young Randolph was still in a kneeling position, his head blown almost off.

It was a shocking bit of savagery on the part of the Hatfields, but the officials of Pike County didn't seem to have any idea of how to deal with it. Circuit Judge George Brown impaneled a grand jury that, after ten days of deliberation, returned indictments against twenty men, including Devil Anse, his brothers and sons, and various allies. Four days later Judge Brown issued warrants for seventeen others as witnesses for the state. He might as well have saved his time. When court convened in February 1883, the sheriff reported that he had been unable to arrest any of the indicted men. Even if he had had extradition papers, it is doubtful that he would have gone over into West Virginia to get the Hatfields.

Afterward, the Hatfields still came over into Kentucky, but they came in numbers, and armed. The McCoys did the same when they ventured into West Virginia. This state of affairs continued for five years.

The killing of the McCoy boys seems to have slaked Devil Anse's desire for revenge. Randal McCoy was another story. If the sheriff would not or could not control the Hatfields, perhaps the courts could. Randal finally got in touch with Perry Cline, a Pikeville lawyer who had served in the state House of Delegates and as jailer and deputy sheriff. Cline had reportedly had some unfortunate dealings with Devil Anse over some land and may have welcomed a chance to get even. Furthermore, he still had political ambitions, and a publicized case against the Hatfields, the West Virginia savages who had murdered fine Kentucky boys, might be politically profitable.

Devil Anse had stayed out of the courts for almost five years since slaughtering the McCoy boys and didn't take kindly to the prospect of going to jail now, since he was involved in efforts to develop his holdings in Logan County and did not need adverse publicity or a long prison term. When he heard that Randal was conferring with Perry Cline, he was worried. When he got word that Randal was planning to go into Pikeville, Anse assumed it was to see Cline and decided that he had better stop him. He sent members of his clan across the Tug to ambush McCoy on his way to town. Fortunately for Randal, the gunmen mistook two other men for Randal and his son Calvin and promptly shot and killed John and Henderson Scott, nephews of Randal who had been visiting. (Should these be counted as feud deaths?) Randal and Calvin, leaving home later, rode into town without incident. Devil Anse was upset when he found that his gunmen had killed a couple of strangers.

Once more, the Hatfields had blood on their hands, though no one could prove that they had killed the Scotts. Within days, Cap Hatfield and his friend Tom Wallace added to the trouble. The Hatfields disliked Nancy, Johnse's wife, for browbeating him, which seemed to belittle Hatfield manhood. They suspected that Nancy and her sister Mary, who was married to Bill Daniels, not only carried rumors and gossip but had warned the McCoys of danger several times. So one night Cap and Wallace burst into the Daniels home, and while Cap held Bill Daniels and his daughter at bay, Wallace whipped Mary Daniels with a cow's tail, a painful and degrading punishment. That done, he then guarded Daniels and Mary while Cap whipped their daughter. This was gratifying to Wallace; the Daniels girl had lived with him for a while but had left him and had laughed at his pleas that she return. The Daniels family could identify their assailants if they could find someone to arrest them. They never did.

Then Jeff McCoy, in the fall of 1886, killed Fred Wolford, a Pike County mail carrier, while at a dance (this had nothing to do with the feud), and decided to visit West Virginia for a while. He went to the home of his sister Nancy, Johnse's wife, and there heard of the whipping of his sister Mary and her daughter by Cap Hatfield and Tom Wallace. This infuriated Jeff. He let his temper get the better of his common sense and went after Cap and Wallace. With the help of a friend, Josiah Hurley, he went to Wallace's home, found him working in the field, captured him, and set out to take him to jail in Pikeville. But as they went through the woods, Wallace bolted and escaped. Jeff and Hurley followed him to Cap's cabin and shot the place up, but to no avail, the cabin being too sturdy to take by force.

Cap returned, saw how they had shot up his cabin, and set out to capture the offenders. With a group of helpers, he overtook the two, captured them, and started out with them for Logan. When they stopped at a home along the way, Jeff escaped and made for the Tug Fork and Kentucky. With Cap and Wallace banging away at him, he made the creek, jumped in and, swimming most of the way under water, made the Kentucky shore. But as he attempted to pull himself up the bank, he was shot and killed by Cap.

Devil Anse wrote Perry Cline and said that he was sorry about the killing, that he had no animosity toward relatives of Jeff, and blamed all the commotion on Nancy (McCoy) Hatfield, and Mary (McCoy) Daniels.

Anse had reason to hope that it would all blow over. It was a violent time throughout the Big Sandy Valley, and much of Kentucky. There was, as Otis Rice points out, far more concern among Kentuckians living along the West Virginia border about bands of criminals who operated from both states, preying on the public with impunity, than about the Hatfields and McCoys, who preyed only on each other. Far more serious feuds had been or were tearing apart several other Eastern Kentucky counties, so that regional, state, and national newspapers tended to ignore the Hatfield-McCoy fuss.

But while Anse was willing to stop the trouble, Perry Cline had no such aim. In the governor's race of 1887, Cline promised to deliver the McCoy vote to the Democratic candidate, Simon Bolivar Buckner, who promised in return that if elected he would try to bring the Hatfields to justice.

The idea of facing the authority of the state of Kentucky did not appeal to the Hatfields, and on August 29, 1887, Nat Hatfield dropped a note to Perry Cline:

My name is Nat Hatfield. I am not a single individual by a good many, and we do not live on Tug River but all over this county. We have been told . . . that you and your men are fixing to invade this county for the purpose of taking the Hatfield boys . . . we, forty-nine in number at present, do notify you that if you come into this county to take or bother any of the Hatfields we will follow you to hell or take your hide, and if any of the Hatfields are killed or bothered in any way, we will charge it up to you and your hide will pay the penalty. . . . we have a habit of making one-horse lawyers keep their boots on and we have plenty of good strong rope left. We have no particular pleasure in hanging dogs, but we know you and have counted the miles and marked the tree.

Undeterred, Jake and Larkin McCoy went over into West Virginia to capture Cap Hatfield and Tom Wallace, who had whipped their sister Mary and her daughter. They caught Wallace and took him to Pikeville, but within a week he escaped from jail, probably with the help of the jailer. This irritated the McCoy boys, and in the spring of 1888 Wallace was found dead in a West Virginia field.

Perry Cline, ignoring the increasing hostility, took some indictments against the Hatfields and traveled to Frankfort to ask Governor Buckner to keep his promise. Buckner made a formal request of Governor E.W. Wilson of West Virginia to extradite Devil Anse and nineteen of his clansmen to Kentucky for the murder of the three McCoy boys. Buckner then announced that the state of Kentucky would offer a reward of $500 for the delivery of Anse to the Pike County jail. Upon the advice of Perry Cline, Buckner named Pike County deputy sheriff Frank Phillips to receive the prisoners when and if Governor Wilson delivered them.

Governor Wilson was in no hurry to act. There were a lot of Hatfields and Hatfield supporters in the state, and they flooded the governor's office with requests that the Kentucky request be ignored. Tired of the delay, Perry Cline obtained warrants for twenty of the men mentioned in the indictments, gave them to Frank Phillips, and told him to see what he could do. Considering the awesome reputation of the mountain feudists for marksmanship, it is remarkable to note how much Phillips was able to do.

He was not your ordinary deputy. Kentucky Adjutant General Sam Hill described him as "a handsome little fellow, with piercing black eyes, ruddy cheeks and a pleasant expression, but a mighty unpleasant man to project with." Phillips was reputedly a great hand with the women, given to drink, and possessed of a quick temper. He set out for West Virginia and a week later returned with his first prisoner. It was none other than old Selkirk McCoy, who had earned the McCoy hatred by voting with the Hatfields in the case of Floyd Hatfield's hog. They threw poor Selkirk into the Pikeville jail.

Phillips then seemed to get delusions of grandeur and took it upon himself to engage in interstate diplomacy. He wrote to Governor Wilson (on Perry Cline's stationery), enclosing fifteen dollars for warrants against various Hatfields, saying he was acting as agent of the governor of Kentucky. Wilson replied that fees should be sent to the secretary of state. What Wilson did not say was that he had heard that Perry Cline had persuaded Governor Buckner to offer large rewards for the capture of the Hatfields and had then promised the Hatfields that he would use his influence with the governor to reduce or rescind the rewards if they, the Hatfields, would pay him. There was another report that the Hatfields had promised Cline they would stay out of Kentucky if Buckner would cancel the rewards and that Cline had approved their offer. A.J. Auxier, a Pikeville attorney hired to represent the men indicted for the McCoy murders, said the report was correct and that the Hatfields had given him expense money, $225 of which was to be paid to Cline. G.W. Pinson, clerk of the Pike County Criminal Court, made much the same statement. Obviously, Cline was keeping the feud fires hot and playing both sides for profit.

Governor Wilson was not eager to take part in such crooked antics. Neither was Goveror Buckner. But in his address to the Kentucky legislature on December 31, 1887, Buckner indulged in a bit of flowery oratory concerning his determination to suppress the "violent conduct of a comparatively few lawless individuals." The Hatfields took this as a threat against them.

Phillips had already shown that Kentucky authorities were willing to invade West Virginia to bring Hatfields to trial in Kentucky. Devil Anse could not afford to let that happen to him. He knew that if he went into a Kentucky court for killing the three McCoy boys, he would spend a lot of valuable time in prison. He moved to prevent that. On January 1, 1888, Anse called the clan to assemble. They met at Jim Vance's home. There they decided they had to get rid of Randal McCoy and his family, who could testify against them if they were captured and taken to trial, which was becoming more of a possibility with Frank Phillips tearing around.

Anse complained that he was feeling bad, and Jim Vance was named to head the killing contingent. Under Vance's command were Cap, Johnse, Bob, and Elliott Hatfield, Ellison Mounts (mean, not too bright, often called Cotton or Cotton Top), Tom Chambers, Charles Gillespie, and Doc Ellis. They all swore to follow Vance regardless of danger, and Vance himself swore: "May hell be my heaven, I will kill the man that goes back on me tonight, if powder will burn." That afternoon they set out for the McCoy home. They stopped at Cap's for supper. It was getting dark, but there was a bright moon, and they crossed the Tug and rode toward the McCoy home without trouble, on the way passing the polling place where the trouble had started.

Vance ordered his men not to shoot until he gave the signal. Silently, they surrounded the McCoy home where Randal, his son Calvin, his wife Sarah, and their daughters Alifair, Josephine, and Adelaide were sleeping. Vance called for the McCoys to come out and surrender as prisoners of war. Calvin jumped into his clothes, ran downstairs, and told his mother to stay in bed. Then he went back upstairs, while Randal manned a downstairs window. About that time, against orders, thick-headed Johnse fired off a premature shot into the cabin, and shooting began in general. Johnse was the first hit, getting a load of shot in the shoulder.

Vance ran to the side of the cabin and tried to set it on fire. Chambers lighted a pine knot, climbed from a pile of logs to the cabin roof, and tried to poke the flaming knot into the loft, but Calvin fired from below, blowing a hole in the roof, temporarily blinding Chambers and blowing off three of his fingers. But the fire set by Vance fared better and soon was spreading dangerously.

Calvin called on the girls to try to put it out, and they threw what water they had in the house on the flames, but when they tried to get outside for more, Vance warned that he would kill them if they stepped outside. They then threw what buttermilk they had in a churn on the blaze, but the fire still spread.

Alifair opened the kitchen door for air. Seeing the men in the bright moonlight, she called out to Cap that she recognized him. Cap and Johnse called to Ellison Mounts to shoot her. Mounts fired and Alifair collapsed. Josephine screamed, and Calvin, hearing her, called down to ask what was the matter. Josephine cried that Alifair had been shot. Sarah, hearing this, left her bed and ran to where Alifair lay sprawled, halfway out the door. Vance ordered her back into the house and raised his rifle as if to shoot. She knelt and crawled toward her daughter but Vance struck her with his rifle, knocking her to the ground.

"Oh, God," she cried, "let me go to my girl! Oh, she's dead! For the love of God, let me go to her!" Again Vance swung his rifle, breaking her hip. Sarah put out a hand and tried to rise, but Johnse pulled his pistol and beat her over the head until she lay motionless on the ground.

As the fire spread, Calvin realized that something drastic had to be tried. "I'm going to make for the corn crib," he told Randal. "That'll draw their fire. When I do, you go out the front and try to make it to the woods."

It worked. Running, dodging, Calvin almost made it to the crib before a fusillade cut him down. But while the Hatfields were concentrating on him, Randal, carrying his rifle and extra bullets, reached the woods. Vance knew it would be foolhardy to follow him. With the cabin in full flames, they set fire to the smokehouse and rode off toward West Virginia, knowing they had failed badly. They could hear the cries of the girls as they rode away. Mounts, Chambers, and Johnse were wounded. Behind them they left Calvin and Alifair dead and Sarah critically wounded, with an arm and hip broken and her skull crushed.

When Randal came from behind a pigpen where he had been hiding, he found that Adelaide and Josephine had made good their escape and had come back and built a fire, trying to protect their mother from the cold. Neighbors, attracted by the sight of fire in the night, rushed to the McCoy home, horrified at what they found. They carried Sarah to the home of her son Jim. Two days later Calvin and Alifair were buried alongside their three brothers, Tolbert, Pharmer, and Randolph Jr. Sarah was taken by wagon to the home of Perry Cline in Pikeville. There she was tended by her daughter Rose Anna, who left her Aunt Betty's and made the care of her mother her one cause in her morose, lonely life.

Regional newspapers, which had largely ignored the Hatfield-McCoy trouble in their preoccupation with better known feuds, now paid it attention, though often erroneously. The *Courier-Journal* reported that:

In 1882 parties led by a man named Hatfield abducted three boys named McCoy and conveyed them to West Virginia. A reward was offered for the arrest of the Hatfield party, and one of the gang is captured, who is now in the Pike County jail. On Sunday last others of the same party went to the residence of Randolph McCoy and killed his wife, his son and set fire to the house . . . two little girls escaped and succeeded in recovering the dead bodies from the flames. . . . the Pikeville jail is strongly guarded, but fears were entertained that an attempt would be made to release the member of the gang confined there.

The "member of the gang," was none other than poor, old Selkirk McCoy, whose only crime was voting according to his conscience.

The *Cincinnati Enquirer* and later the *Wheeling Intelligencer* declared that:

Alfara, the eldest daughter, was the first to open the door . . . and in the glaring light was shot dead by the fiends outside. . . . Calvin next appeared and he was shot dead. [Randolph's] wife . . . in escaping from the burning building . . . was shot through the head and . . . at last accounts will die. Randal McCoy escaped from the burning house . . . and opened fire upon the attacking party. He is known to have killed one of the gang by the name of Chambers and . . . shot Cap Hatfield in the shoulder, putting the rest to flight.

Pikeville was on fire with outrage against the slaughter on Blackberry Creek. Randal demanded that Sheriff Harmon Maynard take a posse and go after the Hatfields, with or without warrants or extradition papers. Maynard, a cautious lawman, declined. Frank Phillips did not. He had become a terror to the supposedly dangerous Hatfields; in repeated raids into West Virginia, he had captured and jailed Wall Hatfield, Tom Chambers, Elias Mitchell, Andrew Varney, L.S. McCoy (a son of Selkirk), Moses Christian, Sam Mahon, Dock Mahon, and Plyant Mahon.

Gathering a posse, Phillips now rode openly across the Tug and before long came upon Cap and Jim Vance. They were walking, accompanied by Jim's wife Mary, toward Cap's house, when Mary shouted that there was "a whole passel" of men around the hill. Vance and Cap dived behind rocks and opened fire. Phillips and his posse spread out. One of his men got a bead on Vance and shot him in the stomach. Vance cried to Cap that he was killed, but Phillips, an old mountain fighter himself, crawled carefully around to Vance's rear, where he saw that Vance was only wounded. Casually he walked up to Vance and put a bullet through his brain. During this exchange, Cap managed to roll down the hill and escape into the woods.

With Vance's scalp on Phillips's belt, the Hatfields were reluctant to tackle him head-on. They rode up and down the West Virginia side of the Tug as before, but they no longer came over into Kentucky. But on January 19, 1888, Phillips decided that he would take the fight to them, and with a posse he invaded Hatfield territory. Along Grapevine Creek, a branch of the Tug, they ran into the Hatfields and a constable, J.R. Thompson, armed with a warrant for the arrest of the killers of Jim Vance. A firefight broke out. Bud McCoy was the first to fall, shot in the leg. Then Bill Dempsey, a young Hatfield adherent, was shot in the leg, crawled behind a shuck pen, and, when Phillips approached, begged for mercy, explaining that he had been ordered by the sheriff to join a posse to chase the Kentuckians out of West Virginia. Phillips calmly put a bullet through his head.

No one knew it at the time, but the shooting part of the Hatfield-McCoy feud was about over. Instead, the battle was taken over by

courts and lawyers. Later, Pike County Judge Wagner and County Attorney Lee Ferguson went to Frankfort to ask for troops to defend the
county, saying that the violence had little to do with Hatfields or Mc-
Coys but was Pike County against Logan County, Kentucky against
West Virginia. West Virginia state senator John Floyd, in a plea to the
West Virginia governor, made a similar plea, insisting that "the Hatfields are not interested in the difficulty any more than other citizens,
while the McCoys . . . constitute but a small portion of the [Kentucky]
gang." Floyd laid the blame for the continuing hostility on Perry Cline.

The situation was not improved by an increase in press coverage.
Typical was the reporting of Charles Howell of the *Pittsburgh Press*.
Howell spent some time with the McCoys and with Perry Cline and
Frank Phillips but none with the Hatfields, and his stories reflected the
fact. "There is a gang in West Virginia," he wrote, "banded together
for the purpose of murder and rapine. There is a gang in Kentucky
whose . . . principle is the protection of families and homes. . . . An
unresisting family has been deprived of five of its members, a father
and mother of five of their children, their home burned, their little
substance scattered to the wind."

Then the two governors got into it. Wilson of West Virginia insisted that his state had been invaded by Kentuckians who had killed
Bill Dempsey and that he would no longer consider extraditing anyone. Buckner wrote to Wilson that he was sending General Sam Hill
to Pikeville to confer with Colonel W.L. Mahan, Wilson's agent. Both
governors ordered their state troops to prepare for possible duty
along the Tug. Newspapers warned that war between the two states
was imminent. Hill went at once to Pikeville but arrived after Mahan
had returned to West Virginia. Hill reported to Buckner that West
Virginians were responsible for the trouble and that Senator Floyd
had made matters worse by urging Governor Wilson to refuse Kentucky extradition requests. Buckner wrote Wilson insisting that the
Hatfields had caused the trouble and that Frank Phillips had gone
into West Virginia only when he failed to get any response from Wilson to his requests for extradition. And so on.

Before the state troops could clash, Governor Wilson concluded
that further dealings with Buckner were useless and sent Mahan to
Frankfort to demand that Kentucky immediately release the nine
West Virginians who had been seized illegally and were moldering in
the Pikeville jail. Buckner said the courts, not the executive, had jurisdiction over release of prisoners. Wilson ordered Eustace Gibson, a
former congressman, to initiate habeas corpus proceedings in the
U.S. District Court in Louisville. Gibson argued that armed men from

Kentucky had invaded West Virginia and without legal authority taken West Virginia citizens to the Pikeville jail, where they were in great danger of assassination.

Kentucky attorney general Parker Watkins ("Polly Wolly") Hardin argued that since the case involved states, only the Supreme Court had jurisdiction. He also argued that if the court freed the prisoners, they would return to West Virginia and never face trial for their crimes. Judge John Barr held that it was not essentially a case between two states and ordered the jailer of Pike County to produce the nine men to the court in Louisville.

The appearance of the famed "mountain desperadoes" on the streets of Louisville caused great excitement, and reporters swarmed around the jail and the courtroom where the prisoners later were brought. Wall Hatfield, especially, became a favorite of the press and had a great time giving interviews, insisting, among other things, that he had only one wife (some reporter had gotten the idea that he had five) and that Devil Anse and his sons were responsible for the murder of the McCoy boys.

For weeks it appeared that the prisoners would grow old in jail before the court decided who had responsibility and jurisdiction. Eventually the question was taken up by the U.S. Circuit Court and finally by the Supreme Court of the United States, which, in its majesty and with Justices Harlan and Bradley dissenting, upheld the judgment of the lower court that the arrest and abduction of the prisoners were lawless and indefensible but that the authority of the governor of Kentucky was no grounds for charging complicity of the state in the wrong done to West Virginia. The outcome was that the Kentuckians shouldn't have done it, but since they had there wasn't much that could be done about it. Everyone assumed that the cases would go to trial.

Meanwhile, things along the Tug became almost ridiculous. With large rewards offered by West Virginia for the capture and delivery of various McCoys and their allies, and similar rewards offered by Kentucky for the capture of Devil Anse and his cohorts, bounty hunters and private detectives swarmed into the area, intent on getting some of the reward money. They were universally despised, and regional newspapers proposed that rewards be offered for *their* capture, in which case the Hatfields and McCoys would take care of them in short order and after a few good hangings peace would descend on all. This did not deter the detectives, who managed to capture Charles Gillespie, a minor figure in the burning of the McCoy cabin. Gillespie confessed that the assault on the McCoys was designed to "remove every material witness to the murder of the McCoy boys." The detectives also captured Ellison Mounts, who managed to shoot one detective in the leg.

Meanwhile, back in Pikeville, things had taken a curious turn. After the assault on the McCoy home and the murder of Alifair and Calvin, Nancy McCoy, who had never lost her loyalty to her clan, left Johnse and went to live in Pikeville. There she met none other than Frank Phillips. They took to each other and, though both were legally married, started living together. As soon as they could obtain divorces, they got married.

No such happy ending awaited Rose Anna. Day and night she tended her mother, but while Sarah, a remarkable woman, slowly but steadily regained her strength, Rose Anna gradually faded. Sarah sent for a doctor, but he could find nothing medically wrong with Rose Anna, and she finally died quietly in her sleep.

On August 23, 1889, the trial of the Hatfield "gang" began in Pikeville. Ellison Mounts had confessed that he had been party to the murder of the three McCoy boys and named Devil Anse, Johnse, Cap, and Bill Hatfield, Alex Messer, Charles Carpenter, and Tom Chambers as those who fired the shots. Among the nineteen witnesses produced by the prosecution were eight named Hatfield, evidence that family lines were more blurred than writers have claimed.

To the surprise of many McCoys, Perry Cline appeared as defense attorney for Wall Hatfield, possibly in an effort to regain some of the money he had lost to the Hatfields in land deals. Old Randal proved a poor witness, unable to recall many events, but Sarah was articulate and precise. She spoke well of Wall Hatfield, however. Others also spoke well of Wall, but to no avail. The jury found him guilty and recommended life in prison. He appealed, and Judge John Rice granted him a sixty-day suspension of judgment. Alex Messer and Dock and Plyant Mahon were tried together, and they too received life sentences. When asked if he had anything to say about his sentence to life at hard labor, Messer said, "Hit's mighty little work I can do, jedge. Hain't been able to work none on any count for several years." Spectators guffawed, but the sentence stuck. Dock and Plyant Mahon were granted appeals.

The rest of the accused were give life or lesser sentences, and for a while it seemed that the Kentuckians would be denied the hanging they had anticipated. Old Randal was so outraged that he reportedly attempted to raise a mob and take some of the defendants out and hang them, but, as with most of his plans, he failed. He was somewhat mollified when, on September 4, the jury returned a guilty verdict against Ellison Mounts and recommended that he be hanged. Mounts protested that he had been assured that his guilty plea and cooperation would get him a light sentence, and he tried to withdraw his guilty plea. The judge overruled the motion and sentenced him to hang on December 3.

On November 9, 1889, the Kentucky Court of Appeals upheld the convictions of Wall and the Mahons. Wall's life sentence proved to be just that. Six months later he died in the state penitentiary. On December 3, Ellison Mounts was hanged on a hillside in Pikeville. Although state law required that such ceremonies be private and a fence had been erected around the gallows, the position of the gallows allowed the crowd of thousands to look down from the hillside on the final act. As the hood was placed over his head, Mounts cried, with considerable honesty, "The Hatfields made me do it!"

On November 19, 1889, Devil Anse Hatfield was fined $100 for moonshining in U.S. District Court in Charleston, West Virginia. Unlike most moonshiners, he was not given the customary year in prison. On the contrary, he was treated in Charleston as something of a celebrity. Reporters asked his opinion on all manner of topics and hung on his words. The judge treated him with courtesy and respect and provided him with a guard to make sure he was not annoyed by bounty hunters or such low types. Old Anse had killed or caused the murders of practically all of the McCoys but paid none of the price.

By that time, most people had forgotten the feud. Frank and Nancy Phillips, who had become parents of a son shortly before their marriage, were said to deal in the manufacture and sale of whiskey, and on at least two occasions Nancy was in court for such enterprise. Neither she nor Frank mellowed much with age or parenthood. In 1894, at the age of thirty-six, Frank died in a gunfight. According to the *Hazel Green Herald*, he and detective William Blevins were chasing the Ricketts boys, West Virginia gun thugs who "had killed old man Ferrel in Logan County," when the Ricketts ambushed and killed them instead. Three years later Nancy died of tuberculosis.

Perry Cline died in 1891. He was only forty-four. Old Randal and Sarah never went back to Blackberry Creek. Randal got a license to operate a ferry on the Big Sandy at Pikeville. Sarah died in 1894. Randal lived on to the age of eighty-eight, still complaining about the injustices he had suffered, and in 1913 died of burns received when he fell into an open fire. In 1921, at the age of eighty-two, Devil Anse died and was given a big funeral.

The Woman in the Case

One story concerning the French-Eversole War in Perry County is about the woman who caused the trouble, or, more precisely, about the young man whose desire for this woman caused the streets of Hazard to run red with blood, to exercise hyperbole. The young man was a clerk in Fulton French's general store when he met this woman. She drove him crazy. One night he came back to the store to get his hat, and there was this woman with his employer, French. Engorged with jealous rage, the young man decided to get rid of French, went one night to the home of Joseph Eversole, French's chief competitor in the merchandise business, and warned him that French was planning to kill him. Eversole, alarmed, began arming his employees. French, hearing of this, armed his. It wasn't long before the two sides clashed. But it was Eversole, not French, who was killed. The lovesick young man committed suicide.

Isn't that a good story? You could make a movie out of it. There is only one thing wrong with it: It isn't true. It never happened. There never was any mountain temptress, any lovesick young man. A total fabrication. Where the tale started, no one knows.

But there was a French-Eversole War, waged in the years from 1887 through 1894 between the forces of Joseph C. Eversole and B. Fulton French, two bright, tough, aggressive lawyer-merchants who were in business in Hazard, the county seat of Perry County, Kentucky. The war almost destroyed Hazard, which wasn't much to begin with—about two hundred people trying to create a decent society in the isolated heart of Kentucky's Cumberland Mountains, a Main Street ankle-deep in mud half the year, some board sidewalks, a few stores, and a courthouse where judges were often afraid to hold court because of gunplay. There wouldn't be a railroad into Hazard until 1912, a hard-surfaced road until 1925. Life was plain and hard, diversions few, and culture almost nonexistent. People drank a lot.

Like most of the counties of central Eastern Kentucky, Perry was settled in the years following the Revolution, chiefly by Virginians who came up through the Cumberland Gap and toward the center of the new wilderness territory. But instead of continuing into the Bluegrass area—the region of Harrodsburg, Boonesborough, and Lexington—they turned up the Kentucky River into the mountains and in small groups started dropping off and settling down in what are now Lee, Breathitt, Clay, Leslie, and Perry counties. They bore the same family names that can be found around Hazard today—Duff, Bowling, Wooton, Eversole, Combs.

Old Jacob Eversole built a cabin opposite the mouth of Lick Branch around 1800 that remained the family home until 1880. The Campbells went on upstream and settled at the mouth of Campbell's Creek. The Combses came in and settled in what would become Hazard after one of the family, Leslie, decided to stay in the Bluegrass; a grandson, Leslie Combs III, founded the beautiful Spendthrift thoroughbred horse farm. A great-grandson of the Combs branch that settled in Clay County became governor of Kentucky. Another notable Combs was known as Old Danger Combs; he had been and remained a Tory, unhappy that the colonies had left the mother country, later became a Democrat, and fought for the South in the Civil War. So did many of the Bakers, Caudills, and Walkers.

Perry wasn't even a county until 1819, when citizens living in Clay and Floyd counties decided they wanted one of their own and the legislature created Perry, with the county seat at Hazard, both named for Oliver Hazard Perry, the hero of the Battle of Lake Champlain in the War of 1812. John Duff laid out the town, and Jessie Combs was elected county clerk in 1822. He served until his death in 1878, which may be some sort of record. Hazard grew slowly but steadily until the Civil War, with new families—Holbrooks, Napiers, Amises, McIntires, Pratts, and Olivers—settling in town or around the county. The town got to be something of a trading center, and after the war Joseph Eversole, a descendant of the pioneer family, and newcomer Benjamin Fulton French became leading merchants.

But then troublesome events began to take place. Timber had been the main product of the sharp, rocky hills, but there were thick veins of rich coal under those hills, and in the years following the Civil War outside companies began buying up large tracts of land or rights to the minerals under that land. Fulton French served as agent for one of the largest of these companies and soon established a reputation as a tough man and a hard bargainer, more concerned with getting cheap coal for the company than with getting a fair price for the mountain landowners. According to the *Hazel Green Herald* of August 12, 1887, "An English syndicate are buying mineral rights in parts of our county. Poor, blind people, selling their vast wealth for a song, the finest coal land for fifty cents an acre. The same syndicate has bought in Perry County 130,000 acres of mineral rights." Author Harry Caudill wrote later, "When Hazard attorney Joseph Eversole warned landowners that the mineral deeds were tantamount to fee simple conveyances, the purchasers sought to silence him; in the resulting war Fulton French, a lawyer for the land syndicate, was his leading opponent."

French had come up from North Carolina, married Susan Lewis, of a large, substantial Harlan County family, and settled on Cutshin Creek in what is now Leslie County before moving to Perry and going into the dry-goods business. His chief competitor was thirty-five-year-old Joseph Eversole, a member of another large, influential mountain family, a slender, handsome, popular young lawyer and businessman who had married Susan Combs, daughter of the prominent judge, state legislator, and educator, Josiah Combs. In the beginning the two men, both talented and ambitious, were on good terms, but Eversole came increasingly to resent French's sharp buying practices in acquiring land for the syndicate and what he considered French's disregard for the welfare of the mountain people. Like the Eversoles in general, Joe Eversole was a public-spirited man, generous with time and money, interested in improving the quality of life in his rugged mountain community. But, though small, he had a fiery temper and was known as a tough fighter.

Fult French was a hard, grasping man whose concerns were centered on his own pocketbook. As historian Allen Watts, himself a former resident of neighboring Letcher County, says, French was undoubtedly the villain of the piece; Eversole was trying to protect the small mountain landowner.

Eversole's disapproval gradually cooled to a sort of polite hostility, and it took only a disagreement over competition between the two stores to spark the gunplay that was more and more common as a means of settling disputes in the mountains during the post-Civil War era.

Something happened—who knows what?—that persuaded French and Eversole to start arming themselves and their employees. French, in mountain Mafia style, began hiring gunmen. Eversole may have hired some outsiders himself. According to the *Hazel Green Herald* of September 1, 1886: "Some weeks ago their rivalry led to a murderous fight in which French and his friends were driven out [of Hazard]. French began collecting a band with which he will move on Hazard. He makes Mt. Pleasant [Harlan] about thirty miles away, his headquarters. He has recruited seventy men of desperate fortunes. They are paid $2 and $2.50 a day. Eversole, surrounded by an equally desperate gang, is fortified in Hazard. A fierce conflict is imminent." This account may or may not be accurate. French lived in Leslie County; why would he have his headquarters in Mt. Pleasant— Harlan—a long, hard ride away?

The ambush killing of Silas Gayheart, a friend of French's, was the first overt act, but by the time he was shot, in the summer of 1887, mountain gun thugs such as Bad Tom Smith, Joe Adkins, Jess Fields, and Bob Profitt were walking around Hazard brandishing rifles and reportedly working for Fult French. A year or so later Old Claib Jones turned up and, by his own account in his "autobiography," tried to bring peace by killing off one side or the other. It is not clear which side he was working for. He was not the world's most accurate reporter.

The Eversole people always denied killing Gayheart, and there was no apparent reason why they would want to. An ambush killing was always hard to trace; the killers struck and ran, usually killing all witnesses and leaving few tracks in the tangled woodland. There were accusations in Hazard that a dozen men, including two Eversoles, were involved in killing Gayheart, but no one was ever indicted. Fult French, however, sent out his men to hire more gunslingers, and though there had been no overt show of feud warfare, there was a great deal of tension in Perry County throughout the winter of 1887. There was a lot of shooting on the street at night, and people became reluctant to go out after dark. Everyone was edgy.

Then, early one morning in the spring of 1888, Joe Eversole, on his farm out in the county, heard from one of his lookouts that Fult French and a large group of his men had camped the night before on the road from Mt. Pleasant to Hazard and were planning to attack the town. The Eversoles usually centered their forces in Hazard around the "fort" where the Beaumont Hotel later stood, but on this occasion they had withdrawn from the town and gone about their business, apparently feeling safe from action by the French forces.

Calling his men together, Eversole selected a small group to go to Hazard, avoid confrontation, and gather what information they could. He went with the bulk of his forces to the southern section of the county, where he could count on a large body of sympathizers. Within hours, French and his army swooped down, somewhat surprised to find Hazard quiet, with a few people in the stores and almost no one on the street. They took over the courthouse, fortified their homes, and warned the few Eversole men they saw to leave town or face trouble. They left.

Joe Eversole, staying with his men out on South Fork, heard the news and, taking five of his most trusted men, rode toward Hazard. On the way he picked up a dozen more. Late in the afternoon they reached Hazard and attacked the French forces, who fought back in spirited fashion. The fighting went on until dark, but with few results. One French gunman was wounded. Eversole said none of his men was hurt.

Eversole and his men withdrew. Two days later a strange but not atypical thing happened. A reporter for the *Cincinnati Enquirer*, hearing that there was serious trouble in Perry County, took the train to London, hired a horse, and began the exhausting seventy-mile ride over the rugged mountain trails. Not far from Hazard he fell in with a lanky mountaineer, told him the purpose of his journey, and was delighted when the mountain man offered to escort him into Hazard and introduce him to feud members who could give him the facts about the terrible battles.

They were French adherents, and what they gave him was a highly one-sided, wildly exaggerated version of what had been a fairly harmless clash; but by the time it appeared in the *Enquirer*, the mountains were made to appear dripping with blood. The mountaineers were not without a certain sense of humor.

Ten days later, the two sides clashed again. This time there were casualties on both sides. Such sporadic fighting continued through the summer months, until people on both sides grew tired of the feud and began thinking of ways to stop it. Both French and Eversole were probably eager to quit. It was getting to the point where neither could afford to continue. Neither was a wealthy man, and the fighting was ruining their businesses. Some people had left Hazard. Others, out in the county, were afraid to come into town to buy. And the cost of keeping up their armies was beginning to pinch. French sent Joe Adkins to Eversole's store to see if Joe Eversole would like to talk. Eversole said that he would.

The two men met on Big Creek and drew up a formal truce under which both agreed to give up their guns. French promised to hand his over to the judge of Leslie County, who was a cousin, while Joe Eversole agreed to hand his over to Judge Josiah Combs, his father-in-law.

When the news was announced in Hazard, there was a general feeling of relief, but the peace that descended was an uneasy one. Men from both sides now walked the streets, but some were still armed, they still eyed each other warily, and when one side was drinking in a saloon and members of the opposing camp entered, things tended to get rather quiet. Both French and Eversole needed some time to replenish their declining fortunes, but few people in Hazard seemed to believe that the truce would last very long.

And it didn't. French accused Eversole of regaining possession of his guns while Judge Combs was not looking. Eversole replied that French could not regain his guns because he had never surrendered them as he had promised to do. On September 15, 1887, Joe Eversole and Bill Gambrell met on the street in Hazard. Gambrell was a loud-mouthed, gunslinging, part-time preacher, denouncing the demon rum one moment, peddling moonshine whiskey the next. Gambrell made what seemed to be a threatening remark. Eversole told him to keep his mouth shut or risk getting it shut permanently. Gambrell reached for his pistol. Eversole grabbed Gambrell's pistol, pulled his own, and shot him. Gambrell was killed. He was a French man, and the feud was automatically restarted. By November 24 the *Louisville Post* was warning that "Perry County is again in a state of terror. The French and Eversole war has been renewed. Every man in the county almost has sided with either French or Eversole."

In the meantime the level of violence was automatically raised when Bad Tom Smith appeared on the scene. Just when, where, and why he got the name of Bad Tom is unclear, but from the time he was a boy on Carr's Fork, in Knott County, Tom Smith was obstreperous, erratic, usually in trouble. He began his career as a brawler, then became a petty thief, stealing anything, from hogs and horses to merchandise. He would fight anyone and terrorized girls as well as boys in the neighborhood. In 1884, when he was twenty, Tom was walking into Hazard on election day when he saw some of his friends holed up in a livery stable and being fired upon by several gunmen lying in the weeds outside. Picking up a large rock, Tom knocked one of the besiegers unconscious, took the man's pistol and shot the other two, ending the battle, relieving his friends, and winning considerable attention.

But there was another aspect of Tom's personality that needs to be considered: He was an epileptic, in a time and in an area where epilepsy and the seizures or "fits" that marked it were little understood and generally feared or regarded as a sign of insanity. It is likely that Tom was shunned, ridiculed, considered strange, and probably picked on as a boy, inclining him early on to be a fighter. He was big and strong, a little over six feet tall and weighing almost two hundred pounds, just dumb enough to be fearless, just bright enough to be dangerous, and a dead shot.

Fult French knew of Tom's handicap and took profitable advantage of it. Though Tom was married to a Lewis, as was Fult French (he later left her), Fult seemed to give him the dangerous, dirty jobs to do, and Tom did them.

In 1885 he held up and robbed Ira Davidson of his watch. This was a more serious matter than it might appear today—a good watch was rare and expensive—and the Davidsons soon had Tom in court, where he was found guilty and fined. Davidson denounced Tom in very explicit terms, and a few nights later the home of Davidson's mother burned to the ground. When the trouble between Eversole and French began, both sides tried to enlist Tom, but at first he showed no interest. Then he stole a horse belonging to Nick Combs, Joe Eversole's brother-in-law, and the Eversoles had him arrested and hauled into court. Tom threatened to kill lawyers, the judge, witnesses, and anyone else associated with this breach of etiquette. Since the Eversoles had so insulted him, he joined the French forces, and from then on, while the French gunmen were under the orders of Fult French, they were led by Bad Tom Smith.

Tom later gave a much different version of his affiliation with the French forces. "I was a poor boy," he told a Hazel Green reporter on May 23, 1895, while in jail in Breathitt County, "and I worked for a living. I would first work for a French and then an Eversole. . . . Somebody reported that I was acting for the French party. . . . I went to Eversole's store one day and he knocked me down with the butt of his gun, kicked me into the street and ordered me to leave the county. I then went to the French party and after a while they took me in. I fought it through with them. I joined that war on my own account."

Bad Tom fell in with another French gunman named Joe Hurt, a nervous, excitable gunman who admired Tom's toughness, and the two of them were credited with several of the murders committed in 1887 in connection with the feud. Joe went to Tom's home one day on some sort of business, but the two of them started drinking and an argument flared. Tom said that Hurt was no friend, that he had broken into Tom's home and attacked him. In any event, Tom killed him.

The Eversole men were warned to watch out for Tom. The warning was well founded. On April 15, 1888, Joe Eversole, his brother-in-law Nick Combs, and Judge Josiah Combs were riding toward Big Creek. It had been quiet in Hazard for several weeks, and people were beginning to hope that the feud had died down. But as the Eversoles rounded a turn on the road, they were hit by a burst of gunfire from a thick patch of woods above the bend. Joe Eversole was knocked from his horse, his body riddled by eight bullets. Nick Combs was similarly hit. Josiah Combs was nicked and had five bullet holes in his clothes but managed to escape. As he fled, he saw two men, neither of whom he could identify, run from the woods, fire repeatedly into the bodies of the fallen men, and then go through their pockets.

It would later be revealed that the chief assassin was Bad Tom. After his victims fell, as Tom was rifling the pockets of young Nick Combs, Nick became conscious, turned, and asked Tom why he had shot him. Tom calmly pulled his pistol and shot him through the head, explaining to his startled helpers that they could not afford to have a witness hanging around, talking and making a nuisance of himself.

Judge Combs rushed back to Hazard, got together a group of Eversole men, and retrieved the bodies. Despite the increased tensions, they were given a big funeral, with about fifty men with rifles guarding the cemetery ceremony.

After that there was no way to control the killing. With Joe Eversole gone, John Campbell assumed leadership of the Eversole forces. He tried to instill some order and discipline into his haphazard ranks, showing them how to spread their forces in order to attack from many vantage points, and how to concentrate them to focus their fire. He posted guards on important buildings and sentries at the main entrances into town, with orders to shoot anyone approaching who did not know the password. Unfortunately, Campbell left town one afternoon and upon returning that night found the sentry sound asleep at this post. Campbell shouted a command, ordering the man to his feet. The man, fogged with sleep, leaped to his feet and shot Campbell. Killed him.

The famous Shade Combs then decided to take a hand in matters, called a few of the Eversole gunmen into conference, and announced that they were going to stop the feud by assassinating Fult French and his top gunmen. He had it all figured out. His lieutenants listened to his plan and agreed enthusiastically. But they had first to overcome the obstacle of Bad Tom Smith. They never did.

When Shade Combs took command of the Eversole forces, Bad Tom sent word to him that unless he left Perry County, he, and his wife and children would be killed and their house burned. It was then that Shade conceived his plan to ambush Bad Tom, took two trusted lieutenants, and rode out toward the French hideout. But they were the ones who were ambushed. One of his men was killed, and Shade fled. Worried for the safety of his family, Shade stayed close to home for several weeks until one afternoon he went out into the yard to play with his children. There was the crack of a rifle and Shade Combs fell dead. As Mrs. Combs wept and the children screamed, Bad Tom rode by slowly, smiling.

On October 9, 1888, Elijah Morgan, a French man though a son-in-law of Josiah Combs, was killed from ambush as he and Frank Grace were on their way to Hazard to try to bring the two warring sides together and stop the feud. There had been rumors for weeks that he was marked for death, and no one was surprised when he fell. It was generally believed he was killed in retaliation for the death of Shade Combs.

This was too much. Circuit Judge H.C. Lilly asked Governor Buckner to send troops to Perry and Breathitt counties to enable him to conduct trials. "French has thirteen or more men, well armed," he lamented. The governor replied that he didn't think thirteen gunmen should be able to terrorize a community and keep the sheriff and judge from discharging their duties. "Fears and alarms," he wrote, had produced "nothing more than a vague apprehension in the public mind." Rather snidely, the governor added that Judge Lucius Little of McLean County was willing to swap courts with him, and the *Hazel Green Herald* sneered that "the lily of the valley is sweeter than the Lilly of the mountains." This was unfair to Judge Lilly, who knew the situation better than did the governor or the Hazel Green editor, and knew how difficult it would be to hold fair trials in a courthouse full of feudists.

Eventually the governor sent the troops, under General Sam Hill, with Captain Sohan in charge. Sohan camped his troops about two hundred yards from the courthouse and offered protection to the court. In his report, he noted that "the judge, in charging the jury, passed lightly over murder."

General Hill's report to the governor was even more discouraging. "Hazard contains about 100 people when they are all in their homes," he wrote, "but only 35 were at home when we reached here. Ten men have died in the past two years and county authorities have failed to act with any degree of promptness or vigor. What this is all about I cannot say." He went on to say that "there are no churches of any kind, few schools, and half the murders are never made known to the public. Many people live in poverty. More than 20 men have been killed in the feud, most from ambush."

Before the troops left, Captain Sohan organized a company of state militia in Hazard. This might have served to dampen the feud, for the people were impressed by the troops, who were proof that the state intended to enforce the law. But most of the militiamen were feudists, and as soon as the troops were withdrawn, the fighting resumed.

Bad Tom was arrested and put in jail, but Fult French intervened and Tom was shortly released. Tom then went to Hindman, in nearby Knott County, and there, apparently on orders from French, shot and killed Ambrose Amburgey. This probably had nothing to do with the feud. Just a disagreement that had to be settled.

But Tom's high jinks were getting too much for even the timid folks of Hazard, and the grand jury meeting in the fall of 1889 handed down multiple indictments against him, though without troops the indictments were useless. As the November 1889 term of court convened, Judge W.L. Hurst was named special judge. He was warned to leave town. Eventually he did, but before he left, what became known as the Battle of Hazard Courthouse took place.

It was becoming apparent that Fult French ruled Perry County. The Eversole forces were badly depleted, and those surviving found it dangerous to oppose Bad Tom and his bloody bunch. Ira Davidson, an Eversole man who was Circuit Court clerk, was heard to say that the sheriff should bring Bad Tom and Joe Adkins to justice. Ira got word that he would be killed if he stayed in Hazard. He took his family and left. Abner Eversole, county school superintendent, was ordered to leave or be killed. He left. The grand jury indicted Bad Tom, but he ignored it.

But at the fall 1889 meeting of Perry Circuit Court, the Eversole forces decided to take a stand against the French thugs and demand that the court do something about the murders. Both sides had collected as many men as they could round up—twenty or thirty on each side—and they milled about the courthouse waiting for someone to start something. They didn't have to wait long. A man named Campbell, who was with a group of French men on Graveyard Hill, above the courthouse, began shooting, probably because he had been drinking. A storekeeper named Davidson saw him, got his gun, and killed him.

Wesley Whitaker, an Eversole man, and Henry Davidson of the French forces got into an argument near the courthouse. Whitaker drew his gun, but Davidson ran and hid in the home of Jess Fields, another French warrior. They banged away at each other, but both were drunk and no damage was done. But the idea caught on with the crowd on Main Street, and soon the shooting became general. The Eversoles grabbed control of the courthouse. The Frenches took possession of the jail, only a few feet away. Jess Fields and Joe Adkins, who were in the courthouse, jumped out a window and made a dash for the jail, where they joined their fellow feudists. For hours the two forces blasted away at short range, doing remarkably little damage except to the courthouse, which was almost blown apart. Indeed, before it later burned, some citizens proposed that it be torn down, since it was so riddled with bullet holes that "it wouldn't hold corn shucks."

Bad Tom and Jess Fields dug in on Graveyard Hill, where they could fire down on the courthouse, and for the next eighteen hours the firing went on fairly steadily until, around noon on the following day, the Eversoles ran out of ammunition and were forced to retreat.

In this so-called "Battle of Hazard" only two men were killed and only a few wounded. Bad Tom, lying in a small depression intended as a grave, rested his rifle on a flat tombstone and kept up a steady fire. At one point Jake McKnight, an Eversole man, started across the street. Tom shot and killed him. As they ran low on bullets, the Eversoles tried to get away along the bank of the Kentucky River. Bad Tom, Jess Fields, and Bob Profitt went after them, hoping to wipe out the whole force and end the war, but Green Morris lay behind a fallen log on the river bank and shot both Fields and Profitt, wounding Fields painfully but not seriously. The other French gunmen held back, and the Eversole men got away.

Court had adjourned, anyhow, but on the night of the fourth of July 1890, someone burned the courthouse, though most of the records were saved. Then another of the Eversole men, Bob Cornett, who had gone home and was trying to get some logs down to the sawmill, was shot and killed from ambush.

Again there were demands that the French gang be brought to trial, but Judge Hurst, who had been holding court, was told to leave town or die, and left. That was the last straw. Circuit Judge Lilly wrote again to Governor Buckner, stating flatly that he would not try to hold court until the governor furnished him with protective troops. Governor Buckner again sent in the troops, this time under Captain Garthers (Gaither?) from Louisville. The captain rounded up a dozen gunmen from both sides and saw that they were tried for their crimes.

At first Fult French tried to impress Gaither, presenting himself as a community leader concerned only with peace and development of the economy. Gaither was not taken in. Among those brought to trial was B. Fulton French. As can be imagined, the most famous defendant was Bad Tom Smith. Some of Bad Tom's friends sent word to the court that Bad Tom would never be tried and that anyone who attempted it would be killed. Gaither was not frightened; as a matter of fact, so many of the dangerous French gunmen had been arrested that there were not enough left to attempt a rescue.

Tom was arrested, given a hearing, and taken to Pineville for trial. Pineville at the time was a fairly rough mountain town, but the appearance of the famous Bad Tom created a minor sensation, and crowds lined the street to the courthouse to see him brought to the jail. But it was the same old story in a different setting. Tom was tried, found guilty, and sentenced to life in prison. But he was granted an appeal and left. He was not retried. The authorities just seemed to forget it.

For all intents and purposes, the French-Eversole War was over. If there had been a winner, it was probably Fult French, but it was an empty victory. He was tried and acquitted and left Perry County. He didn't go very far. When the notorious Curtis Jett of Breathitt County was tried in Jackson for the murder of attorney J.B. Marcum, who should be among the defense attorneys but B. Fulton French, to whom some in the court referred as Judge French. Later French went to live in Clark County. He was tried in 1896 in Breathitt Circuit Court for murder, and acquitted, but his crimes caught up with him.

The Eversole ranks had been riddled. But Hazard was the real loser. General Sam Hill, sent by Governor Buckner to make an assessment of conditions in Hazard, reported that the place, "a dirty, shabby little excuse for a town," had been shot to pieces. But eventually a lot of people who had left to avoid the violence began returning, repairing their homes, taking up their farms or businesses.

The bitterness, however, lingered, and many people were killed after the feud proper had died down and the feud leaders were dead or departed. The following, for example, is reprinted from the *Carrollton* (Kentucky) *Democrat* of November 2, 1889, under the heading "A Mountain Murder. Sad News for a convicted moonshiner. Home destroyed and Father shot in cold blood":

Among the moonshiners confined a few days ago in the Covington jail was Wm. Loomis. At the last term of the . . . court he was fined $100 and sentenced to sixty days in jail. Recently he was pardoned by the President and was awaiting money to defray expenses to his home in Perry County. His father was arrested at the same time, but receiving a lighter sentence he went directly home after he had served his thirty days. After he left the nearest railway station he was compelled to walk eighty miles . . . through a mountain region infested with lawless cut-throats. His son received a letter the other day stating that his father had been shot and was at the point of death. When his father reached home in Perry County he found a sad state of affairs. His home, which contained his wife and son, had been riddled with bullets, and his barns and outhouses destroyed by fire. He immediately sold his farm and started to leave the county. . . . as he was departing he was shot from ambush by unknown parties. He was picked up and carried home where he was guarded to keep from being shot again. The gang threatened to exterminate his whole family. He had a quarrel with two men, one named Bill

Smith, the other Jack Morris. They belong to the Eversole party, which has battled with the French faction. [This may have been a mistake; Bill Smith was the brother of Bad Tom Smith.] The jailer of Perry County had warned Loomis not to come back . . . as his life would be in danger. Loomis [this apparently refers to the son] is willing to take chances with the crowd. He wants to get up there and rescue his mother and sisters.

In 1894, to general surprise, Judge Josiah Combs returned to Hazard. He was not happy elsewhere, he said. His roots, his people, his memories—good and bad—were in and around Hazard, and he was determined to spend his declining years there. He did not have many left to spend. As he stood talking to a friend in front of the courthouse on the morning of September 20, 1894, a shot came from a cornfield across the way, and Judge Combs, without a word, staggered to his home and fell in the doorway, dead.

The cornfield gunman stood for a few mements, saw Combs fall, and then walked slowly to the rear of the field, where he joined two others, all with their faces blackened. Recovering from their shock, several men pursued them and identified Jess Fields, Joe Adkins, and Boone Frazier. Fields and Adkins were finally caught, indicted, and tried in Knox Circuit Court.

The trial attracted wide attention, partly because the noted Colonel W.C.P. Breckinridge and B. Fulton French were among the defense attorneys. Nevertheless, both Fields and Adkins were sentenced to life in prison. Adkins served only eight years, however, before he was pardoned. He was later reported to have left the country. Frazier was never caught.

Strangely, a year later, in the fall of 1895, Fulton French himself was indicted in Perry County for complicity in the murder of Judge Combs. He was tried in Breathitt County and acquitted, though Bad Tom Smith, confessing just before he was hanged, charged French with planning the Combs murder. Tom said he would have taken part in the killing himself but had been shot in the arm and was not feeling well.

Bad Tom's hanging was precipitated by his own troubles, this time with his wife, whom he described as "an Eversole woman." He was tired of Hazard anyhow, and after leaving his wife he went to live in Breathitt County. For a while it seemed that he might be turning over a new leaf, but old habits die hard. He took up with a woman named Katherine McQuinn, who ran a house on Smith's Branch of Quicksand Creek of which there were scurrilous reports. Actually, Mrs. McQuinn was the victim of a minor indiscretion but had paid dearly for it.

Katherine McQuinn was a handsome woman and high-spirited. But her good looks attracted the attentions of a young clerk in the Day Brothers store in Jackson; she welcomed the attention, and they began a furtive affair. Not furtive enough. Mr. McQuinn came home one day and caught them in bed. Instead of shooting one or both of them, he fled from the house and ran up and down the streets of Jackson, screaming and moaning, until it became obvious that the shock had completely unsettled him. He was sent to the Eastern Kentucky Lunatic Asylum, where he died. The young clerk, distraught at the fate of Mr. McQuinn and racked with guilt, committed suicide. (It is possible that a garbled account of this event became the basis for the legend of the woman who started the French-Eversole War.) Katherine was left to face alone public disapproval and hard times. She supported herself by running a boardinghouse of sorts where few questions were asked. And it was to her establishment that Bad Tom Smith, in the fall of 1893, brought his cargo of trouble.

Tom could not keep out of trouble. Perhaps he didn't try. He seemed comfortably ensconced with Mrs. McQuinn, safe from the law and surviving enemies, but he took to drinking heavily and finally overplayed his hand. It was during a particularly energetic drinking bout that he shot and killed a Dr. John Rader. That was a mistake. Jackson was not Hazard, and Bloody Breathitt was not Perry County. Tom was arrested, tried, and sentenced to hang. The Breathitt jury was not fooling. This time there was no appeal. Tom made one futile effort to saw his way out of the Jackson jail, but another jail inmate informed on him, and he was caught. On June 28, 1895, he was taken to the courthouse lawn and hanged.

His death was almost as untidy and bizarre as his life. There was much controversy over how the scaffold should be built, the kind of rope that should be used, and other social niceties. Sheriff Breckinridge Combs became impatient with the advice he was receiving. Bad Tom had asked to be baptized, but some people objected, saying it was a ruse to let him escape. Sheriff Combs announced that he would allow the baptism by the Reverend John Jay Dickey, the circuit-riding Methodist minister, founder of the Jackson school and editor of the *Jackson Hustler*, the community's first newspaper. The Reverend Dickey was helping Tom write his life's story, the sheriff announced, and would sell copies of it for twenty-five cents on the day of the hanging.

Reporters nagged Combs about the exact time of the hanging, but he brushed them off. "I don't know what time I will spring the trap," he said.

I was down to see the governor about that this morning, and he was sorter of the opinion that it had best be done right about sunrise, because if it was put off the crowd would be bigger and there'd more likely to be trouble. I kinder insinuated to him that a fellow ought to live just as long as the law allows, and it would be fair to all sides to split the difference and let him die twixt twelve and one. Anyhow, I can hang him when I please. It's me that's got the say now, but I thought as he's the highest chief I'd let him think about it. There won't be any trouble hanging him unless some fellow takes a notion to shoot him off the gallows. The only time there's going to be trouble is when Smith is dead and the roughs from the upper counties get drunk and there'll surely be some shooting.

I'm might afraid I'm going to have trouble getting the right kind of rope. I telegraphed to Louisville for a rope, but the jailer didn't have any, and today when I was in Lexington I didn't have time to see about it. I can't get anything but an inch rope here, and I don't want to hang the poor fellow with that kind of stuff. He ought to at least have a decent rope.

I don't know about that roof. I don't know as I'll put it on or not. Anyhow, it's nobody's business if I do. I'm running this thing, and I am going to do just as I please about it.

Tom didn't spend a good last night. For one thing, the jail was full of people singing, praying, and taking down Tom's every word. To make matters worse, Tom was reported to have had a "terrible fit," undoubtedly an epileptic seizure. His wife relented and came from Knott County with their three children to see him, causing a great deal of excitement. The unfortunate Katherine McQuinn could not attend, being in jail herself, charged with conspiring to kill Dr. Rader.

Tom was accompanied to the gallows by his brother Bill and his sister Mary (or Minnie), who then retired to the jail during the gruesome hanging and was comforted by the jailer's wife. Gallows had been erected on the Breathitt County Courthouse lawn, and from daybreak people had been pouring into Jackson for the grisly festivities. A crowd had come over from Knott County, home of the Smiths. Reporters from Lexington, Louisville, and Cincinnati sat on the courthouse steps, looking self-important. Several times during the morning members of the Smith family had gone up to the jail for a few last words with Bad Tom, their black sheep. All reported that throughout the ordeal Tom remained calm.

Sheriff Combs brought Tom from the jail at noon and walked with him through the press of people who crowded around the gallows, built only a few yards from where the lynch mob had taken the cursing, struggling Hen Kilburn and hanged him during the bloody Breathitt County feud. Some reporters estimated that three thousand people were crowded into the square, but Tom seemed to take little notice of them as he climbed the steps to the gallows.

Tom turned and spoke to the sheriff, who nodded in reply, and a total silence fell over the crowd, except, according to one account, for the crying of a baby here and there. A hanging was an unusual affair in those days, a major attraction, and whole families traveled miles to attend.

Sheriff Combs had an idea Tom would make a last-minute confession and warned reporters to be ready to take down every word. When Tom was ready, Combs announced that Tom was going to talk with the reporters. A reporter for the *Cincinnati Enquirer* shouted to ask him if he wished to make a confession. Tom turned to Sheriff Combs and in a low voice said he did. He said he would tell everything, or as much as he had time for. Combs told him he had plenty of time. Tom nodded, wiped his forehead, and began.

"I am guilty of the crime," he said.

I killed Dr. Rader. It was nobody paid me to do it, and I'll tell you how it was. I met Dr. Rader in town that day, and he says to me, "I want to court a girl, and I want you to help me do it." I told him all right, and we went out to Mrs. McQuinn's house, and I went and got the girl, Louise Southwood. Then we all got drunk. Rader wanted the girl to go to bed with him, but she didn't want to and ran away from him. He went out and brought her back. I just recollected hearing him persuading her. I was so drunk, Mrs. McQuinn and Bob Fields pulled off my shoes and put me to bed, and I went to sleep. After a while Mrs. McQuinn came to the bed, and told me that Rader had been over to my bed twice and said he was going to kill me. I knew he had a pistol, for he had told me about it being such a good one. Then Mrs. McQuinn told me that if I would kill him she would say she done it and I would come clear and they wouldn't do anything to her. I was so drunk, and I just got up and shot him. I shot twice, but I never could tell where the other bullet went. Me and Katherine then looked at Rader lying on the bed, and covered him up again and took his money. That's all there was to it so far as I know. I wasn't paid for it that's certain. It was whiskey and bad women that brought me here and I want to tell you boys to let them alone. Oh, God, save my poor soul! I wish I had never been born.

Previously, in court, Tom had claimed that Mrs. McQuinn had done the actual shooting.

Detective George Drake, who was on the scaffold for the occasion and was accorded the status of a celebrity, came over to speak to Tom. Drake was an unattractive character, a sometime deputy U.S. marshal, bounty hunter, railroad detective, once a security guard at Lexington's Phoenix Hotel, and deputy sheriff if anyone wanted one. He was reputed to have once chased and brought to jail eleven killers in a month, had captured Breck Roberts when he escaped from the Breathitt jail, captured John Henry and Hub Jackson for boxcar break-ins, and had chased Wick Tallant all the way to Texas and captured him for some mischief. In friendly fashion, he asked Tom if he wanted to continue, and Tom nodded he did. He said he would like a drink of water.

After jailer Tom Centers brought him a cup of water, Tom said, "Yes, I want to name them all but I can't tell the dates and how I killed them. This would take too long." Sheriff Combs said he could have all the time he needed, for him just to tell it in his own way, and Tom began again.

Tom said that Joe Hurt was the first man he killed, simply because Hurt supported the Eversoles in a local election. (He had earlier said that Hurt had come to his home drunk and attacked him, forcing him to shoot in self-defense.) Joe Eversole and Nick Combs were the next victims. He admitted killing them both from ambush and added that he took about thirty dollars from Joe Eversole's pockets as he lay dead. John McKnight, Tom added, was killed in the Battle of the Perry County Courthouse. Then he and Jack Combs ambushed Bob Cornett. And finally he repeated his account of the murder of Dr. Rader. He did not mention the murders of Shade Combs or Ambrose Amburgey.

After this, Tom talked for a minute to his sister Mary, who, with the help of the sheriff, had climbed the steps to the scaffold and stood quietly while her brother finished his bloody accounting. Then she went to him, took his hand, and patted his face. "Tell nothing but the truth," she said, and turned away. Then she came back, and put her arm around him. Holding her head high, she said, "Tom, face God like a man."

Tom watched her walk back to the edge of the scaffold and went on to tell about working for Fulton French but said that he was never paid except with clothes and a little money when he asked for it. Several reporters pressed in to ask him further questions, but he ignored them. Then he turned to the sheriff and said that he was ready to address the crowd. His previous remarks had been to reporters, for the record.

"Go on, Tom," said Combs. Tom turned and raised his hand, quieting the crowd again. Slowly he stepped to the front of the scaffold, looked out over the crowd, and said:

Friends, one and all, I want to talk to you a little before I die. My last words on earth to you are to take warning from my fate. Bad whiskey and bad women have brought me where I am. I hope you ladies will take no umbrage at this for I have told you the God's truth. To you little children who were the first to be blessed by Jesus, I will give this warning: don't drink whiskey and don't do as I have done. I want everybody in this vast crowd who does not wish to do the things that I have done and to put themselves in the place I now occupy, to hold up their hands.

Every hand shot up. "That is beautiful," said Tom. "It looks like what I shall see in heaven [which seems optimistic]. Again I say, live better lives than I lived. I die with no hard feeling toward anybody. There ain't a soul in the world I hate. I love everybody. Farewell till we meet again."

Mary went across the scaffold, hugged Tom, and kissed him a last time. Then with the help of Sheriff Combs, she went back down the steps and, as the crowd parted to let her through, walked back to the jail to await her brother's body. She was joined by other members of the Smith family.

Bad Tom now launched into a long and loud prayer. On the scaffold several preachers, including the industrious and compassionate John Jay Dickey, prayed with him, as Bad Tom cried out for mercy and forgiveness. He then asked Dickey and a Reverend Hudson to sing a hymn, "Guide Me, Oh Great Jehovah," and thousands in the crowd joined in. As the song ended, Bad Tom again dropped to his knees and prayed for mercy. As he rose, Sheriff Combs took him by the arm and told him it was time. "Oh, just one more dear hymn," asked Tom, and Combs consented. Again the ministers climbed to the scaffold and sang "Near the Cross" as the crowd, knowing the end was near, grew quiet. Sheriff Combs, white-faced and shaken, motioned to his deputy to hand him the leather straps with which he fastened Bad Tom's legs and arms. Tom gritted his teeth and cast a last look at the hills standing bare and grim beyond the town. As the hood was drawn down over his head, he took a deep breath and shouted, "Save me, oh God, save me!"

At this, Sheriff Combs nodded, a deputy pulled the lever, and Bad Tom Smith fell nearly five feet before the noose caught him. The sound of his neck breaking could be heard above the crowd's gasp of horror. Many women whimpered and fainted. Suddenly the carnival atmosphere gave way to the grim reality of a man's death.

Bad Tom fell through the trap at 1:45. He was allowed to hang for seventeen minutes before he was taken down and placed in the coffin waiting nearby. His brother Bill drove the last nails into the coffin and went to the jail to get Mary, who walked with considerable dignity beside her brother to the wagon on which the coffin rested. Almost five hundred people accompanied the body on its fifty-mile journey to the Smith home on Carr's Fork in Knott County, where Bad Tom was buried.

Following the funeral, Tom's widow, who had stuck to him throughout his tempestuous career, his loving, sturdy sister Mary, and Susan Eversole, widow of a man Bad Tom had brutally murdered, sat for a long time on the porch of the Smith home, talking. They were discussing the future of the now-fatherless children of Bad Tom. If this seems unusual, keep in mind that Tom's widow had been an Eversole. Furthermore, Susan Eversole, like her late husband, was a strong, responsible, and deeply moral woman and undoubtedly felt a deep concern for Tom's children. So it is not too surprising that, as the day wore on, the women agreed that the comfortable Eversole home in Perry County would be the best place for the children to grow up. The next morning, when Susan boarded her wagon for the long drive home, the children of Bad Tom Smith, drained of tears but still confused and frightened, rode with her.

It had been an unselfish decision by the Smiths, who, despite Tom's wild journey through the world, were poor but good, solid people. Even Tom, despite the bloody trail he left, deserves some understanding. Aside from the epilepsy that brought him ridicule and abuse, Tom had never been too bright and was easily influenced, often by those who used him for murderous purposes. Compared to Joe Adkins and Jesse Fields, who were simply killers, Tom was something of a victim.

It is too easy to designate a feudist as a villain, but if a villain is needed in this tale, Fulton French will do. As historian Allen Watts has pointed out, this was, particularly on the French side, a business feud. French was working for the big land companies against the small mountain landowners. Joe Eversole had a lot of power in Perry County because he was, in the final analysis, working for the common people; so was Josiah Combs, a true patrician. But they were no match for the financial power of French and of those backing him.

And if there was a heroine, it was surely Susan Eversole. One of the redoubtable Combs clan, she never wavered in the face of danger and tragedy. She saw her father killed, she saw her husband killed, she had to send her children away to live with relatives to escape the violence, but she never lost her courage, dignity or sense of morality.

One last episode remained to be played out as a finale to the French-Eversole war. Fult French, though wealthy and a fairly prominent attorney, feared that he might still have enemies and took to wearing a bullet-proof vest. Conscience is a merciless master, and he was still wearing it in the winter of 1913 when, in the entry hall of a boarding house in Elkatawa, he ran into Susan Eversole, the deaths of whose husband and father he had probably ordered. Mrs. Eversole was still in black, as was the custom of the time for widows, and was accompanied by her son Harry, a slender, one-handed man (he had shot himself in the hand, necessitating amputation). Startled, Susan stumbled slightly. French drew back with a slight bow. "Good morning, Mrs. Eversole," he said and put out his hand. Susan stared, then turned her back on him. French turned to leave, but Harry pulled a pistol, and French bolted out the front door and jumped a low fence surrounding the yard. As he did, Harry shot him, hitting him just below the vest, apparently puncturing his liver or spleen. Harry's second shot missed, and French kept running. Since the shot had not killed French, Harry could not be tried for murder, so the judge fined him $75 for disturbing the peace. Susan paid the fine.

But in the strange if slow way in which the mills of justice sometimes grind, Fulton French died of the wound more than a year later.

A Nice Little College Town

Driving through Morehead, Kentucky, with its imposing university and attractive medical center, it is hard to imagine that there was a time when a feud almost destroyed this town and its county. For the Rowan County War has been almost lost to memory. Few people write letters any more, or keep diaries. The telephone has made written records almost archaic. That is too bad, because time tends to erase the footprints we leave on earth, and we need our records.

Recently the state built a bypass around Morehead that did, as intended, relieve downtown streets of traffic congestion. The trouble with bypasses is that too often they bypass the past. As Thucydides said, we need an exact knowledge of the past as an aid to our interpretation of the future.

The Morehead bypass erased a lot of footprints. For much of its course it was built on the bed of the Chesapeake and Ohio Railway tracks, and to accommodate its right-of-way several old buildings were torn down, some of them more historic than most local people realized. The Rains Hotel, for example, and what was once the American House and Saloon, went down. They played important roles in that unhappy chapter in the history of Morehead and Rowan County that has come to be known as the Rowan County War. War is a better term for that grisly episode in Rowan County's history than the word feud, which many people employ.

Perhaps the clash between the Martins and the Tollivers could be said to constitute a feud. At any rate, it lasted more than three years, and historian David Williams counted twenty men killed and sixteen wounded in that time. Like other mountain feuds, it forced the governor to send troops into the county to restore order and permit the courts to operate. General Sam Hill, in charge of the troops, got so disgusted with the place that he suggested to the governor that he do away with Rowan County altogether and let surrounding counties absorb it. Fortunately, this was not done, and Morehead licked its wounds and survived.

Rowan County is typical of the northeastern section of Kentucky between Lexington and Ashland—hilly, wooded country drained by the north-flowing Licking River. About a third of the county is suitable for farms, a third is owned by the government, and much of the county is part of the Daniel Boone National Forest. Cave Run Lake lies along the southwestern border of the county and is a popular boating and vacation spot.

The first settlers came from Virginia in the years following the Revolutionary War, most of them claiming land grants for wartime service, but it was not until 1856 that Rowan was carved out of Fleming and Morgan Counties. It was named for John Rowan, a Kentucky legislator best remembered as the builder of Federal Hill, the picturesque Bardstown home now known as My Old Kentucky Home, where Stephen Collins Foster is supposed to have composed what became the state song.

The rural nature of Rowan County changed in the latter half of the twentieth century in response to the growth of Morehead State University, development of St. Claire Medical Center, and the growth of boating and tourism around Cave Run Lake. Before that the county had attracted unwanted attention because of a burst of violence.

What became known as the Rowan County War, or the Martin-Tolliver feud, was hardly a conflict of heroes. John Martin, though a member of a prominent Republican family, had had his run-ins with the law and had been arrested in 1877 for horse-stealing. Democrat Craig Tolliver, leader of the Tolliver clan, was big, ruthless, and clever but had little regard for law that got in his way. The Tollivers had come into Kentucky from North Carolina, most of them settling in Carter and Elliott Counties. Hugh Tolliver, Craig's father, was shot and killed by robbers who were after a large sum of money he had received from a North Carolina land sale, and Craig learned at an early age to carry a gun.

When Craig became involved in the feud, he and his family were living in Farmers, the county's largest town, with a population of more than 1,000, the site of several sawmills and the center of regional farm trade. Morehead, about eight miles to the northeast, had around 700 people and was important only because it was the county seat. But several families, including the Logans and Powerses, had big plans for Morehead and regarded Tolliver as an interloper who wanted to use the town for his own political and economic profit.

Yet, as Fred Brown (co-author with Juanita Blair of *Days of Anger, Days of Tears*, probably the best work on the Rowan County feud) says, "There are no devils here, just men." But some of the men were more devilish than others and took advantage of the confusion in a tough rural community. Tangled political and business rivalries spawned a condition approaching chaos, and in the summer of 1883 Craig Tolliver decided this situation offered opportunity. It took him only about a year to take advantage of that opportunity, and for several years afterward he tended to act as though he owned the place. And since Morehead was the county seat, he held authority over much of the county as well. His reign was ended, as was his life, by a lawyer who did not seem the type to unseat the powerful but who finally decided that he, and the town, had had enough.

Strangely, the trouble began over an election that should have had little direct effect on Rowan County. In 1874, nine years before the real trouble started, Democrat Thomas Hargis ran against Republican George Thomas for circuit judge. Thomas's backers charged that Hargis was not old enough for the office and had never passed the bar. When Hargis went to get supporting records from the county clerk, he found that they had been torn out of the record books. He cried foul, and the contest became bitter. The bitterness grew when Hargis lost by twelve votes.

The scars from the race remained deeper in Rowan than the usual Democrat-Republican differences and finally broke into open violence ten years later during the race for sheriff between Republican Cook Humphrey and Democrat Sam Goodin (or Goodan, or Gooden; Williams and author Fred Brown prefer Goodin). The August election day was marked, as usual, by drunkenness, gunfire, fist fights, and vote buying; the secret ballot had not been adopted in Kentucky, and people voted in public, their votes called out as they were cast, thus assuring that they would vote as they had been paid to. Free whiskey encouraged voting. And fighting.

But the violence that fueled the feud resulted from an accident of several days before. There had been a dance in Morehead, and during the evening Lucy, the wife of William Trumbo, got tired, excused herself, and went upstairs to what she thought was her room. It was not. By mistake she got into the room of H.G. Price, a wealthy timber dealer and owner of the steamboat *Gerty*. When Price returned to his room, he was pleased to find on his bed what seemed to be a bonus, and he attempted to make the most of the situation. Mrs. Trumbo screamed, fled, and told her husband of her horrible experience. This should not have been cause for trouble, but it was. Lucy Trumbo was a sister of Elizabeth, wife of prominent businessman H.M. Logan; she was also a cousin of Lucy Martin, John Martin's wife. Both the Logans and the Martins were families to be reckoned with.

On election day Trumbo sought out Price and demanded that he apologize publicly to Lucy. Price replied—not dishonestly—that he had done nothing wrong, had found Lucy on his bed, and had done what any man would have done under the circumstances. A fight broke out. Friends of the men joined in, to the cheers of drunken onlookers. When John Martin joined the fray, he was slugged by John Keeton. Allen Sutton, Morehead town marshal, demanded that the hostilities cease but was hit with a rock for his trouble. Acting sheriff John Day arrived and pulled a pistol to back his call for order. Instead, either on the street on in a barroom, Floyd Tolliver, brother of Craig Tolliver, swung at John Martin and knocked him cup over tea kettle. Outraged, Martin drew his pistol. Tolliver followed suit, and they banged away at each other. Bystanders joined in, and when the smoke cleared Martin was wounded, Solomon Bradley, a Martin follower and father of seven, was dead, and Adam Sizemore, who has gone down in history only as Adam Sizemore, was wounded. Floyd Tolliver was charged with killing Bradley and wounding Martin, and Day was charged with wounding Adam Sizemore. Tolliver denied shooting anyone, and a grand jury, unable to tell where the truth lay, indicted them all—Martin, Tolliver, and Sheriff Day.

A December court date was set, but shortly before they were due to face justice, Martin and Tolliver ran into each other at the Gault House, a Morehead hotel. As usual, they were drinking, and soon hot words were exchanged. Both reached for pistols, but as Tolliver raised his gun, Martin fired off a fatal shot while his pistol was still in his pocket, ruining his coat and killing Floyd. As he lay on the barroom floor, Tolliver whispered to his friends, "Remember what you swore to do. You said you'd kill him. Keep your word."

This was enough to cause Martin concern, and he was probably not too unhappy when he was arrested and put in jail. But reports that Craig Tolliver, Floyd's brother, was saying that he would kill Martin as soon as he stepped from jail, persuaded County Judge Stewart to order Martin transferred to the Clark County jail in Winchester. The Tollivers were furious when this was done, but Craig advised them to be patient. "There's another day coming," he said. "We can wait."

When Judge Stewart heard this, he decided it would probably mean death for Martin if he were returned to Morehead just then, and he ordered an indefinite postponement of the trial. This was too much for Craig Tolliver. He called a meeting of the clan. Someone proposed a raid on the Winchester jail; they could swoop down, knock out the jailer, grab Martin, and kill him on the way home. It sounded simple, but Craig was opposed. He had a better plan.

On December 9, 1884, Jeff Bowling, a Tolliver henchman and town marshal of Farmers, was handed an order, probably forged by Craig Tolliver, directing him to go to Winchester and order the jailer to hand over Martin, who would then be taken to Morehead. No one could be blamed if, on the way back, he was killed. Bowling, a Tolliver ally who was not above bloodshed (he had knifed James Nickell in the fall of 1882) seemed happy to be a part of the party.

Bowling recruited four deputies and set out for Winchester, where he presented his order to the jailer. Since it carried the (forged) signatures of two justices of the peace, the jailer saw no reason not to release Martin to them. Martin saw plenty of reason. He begged the jailer not to do it, pointing out that his wife, who had just visited him, had told him that Judge Stewart had postponed the trial indefinitely because of threats made by the same men who had sent Bowling. He begged the jailer to get in touch with Morehead officials before complying with the forged order. But the jailer, not familiar with the Morehead climate, decided to obey the order and handed Martin over.

Martin's wife had just boarded the train back to Morehead when her husband arrived, unseen by her, and was placed in the car behind the one in which she was riding. Night fell. The train whistled toward Farmers, where Craig Tolliver and a dozen of his men were waiting. As the train pulled into the station, five Tolliver men held the conductor, engineer, and fireman at gunpoint while six others entered the passenger coach where Martin sat, shackled and handcuffed. Seeing them, Martin tried to run but was immediately shot. Mrs. Martin, hearing the shots, was seized, she said later, "with an undefinable dread" and ran back to the car where her husband lay shot and bleeding. A tough man, he lived until the train reached Morehead and even managed to walk, with help, across the street to the Powers Hotel. He died at around nine o'clock the next morning.

The news of the killing spread through the county, and from that day on open war existed between the Tollivers and their followers and the Martins and their friends. The Tollivers, Bowlings, Youngs, Goodins, and Days were Democrats. The Martins, Humphreys, Logans, and Powerses were Republican.

Craig Tolliver, tall, heavily muscled, and handsome in a brutal way, gradually gained control of Morehead, chiefly by getting himself elected town marshal and by threatening those opposed to him. Dr. Ben Martin, father of John, was a substantial, fairly well-to-do man. The Martins had on their side Cook Humphrey, the Republican sheriff, and Humphrey was one of the few men in Rowan County who was not afraid of Craig Tolliver and his brothers, Bud and Jay, and cousin Andy.

In an effort to even the odds, Humphrey named Stewart Baumgartner from neighboring Elliott County as his deputy. This was probably a mistake. Baumgartner, despite Humphrey's words of recommendation, was a trigger-happy thug and troublemaker. This was academic, however, for he was soon killed. The first casualty, though, was County Attorney Z.T. Young, who was shot but not killed as he rode along Christy Creek, northeast of Morehead. The Tollivers laid the blame on Baumgartner, and a week later, on March 17, 1885, he was shot and instantly killed as he, too, rode along Christy Creek, at almost the identical spot where Young had been shot. No one was ever arrested, but a few weeks later police in Flemingsburg, a small town in an adjoining county, arrested an itinerant gunman who admitted that he and two others had been hired, at fifty dollars a head, to kill Young and Jeff and Alvin Bowling.

Humphrey was not through. In late April he appeared on the streets of Morehead in company with Ed Pearce (or Pierce), a reputed killer, and a handful of Martin sympathizers, all heavily armed. Pearce was not your usual deputy. Short, red-haired, and with a bushy red beard, Pearce came from Greenup, where he was said to have a half-dozen murders to his credit. The Tollivers were alarmed. They sent word to Craig, who was in Elliott County at the time, and he hurried back, bringing with him several of his kin.

Humphrey and Pearce entered the bar at the Carey Hotel and ran into Jeff Bowling and John Day. Insults were exchanged, Day and Bowling retreated to the Cottage Hotel (also known as the Rains Hotel) across the street, and the two groups began shooting at each other. Humphrey and Pearce ran out of ammunition and retreated to the Gault House. Tolliver reinforcements arrived that afternoon from Mt. Sterling and besieged the Martin faction. Rifle bullets ripped through the hotel and ricocheted around the town, terrifying noncombatants. Badly outnumbered, Humphrey and Pearce slipped out the back door and retreated to the Martin home.

Tollivers took over the town, walking up and down Main Street armed with rifles. People were afraid to come out of their homes. County officials caught the train for Frankfort, where they appealed to Governor J. Proctor Knott for help.

In the following weeks a number of people, including Dr. R.L. Rains, Circuit Clerk James Johnson, Robert and James Nickell, and James Thompson announced that they were moving to Mt. Sterling until conditions improved. Others left for good. Dr. Ben Martin, saying that he had been threatened by Craig Tolliver, sold out, took his sons Will and Dave, and moved to Kansas, leaving Mrs. Martin and their daughters at the Martin home until he could send for them.

But the Tolliver noose was not quite tight. Hiram Pigman, H.M. Logan, and D.B. (Boone) Logan, lawyers and businessmen, joined county officials in asking Governor Knott for help. Governor Knott responded by sending Adjutant General John Castleman to Morehead to see if he could determine the cause of the continuing violence. Castleman reported, in effect, that law enforcement in Rowan County was weak because it was in the hands of lawbreakers and that no one seemed especially interested in seeing law enforced. As a result, the leaders of the two camps were summoned to Louisville, where state officials worked out what they thought was a workable compromise. It was not.

Cook Humphrey, H.M. Logan, and Judge James Carey represented one side, generally Republican, while Craig Tolliver and Dr. Jerry Wilson represented the Democrats, if they can be so labeled. On April 11 both sides agreed to lay down their arms, obey the laws, and not attack the other. The agreement granted amnesty to all concerned for the riot. This, of course, pleased and encouraged the battlers, and for a while it seemed that the truce might hold. But not for long. General Castleman, at the conclusion of the truce talks, predicted that the truce wouldn't hold. He was right.

Back in Morehead, Craig Tolliver, supported by County Attorney Z.T. Young, was elected town marshal over Robert Messer. Messer was then elected constable, with Tolliver backing. Ed Pearce, the Greenup gunman, was arrested in Greenup County and tried in Bath County for robbery. He was found guilty and sentenced to twenty years in prison, but before he left he sent for Z.T. Young and told him that H.M. Logan and Sue Martin had offered him and Ben Rayburn money to kill Young as well as Jeff and Alvin Bowling. Pearce later recanted, saying that Craig Tolliver had threatened to have him killed before he reached prison if he did not lie.

On June 11, Alvin Bowling was indicted in Mt. Sterling for the murder of a man named Gill. Ed Pearce, at the trial, testified that John Martin and Cook Humphrey had made a deal: Humphrey would collect the county taxes, Martin would then rob him and take the money, and together they would go West. The Morehead police judge, a Tolliver man, then issued a warrant for Humphrey, who was at the Martin house at the time. (Pearce later recanted this charge, too.)

Then began a period of open lawlessness. Tolliver heard that Cook Humphrey and Ben Rayburn were at the Martin home, and early on the morning of June 28, 1885, after surrounding the house during the night, the Tollivers attacked. Said Mrs. Martin:

Craig Tolliver and his gang came to my house early in the morning after Cook Humphrey and Ben Rayburn. At the time there was no one living at my house except women . . . myself, my daughters Susan and Annie, my little daughter Rena and my married daughter, Mrs. Tusser. My husband had gone to Kansas. He had received warning that he would be killed if he did not go, and we women folks persuaded him to leave. My sons, Will and Dave, had also been threatened, and they, too, had gone to Kansas.

It was Sunday when the Tollivers came. Cook Humphrey and Ben Rayburn were at my house. The Tollivers found out he was there because the night before he had slipped in to Morehead after his Winchester. . . . they saw him and the next day they came after him. They hid in the bushes around the house. In the party were Craig Tolliver, Mark Keeton, Jeff Bowling, Tom Allen Day, John Day, Boone Day, Mich and Jim Ashley, Bob Messer and others I did not know. Tolliver was town Marshal of Morehead and claimed he had warrants for the arrest of Humphrey and Rayburn on the charge of attempting to assassinate Taylor Young, but they never had any warrants.

It was a lopsided fight. "The Tollivers came in the yard and demanded that Humphrey and Rayburn surrender," said Mrs. Martin. "Craig Tolliver slipped into the yard and got inside the house. He was creeping up the stairway when Humphrey discovered his presence, seized a shotgun and discharged it into his face. Tolliver fell back down, and his friends rushed in and dragged him out of danger. He was badly scarred but alive. A half-grown boy was at work in the field, he approached the house and two shots were fired at him. The word got to Morehead but no one dared go to relief."

Sue Martin, a spunky sort, made her escape but was met by Tolliver, his face covered with blood, who threatened to kill her if she went to Morehead. She made a dash through the bushes. Tolliver fired at her, but she escaped and hid in a ditch until nearly night, when she made her way into town. But when she reached the courthouse she was arrested by a deputy sheriff and put into jail. The Tollivers threatened to set the Martin house on fire if Humphrey and Rayburn did not surrender.

"At about four oclock," Mrs. Martin reported, "Rayburn made a run for the bushes. Several hundred shots had been fired. The two men, Rayburn and Humphrey, rushed out the eastern door, leaped the fence and dashed across the cornfield toward the mountain."

The two men had gone about a hundred yards when Rayburn was hit. He rose, was hit again, fell and did not rise. Humphrey made it to the woods, and the gang, knowing he had a Winchester, did not pursue. The Tollivers then set the house on fire. Mrs. Martin and the girls ran out as the house and all its furniture went up in flames. Annie made her way into town, where she was arrested and put in jail with her sister Susan. Mrs. Martin and the other girls spent the night under a tree.

The next night Major Lewis McKee got off the train with 150 men and marched up the street to encamp on the courthouse lawn. The Martin girls were released from jail. There were no charges against them.

Craig Tolliver claimed that he had warrants for the arrest of Humphrey and Rayburn and had a right to use as much force as necessary to arrest them. But on July 3, A.J. McKenzie was appointed temporary sheriff, and a few days later Craig Tolliver, Jeff Bowling, John Trumbo, Boone Day, Robert Messer, James Oxley, and H.M. Keeton were arrested for the murder of Ben Rayburn. It looked bad for them. It wasn't. They had to be given an examining trial before two magistrates. One was a Tolliver man, the other a Republican. The Tolliver magistrate declared that no cause for trial existed, and since it took two to vote for trial, all of the accused went free.

Jeff Bowling went to Ohio, where his mother-in-law had married a wealthy farmer named Douglas who, after a short time, turned up dead. Bowling was tried and sentenced to hang but got the sentence commuted to life, was paroled, and moved to Texas.

Meanwhile, back in Morehead, Craig Tolliver, now Marshal Tolliver, moved to consolidate his gains. C.W. Collins, a Tolliver man, was appointed temporary jailer. H.C. Powers sold his Powers Hotel to Craig. Some say he was forced to sell, since he got only $250 for it. Craig renamed it the American Hotel, opened a saloon, and again changed the name, to the American Hotel and Saloon. The law required that such enterprises be licensed, but since he was the law, Craig saw no reason to bother with such details. He also opened a dry goods store. Not long after the hotel sale, a mob stormed Powers's home and shot it full of holes. Powers had had trouble with Jay Tolliver. He left town.

Following the fight at the Martin farm, Cook Humphrey resigned as sheriff, and William Ramey was named to the post. He was an honest officer but in no position to challenge the Tollivers, and late in the summer of 1885, when the court was clearly unable to function, Governor Knott again sent in troops. A few of the alleged killers were put on trial, and though only minor sentences resulted, many of the culprits decided to leave the county. A kind of peace settled over the town, and on August 8 the troops went home.

On the same day, Craig Tolliver was indicted for beating Sue Mar-

tin, John Day for burning the Martin house, and Humphrey and Pearce
for conspiracy to kill. On November 10, 1885, Pearce was given seven
years for a robbery in Greenup County. Alvin Bowling got twenty-
one years for killing his father-in-law. The records imply that the others went free.

As usual, the peace was brief. In the following months, Wiley
Tolliver was killed by Mack Bentley, and John G. Hughes was killed
by an organization of men calling themselves Regulators, formed
when law enforcement broke down. Early in 1886 Whit Pelphrey was
killed by Tom Goodin, brother of S.B. Goodin, brother-in-law of Bud,
Craig, and Jay Tolliver.

A curious note: Toward the end of 1885 Craig Tolliver went to
Cincinnati, where he was arrested and jailed for robbery but tried
and acquitted. While he was awaiting trial, he was shot by Asbury
Crisp "in a fit of jealousy." Apparently Craig had been romancing the
wrong woman. He got home in time for the elections, which caused
trouble, as usual.

Though no longer sheriff, Cook Humphrey still rode at the head
of a considerable force of men, and occasionally they would parade
through Morehead as if to challenge the Tollivers. On July 2, 1886,
Craig Tolliver handed Sheriff Ramey a warrant for the arrest of Cook
Humphrey, who was in town for court day. Ramey found Humphrey
at the store of H.M. Logan and attempted to arrest him. Humphrey
apparently laughed at Ramey, one or the other drew a pistol, friends
of both joined the fight, and bullets raked the street. When the firing
stopped both the sheriff and his son were seriously wounded, and
W.O. Logan, the young son of H.M. Logan, was dead.

Both sides retreated to their headquarters, and the town braced
for another all-out fight. But the county judge, afraid of the gathering
violence, had again wired Governor Knott for help, and as people
peered from behind blinds, the state militia again marched down
Railroad and Water Streets to the reassuring notes of the bugle. They
remained through the session of Circuit Court.

Once again an effort was made to bring some sanity to the situation in Morehead. When Circuit Court convened, the state was represented by Asher Caruth, Commonwealth's attorney of Jefferson Circuit Court in Louisville. Caruth took a long look at conditions and
tried to find a compromise. In a letter to Circuit Judge A.E. Cole of
Rowan Circuit Court, Caruth recommended that all charges against
Craig Tolliver and Cook Humphrey be dropped, and that in return
both men be required to sign an oath that they would leave the county, never to return except to attend a family funeral, and then only for

the day of the ceremony. They would further be required to agree that, should they violate the agreement and return to Morehead, all charges against them would again be prosecuted.

Both men agreed. Tolliver signed the following document:

Asher G. Caruth
Commonwealth's attorney pro tempore
14th Judicial District:—
  I request you to suspend any further proceedings in the cases now pending in the Rowan Circuit Court against me, and promise that I will remain away from the county of Rowan permanently. Should I ever return to said county I am willing that the cases shall be redocketed and the trials proceed. I will leave said county on or before the 8th day of August 1886. In this agreement I reserve the right, in the event of the death of any of my immediate relatives, to return to attend their burial, but I must immediately thereafter leave the county to permanently remain away.

[signed] Craig Tolliver

Attest: D.B. Logan.

Cook Humphrey signed an identical document. It is interesting to note that Caruth had the documents attested by D.B. Logan, indicating that he was one in whom the authorities placed some trust.

Caruth's efforts were well intended but naive. All the agreement did was relieve Craig Tolliver of the charges against him. Its fatal flaw lay in the assumption that both men would keep their word, which was a total misunderstanding of Craig Tolliver. Cook Humphrey, true to his word, left Rowan, saying he was going out West to start a new life. As far as the record shows, he kept his word. He returned to Morehead only after Craig Tolliver was dead, and then briefly on business. One version of the feud holds that Humphrey returned to marry Sue Martin, but there is no record of the marriage.

The Caruth agreement played directly into the hands of Craig Tolliver, who saw his opportunity and took it. With Humphrey out of the way, the anti-Tolliver faction crumbled, and after staying in Cincinnati until the indictments against him were dismissed, Tolliver rode back into Morehead and took over. He had agreed, of course, that when he returned, the cases against him would be redocketed, but there was no one who dared redocket them. Craig established himself as county judge, and though D.B. Logan managed to get elected police judge, John Manning, a Tolliver ally, was elected town marshal.

His enemies charged that Tolliver was operating the town without regard for law; his saloons were open and operating without the formality of licenses. He was accused of running the American Hotel as something of a whorehouse, but no one brought him to court on the charge. If anyone gave Craig trouble, the troublemaker was notified that the date of his funeral had been chosen; he usually chose to leave before that date arrived. But, as if to rebut his enemies, on June 6, 1887, Craig applied for a liquor license for the American Hotel.

Curiously, during all of this violence, Craig Tolliver maintained a home near Farmers, where his wife and children lived unaffected by the furor in Morehead. Mrs. Tolliver was said to be a mild-mannered woman, loving wife, and attentive mother, and Craig was known as a loving father and husband. Mrs. Tolliver apparently did not inquire too closely about his work.

And it should be noted that not everyone in Rowan County, by any means, was opposed to Tolliver. The citizens of Farmers, the county's largest town, were satisfied with the way Craig ran things, as were most of the Democrats living out in the county. And the more fun-loving element in Morehead did not object to the wide-open manner in which the town was being operated.

But the lawlessness was taking a toll. At night, the Tolliver faction made a practice of shooting up the town, not to injure anyone necessarily but to show that there was no one to stop them. Gradually, business in Morehead withered. In 1883 H.C. Powers had planned to build a new opera house. A new high school was begun, and there had been talk of a new church. But between August 1884 and July 1887, twenty men were killed and more than half of the town's population left. In 1885 Morehead listed more than 700 citizens; by 1887 that had shrunk to 296.

Many of those who remained were enemies of the Tollivers, and Craig Tolliver seemed determined to get rid of them. Mrs. Martin was indicted for sending a poison turkey to a friend of the Tollivers. H.M. Keeton, Morehead constable, was shot and killed by Bud Tolliver. W.N. Wicher was shot and killed by John Trumbo, a Tolliver ally. In February 1887, Dr. Henry S. Logan, R.M. McClure, John B. Logan, W.H. Logan, and Lewis Rayburn were indicted for conspiring to murder Judge A.E. Cole and Z.T. Young, both known to favor the Tollivers. All the indicted men were hustled off to the Lexington jail for "safekeeping."

The indictments were part of a pattern. Craig Tolliver had apparently decided that D.B. Logan was the man in the county most likely to give him trouble. He began to move against him but overplayed his hand in a bit of viciousness that outraged the county.

While John Logan remained in jail in Lexington, his two sons were released on bail and returned to their home a few miles outside of Morehead. Eighteen-year-old Jack Logan was studying for the ministry; twenty-five-year-old Billy was ill with tuberculosis. Knowing that the boys would be their father's chief witnesses at the trials of the Tollivers and their allies, Tolliver decided to get rid of them. On June 7, 1887, Hiram Cooper, a vagrant drunk and Tolliver hanger-on, swore out a warrant charging the two Logan boys with conspiring to murder him. Craig Tolliver issued the warrants to marshal John Manning, who rode with a posse of ten men out to the Logan home. In the posse were Deputy Sheriff Hogg, Hiram Cooper, and Jay, Bud, Cal, and Craig Tolliver.

The Logan boys had their first warning of danger when the posse began shooting out all the windows of the house. Terrified, the boys crept upstairs, but when John "Bunk" Manning and Craig Tolliver went after them, Jack grabbed a shotgun and shot Manning, injuring but not killing him. Tolliver helped Manning outside, and the posse set fire to the house. Deputy Hogg then went into the house and told the boys to surrender or burn to death, assuring them that Craig Tolliver had promised that their lives would be protected. With this assurance the boys came out with their hands up.

It made little difference. They were going to die one way or another. Once outside, their hands were tied, they were marched to a spring about fifty feet from the house, and there their bodies were riddled with bullets. Manning then trampled the bodies, probably trying to make them unidentifiable, and the posse rode back to Morehead. On the outskirts of town, Craig Tolliver halted the posse and ordered every man to swear that the boys had been armed, had been shot resisting arrest, and that their killing had been absolutely necessary.

The next day D.B. Logan, along with Hiram Pigman and Apperson Perry, went to the Logan home and retrieved the boys' bodies for burial. When they returned to town they received warning that they would be killed if they attended the boys' funeral. D.B. Logan was told to leave Rowan County. He was promised that if he left peacefully his wife would be made a domestic servant in a Tolliver home so that she might support their children. That was too much for Boone Logan.

He, Pigman, and Perry quietly began enlisting the support of citizens throughout Rowan County who were outraged by the Tolliver conduct. Logan made it a point that the three of them were never to be seen together, and for several days they met secretly, often in the evening. Logan swore out warrants for all members of the murderous posse but could not get them served.

The Tollivers had every road patrolled, but on the night of June 16 Boone Logan and Ap Perry managed to slip through the cordon and catch the train for Frankfort, where Logan obtained an audience with Governor Knott. In precise, legal detail, he recounted the crimes and depredations of the Tollivers, pointing out the murders of his own kin, the unreported or unsolved killings, and the flight of most of its inhabitants from Morehead. It was an impressive presentation. There was only one trouble: Knott had heard it before and, as he reminded Boone Logan, he had several times sent troops into Rowan County, had spent more than $100,000 of the taxpayers' money, and had accomplished nothing. As soon as the troops left, the violence commenced all over again. Troops, he said, could do little in the face of corrupt officials, lawless lawmen, corrupt juries, and corrupt judges. The people of Rowan County, he added, would have peace and justice as soon as they threw out the crooks and elected honest men.

"Well then," said Logan, "will you lend me fifty or a hundred rifles from the state Armory? It is hard to elect honest men when the dishonest men have guns and use them to keep people from the polls, and to make them afraid to run for office."

Again Knott offered sympathy, but pointed out that state law would not permit him to give away state property or arm private citizens. "You are going to have to settle your own affairs," he said. "You know, of course, that a private citizen can arrest a man if a warrant is issued charging him with a felony?"

Boone felt frustrated and angry but held his temper in check. The governor's suggestion seemed to encourage armed action.

"Governor," he said finally, "I have but one home. From this I have been driven by these outlaws and their friends. They have murdered my kinsmen. I have not before engaged in any of their difficulties. But I now propose to take a hand and retake my fireside or die in the effort."

With that, Boone Logan left the governor's office and walked across the Capitol lawn to the train station. He had not gotten the help that he had hoped for, but he had learned what he must do. He caught the train to Cincinnati, where he bought fifty Winchester rifles, assorted shotguns and pistols, and two thousand rounds of ammunition. He then returned to Morehead and called his forces together.

To Boone's surprise, he found that he, Pigman, and Perry could count on over one hundred men to stand with them against the Tolliver crowd. He and Pigman divided these into four squads, each under an appointed leader, and gave each instructions for the coming showdown. Somehow he managed to get warrants issued for Craig,

Jay, Andy, Bud, and Cal Tollier, Bunk and Jim Manning, Bill, Tom, and Boone Day, John Rogers, Sam Goodin, and Hiram Cooper for the murder of the Logan boys (Boone Logan may have forged these himself) and finally persuaded Deputy Sheriff Hogg to serve the papers at an appointed time on the morning of June 22.

On the night of June 21, Logan and twenty of his men rode to Farmers (Otis Rice says the guns were shipped to Gates Station), where they took delivery of two wooden crates labeled as farm merchandise. They then rode back and joined the rest of their group a mile south of Morehead. The rifles and bullets were handed out. The four squads were directed to take positions at points north, south, east, and west of town and fan out to the right until they made contact with the next squad, thus encircling the town. At eight o'clock the next morning, Sheriff Hogg would serve the papers on the Tollivers at the American Hotel, giving the operation some pale patina of legality. Then Boone Logan would give the signal for the attack, which would begin as soon as he called on the Tollivers to come out and surrender. He did not anticipate that they would surrender peaceably.

During the night the Logan forces surrounded the town and slowly closed in. But no good plan ever goes according to blueprint. Somehow, either because Deputy Hogg got cold feet or because Craig Tolliver in the American Hotel became suspicious when a man named Byron ran across the street carrying a rifle, the fight started before the warrants could be served.

Logan called for Craig Tolliver to come out and surrender. Craig replied with a burst of gunfire, and was at once joined by a dozen of his followers. Logan's men rose up from bushes and ditches and from behind railroad cars and lumber stacks and closed in. If they had been decent shots, they would have slaughtered the Tolliver gang in the first minute. They weren't. But they did hit Bud Tolliver in the knee with the first fusillade. He crawled into the garden behind a nearby home. Jay and Craig, caught in the open, made a run for the Gault House but were caught in a crossfire before they could reach it. Jay headed for a row of bushes but was hit before he could make cover. Craig raced for the railroad station but was downed by a bullet in his leg. He got up and made it across the tracks, where a dozen men closed in on him, and he was hit again. Again he got up and tried to run, but this time a bullet knocked him down for good. Some say that, knowing he was doomed, he pulled off his boots, having always sworn that he would not die with his boots on. As he sat up, possibly to pull off the last boot, two bullets blew his skull apart.

Little fourteen-year-old Cal Tolliver stood in the road in front of the hotel, blazing away with two .44s, with twelve-year-old Cate standing bravely by his side; the Tollivers may have been bullies, but there were no cowards among them. When Craig went down, Cal ran to him and took his watch and wallet and ran again toward the hotel. He got a bullet in his buttocks as he dived under a house, a painful but not fatal wound. Cal was only a boy, and small for his age, and Boone Logan gave the order not to kill him. The same went for little Cate.

A barrel of whiskey in the hotel storeroom exploded in the blaze started by a stray bullet, and the fire spread to the nearby livery stable. Jay Tolliver was found and killed in a weed patch. Three men found Bud behind a store and killed him. Andy Tolliver managed to get away, but he had been hit twice and later died of his wounds. Hiram Cooper hid in a wardrobe in Z.T. Young's hotel room, but Logan's men found him, dragged him out, and killed him. The battle lasted for the better part of two hours. The Tollivers never had a chance. While the battle was raging, mainly along Railroad Street and between the depot, the American Hotel, and the Gault House, the train approaching from Farmers was halted to protect the passengers from stray bullets. When some women passengers asked why they were stopped, it was explained that a gun battle was in progress but that the train would proceed as soon as it was over.

The bodies of the Tollivers were put on a wagon and hauled down the road to Craig Tolliver's home, where Mrs. Tolliver, trying to control her grief, called for her kinsmen to come and, in keeping with custom, help to wash and prepare the bodies for burial. The others were left on the courthouse lawn for relatives to come and claim.

Boone Logan called a meeting at the courthouse and announced that he had acted in accordance with instructions from Governor Knott, which was true in a sense—a very broad sense. Actually, what he had done was not only illegal but brutal murder, though probably the only logical response to the Tolliver tactics. He warned that law and order would prevail and that orderly elections would be held in due time. He also announced the formation of the Law and Order League, which kept the peace until state troops under Colonel W.L. McKee arrived—somewhat tardily, Logan thought—on August 1.

Most people seemed pleased. A week after the battle, some of the young people of the town gave a dance. It was the first social event of its kind to be held in Morehead in three years.

But the trouble was not over. A lot of Tolliver sympathizers were still around. They looked on Logan and his crowd as murderers and as cold-blooded as the Tollivers. Others saw them as vengeful Republicans who had killed good Democrats. Z.T. Young, probably bitter over the defeat of the Tollivers, indicted Pigman and Perry for the murder of Craig Tolliver. After a seven-day trial, the jury was instructed by Judge A.E. Cole, a Tolliver faithful, to bring in a guilty verdict. The jury refused. Without leaving the jury box, it agreed on a verdict of not guilty, an indication of the division within the county. Boone Logan, for some reason, was not tried.

General Sam Hill, sent to Morehead by Governor Simon B. Buckner to report on affairs there, made his report to the governor on November 22, 1887. In it, he recommended that the act establishing Rowan County be repealed, that the county be made part of another judicial district, and that all persons indicted for violence on June 22, 1887, be pardoned. He also recommended, in pointed language, that Judge Cole's conduct on the bench be made the subject of legislative review and that he be replaced with a judge from an adjacent circuit.

The subsequent legislative investigation of Rowan County resulted in four formal conclusions that were submitted to the legislature. The findings were that:

(1) County officials were not totally inefficient, but most of them were "in the warmest sympathy with crime and criminals," going so far as to "rescue criminals from the custody of the law." The investigation singled out Judge Cole for siding with the Tollivers, but doubted that "any judge in the Commonwealth could . . . have enforced the law in that county." Attorney General Hardin heaped coals of fire on the Rowan grand jury which, he said, "was organized, I know, to shield the strong and guilty and punish the weak and helpless."

(2) There was a "want of moral sentiment" in the county.

(3) "The portion of the county attached to law and order has been so long domineered by the criminal element that they are incapable of rendering any assistance in maintaining the law, so greatly that a reformation cannot be hoped for if left to their own resources."

(4) "During the social chaos since August, 1884, spirituous liquors have been sold, with and without license, adding fury and venom to the minds of murderers."

The investigation did not propose, however, that the county be abolished, as General Hill had recommended, though his report had not gone unnoted. But suddenly the people of Rowan saw how poorly they were regarded and what their reputation might cost them. They moved to change their image, and one of their first moves was to encourage development of the Normal School. Allie Young, Z.T.'s son, became a state senator and was instrumental in gaining financial support for the school that eventually became Morehead State

University. Perhaps the school can be said to have grown out of the feud.

Morehead recovered, to become a regional market and educational center. Interestingly, a niece of Craig Tolliver, Cora Wilson Stewart, became nationally known for her leadership in establishing "moonlight schools" for regional adults, the first organized move toward adult literacy education. Another Rowan Countian, Dr. Louise Caudill, began a clinic that grew into the hospital that is now a regional medical center and the second largest employer, next to the university, in the county.

Boone Logan did not stick around to see how the drama played out. He had had enough. He moved with his family to Pineville, where he became one of the most respected and probably one of the wealthiest men in that growing county. He organized financing for and built the Pineville Hotel, luxurious for its day. With his son Ben he owned the Pineville Water Supply Company and was president or director of five coal companies, the K-A Bridge Company, and the Pineville Investment Company. His sister became the mother of the well-known Bell County attorney Logan Patterson. His grandson, another Boone Logan, married Pauline Asher, of the prominent Asher family descended from the pioneer Dillion Asher.

Daniel Boone Logan died in St. Petersburg, Florida, in November 1919 and is buried in Pineville. There remains no trace of him in Morehead—except perhaps Morehead itself.

CLAY COUNTY
The Hundred-Year War

The Incident
at the Courthouse

The sun had pushed its way above the jagged hills of Clay County, melting the mists over the waters of the South Fork of the Kentucky River, sucking up the fog from the dark hollows when, on the morning of June 9, 1899, Bad Tom Baker and thirty of his mountain kinsmen and followers rode into the Clay County seat of Manchester, Kentucky. People along the road into town and along the steep street leading to the hilltop courthouse watched with uneasy glances as the silent men rode up Anderson Street, turned and stopped in front of the two-story courthouse where soldiers, members of the Kentucky State Militia, stood in small groups around tents pitched on the courthouse lawn.

The soldiers shifted uncertainly as the horsemen drew up and formed a ragged line on either side of their leader, who sat for a moment, not speaking, looking with what seemed to be amused contempt at the youthful militiamen. He, Thomas Baker, sometimes called Bad Tom, was the reason the soldiers were there, just as the soldiers were the reason he was there. With an unhurried glance right and then left, and a nod as if in approval of what he saw, Baker dismounted, hitched his horse to the top rail of the low fence, and turned toward the courthouse.

Twice in recent months Tom, leader of the Baker clan in its lingering feud with the Howard and White families, had been accused of brutal murders, the most recent the killing of Deputy Sheriff Will White. In keeping with mountain custom, county officials had sent word to Tom, his son James and his brother Wiley to come in and face trial. Tom had declined the invitation, repeating his belief that he could never hope for a fair trial in courts that he said were controlled by his feud enemies, the Howards and Whites. Local lawmen, knowing that the Bakers could summon fifty men in minutes to defend the clan if need be, were not eager to go up on Crane Creek and bring Tom in.

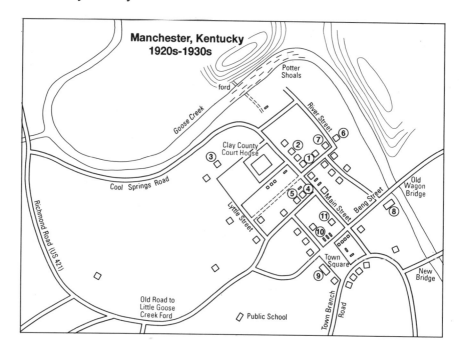

Map 2

Based on information from Jan R. Walters provided by Tom Walters.

1. Bill Marcum house, later a boarding house where Big Jim Howard lived in his last years.
2. Beverly White house, from which Tom Baker was shot.
3. County jail
4. Dr. D.L. Anderson home
5. First National Bank
6. Pitt Stivers home
7. Rev. Francis R. Walters home
8. Livery stable
9. John A. Webb Hotel, owned before 1896 by Calvin Coldiron
10. Dr. Monroe Porter's drugstore
11. Post Office

But Tom had also sent word that he would come in if Governor William O. Bradley would send troops to protect him and guarantee him a fair trial. He added, however, that he would not be put into "that stinking rathole of a jail"; he demanded a room in the nearby hotel. And he warned that he and his men would surrender their guns only if the Whites and Howards were disarmed first. Col. Roger D. Williams, in charge of the troops, had sent word the previous day that this would be done, and now in the humid morning of the mountain summer, Bad Tom Baker and Colonel Williams faced each other, polite but unsmiling, on the walkway leading to the courthouse.

Whatever he had expected, Colonel Williams confronted no cartoon stereotype of the shifty-eyed, tobacco-stained hillbilly. Almost six feet tall and solidly built (a young woman who once applied to Baker for a teacher's job described him as "a fine figure of a man"), with dark hair under his slouch hat, a full mustache, and gray eyes that regarded the soldier before him with a level gaze, Bad Tom was no simple ridgerunner. His dark broadcloth suit was rumpled from the ride in from Crane Creek but was in keeping with the styles of the day, as were his white shirt and black bow tie. Standing behind him, his son James and brother Wiley were similarly dressed, in contrast to the rough work clothes of the horsemen leaning on the fence, some holding rifles casually in the crook of their arms, most with long-barreled pistols stuck into their belts.

"Mr. Baker," said Williams, nodding politely.

"Colonel."

The officer shifted. He did not relish the role of peace officer.

"I am Col. Roger Williams, Mr. Baker," he said. "I have been ordered by the court to place you under arrest."

"Yes," said Tom, curtly. "I know."

"I also have orders to bring your son James and your brother Wiley into court."

Tom half-turned to the two men behind him. "This is them," he said.

"I'll have to ask you to surrender your weapons and accompany me into court," said the colonel. Tom looked at him without moving.

"They said I wouldn't have to stay in the jail," he said.

"Yes," said Williams, "right here, sir." He led the way to one of the tents pitched on the lawn, furnished with two cots, a lantern, and a table of sorts with a pitcher and wash basin on it. Baker glanced at it, expressionless. The soldiers standing nearby looked nervously at the notorious mountain feudist and his hard-faced followers.

"You'll be flanked by soldiers to protect you at all times," Williams continued. Baker nodded curtly, and again Williams had the unpleasant feeling that he was being put into the position of seeking the approval of this accused killer. His men, he knew, assumed that no one would dare attack the army, but he understood the danger in his position, miles from a road or railroad, his inexperienced troops surrounded by hardened marksmen.

"You may have whatever visitors you like, as long as they are not armed," he said. "We will provide your meals."

Tom shook his head. "Don't bother about it. We'll eat across the street."

Williams started to object but apparently decided against it.

"I'll have to ask you for your weapons," he said. "Your men will have to surrender their weapons when they come on courthouse grounds."

Tom reached under the tails of his coat and brought out a black .44 caliber revolver and handed it to Williams in an offhand manner.

"Where you putting Jim and Wiley?" he asked bluntly. "I want them with me."

"I wasn't told anything about them," said Williams. "I'll have to consult Judge Cook."

Tom looked at him, nodded. "I guess we better go in," he said. And Williams, again feeling that he was taking rather than giving orders, turned toward the courthouse steps. Before they entered, Tom turned and stepped back toward his kinsmen.

"John," he called. "Charlie." Two men pushed their way through the group. "You're going to have to give up your guns," he told them. "Just be sure you get them back before you leave for the day. Don't go out on the streets, out in town, without them. There'll likely be a lot of people in town, being Saturday. Stay away from Bev White and his dog-shit deputies, hear? And Jim Howard. I don't know if he's here. Watch out for him. Tell the boys, any of them need to go back home, do it now before they give up their guns. If they need to go, it's all right.

"I look for General Garrard to be here directly," Tom said. "A.C. Lyttle will be the lawyer for Jim and Wiley. The general says he's got me one named Robertson, but it may be A.C. I don't know. They're going to ask the trial be shifted to down at London or Barbourville, and the general says we'll get it, so we oughtn't be here more than today. Emily's coming in this afternoon. If I'm inside, you boys look out after her, take her over to the Potter place."

The men nodded, looking at the ground. Tom turned and joined the colonel, and the group walked into the courthouse. As they approached the doors leading to the courtroom they passed the office of Sheriff Beverly White, who looked up from behind the counter where already a half-dozen pistols lay, two in holsters. The colonel put three more pistols down and again led the way down the hall. Tom Baker gave no sign that he recognized the sheriff, whose brother Will he was accused of killing. He hesitated only a second when he saw, standing in the doorway of the tax assessor's office, James "Big Jim" Howard, the man who had killed Tom's father, Baldy George Baker. After two delays and a hung jury (the jury had reportedly voted 11-1 for acquittal), Howard had been found guilty by a Laurel Circuit Court jury but was free on appeal. Taller than Baker, wide in the shoulder, ramrod straight, well-dressed, and handsome, Big Jim Howard was imposing. For a second he stared without expression at the Bakers. Then a soldier came forward to hold the doors to the courtroom, and Williams and the Bakers went in.

Jim Howard turned and went back into his small but neat office. The day was beginning to heat up, and he opened a window and stood for a minute looking out at the tents and soldiers on the lawn. In front of the line of tents stood the much-talked-about Gatling gun that the troops had brought aboard the special Louisville and Nashville Railway car from Frankfort, loading it with a great deal of sweating and cursing onto a wagon at the station in London for the twenty-five-mile trip over the mountain road to Manchester, the county seat of Clay County and the center of the feud that for half a century had slowly engulfed the county and its people.

Along the walk men milled around the gun, admiring it, laughing at the rumor that either the Howards or the Bakers would bushwhack the troops and capture the gun before the soldiers could haul it back to London. They had already sized up the young city boys and decided that if they had to fight their way out of the county they would have little chance against the feudists.

Shortly before noon a smart, one-horse buggy drew up, two horsemen riding before, two behind, and the Baker clansmen stepped back to make way for the dignified, white-haired man who stepped stiffly down. "All right, get back for the general," one man said, and the others made way for General Theophilus Toulmin (T.T.) Garrard, hero of the Mexican and Civil wars, former member of Congress and the state legislature, grandson of a governor, and patriarch of the Garrard family that for fifty years had opposed, in commerce and politics and the degrading feud, the Whites and their followers. From his guard-surrounded, lonely, decaying mansion out on Goose Creek, the general had driven into town to lend his support to his Baker followers, just as old Judge B.P. White had come up to the courthouse to help the Howards, long allies of his family, in case of trouble. Now the general nodded his thanks and made his way into the courthouse.

"Tom going to tell us when to come in?" asked one of the men. Another said someone would. Talking quietly among themselves, the men squatted or sprawled on the grass. Several lit pipes. One, without ceremony, stood up and urinated on a tree near the walk, earning the indignant attention of a young trooper.

"There's a latrine around back," he said sternly. The man finished urinating, looked at him and said, "Go piss in it, then." Red-faced, the soldier glared for a moment, then turned away. There was a muttering among the soldiers. The clansmen smirked.

After what seemed a long time a man came to the door of the courthouse and said, "You can come in if you want to," and the men filed into the courthouse. Inside, a deputy took their guns and placed them on the counter in the sheriff's office. For a moment it seemed there might be trouble when a young man said he'd be damned if he was going to give Bev White his gun, but an older man standing behind him said, "Come on," and the man handed it over.

Quietly, not speaking, the men shuffled into the courtroom, filled the long benches. On the bench, on a platform elevated about eighteen inches above the floor, sat stern-faced Judge King Cook, up from Pineville, in Bell County, to fill in for Judge Eversole, who had asked to be excused because of illness in his family. Most people in Manchester believed that Eversole was simply afraid to hold court with both Jim Howard and Tom Baker in town and their families standing by. For that reason, Judge Eversole had asked for troops to keep order, and Judge Cook had underlined that act by forbidding anyone to come into the courthouse armed.

Now Colonel Williams sat conspicuously to one side of the judge as a reminder to anyone tempted to start trouble. Sitting at the table to the left was General Garrard, the two lawyers he had brought from Lexington to help defend the Bakers, and Tom, who turned and watched as his kinsmen trooped into the courtrooms. The judge rapped for order, A.C. Lyttle asked to approach the bench, and the three lawyers and the prosecutor argued quietly for more than half an hour over the defense request to transfer the trial to another jurisdiction. It was after eleven o'clock when the judge told the Commonwealth's attorney to proceed. For the next half-hour the man argued forcefully that the Bakers could receive a fair trial in Manchester and that if they were as innocent as they claimed, they should be glad to be tried by people most likely to be familiar with the facts.

A.C. Lyttle rose to present the case for changing venue, but Judge

Cook interrupted and announced a recess until two o'clock. Grumbling, the Baker followers filed out. They grumbled more loudly when they found that the sheriff's office was closed and there was no way for them to retrieve their guns. On the walk outside, General Garrard and Tom Baker stood apart from the rest.

"I want to thank you," said Tom.

"Not at all, not at all," Garrard replied. "I suppose I should be getting on out home, nothing for me to do now. Too bad we got such a late start, but I think you'll be able to finish up this afternoon. Lyttle says he has no doubts you'll get a change of venue; Cook doesn't want the trial held here, with everybody in town, afraid of what might happen. But you'll probably have to stay the night here and leave in the morning. I'll be here before you leave. Try to keep your men from getting into trouble. It's my guess there are plenty of men around who wouldn't mind a gunfight."

Tom, Jim, and Wiley ate dinner at the Potter House, smoked for a while, and returned to the courtroom, but were startled to learn that Judge Cook, after observing the Baker clansmen in the courtroom that morning, saw the possibility of an outbreak that could cost lives and ruin chances for a successful term of court, and ordered the court cleared. The Baker followers were outraged, stormed from the building, then came back to kick on the door to the sheriff's office, demanding return of their guns. A bailiff came out of the courtroom and told them the guns would be given back as soon as court adjourned. Judge Cook didn't want any shooting, inside or outside the court.

A.C. Lyttle made a passionate plea for a change of venue, arguing that no man under God's sun could find an impartial jury in Clay County to try Tom Baker and his kin. He pointed out that the county was under the control of the Whites and Howards, and that violence was sure to erupt if the trial of a Baker for killing a White were held in Manchester, troops or no troops.

Looking at the soldiers and the Baker followers talking and gesticulating outside the courtroom window, Judge King Cook needed no reminder of the truth of Lyttle's argument. Inside or within gunshot of the courthouse were the heirs of the long, bloody war that had gripped and scarred Clay County almost from the moment of its founding in 1806, when it was carved out of neighboring Floyd, Knox, and Madison Counties and named for Revolutionary War hero General Green Clay, of the famous Kentucky family.

A rugged, scenic recess in the heart of the Cumberland Mountains of the Appalachian range, Clay County seemed doomed to trouble from its beginnings. In the early days the rough terrain made road-building so difficult and costly that settlers could seldom manage more than rocky trails, though every able-bodied man was required to work on the roads or contribute to their construction. This lack of roads helped to isolate them from the mainstream of America as the tide of settlement swept westward, and made it hard to develop trade with the booming towns of Central Kentucky.

And Clay had wealth to trade. The wide, beautiful hills contained some of the finest virgin timber in the eastern United States—beech, oak, poplar, walnut, hickory, chestnut. Under the dark hills lay coal seams whose value had not been guessed. And along the banks of Goose and Sexton Creeks were wells that yielded water rich with salt, that mineral so precious on the frontier.

It was the salt wells that drew the earliest settlers into Clay County. Jim Burchell, taxidermist and amateur geologist from Manchester, believes that Spaniards and possibly Welsh, who some believe were in the country long before Daniel Boone and his kind, were drawn there by Indian tales of great salt deposits. The first settler who made salt there was James Collins, a long hunter who in 1775 tracked some animals to a large salt lick on what is now Collins Fork of Goose Creek, and the following year returned to stake a claim. Word of his discovery spread slowly, partly because of the Revolution but chiefly because no one realized how much salt was there. But by 1800 settlers were beginning to sink the big salt wells along Goose Creek, and the fledgling state of Kentucky considered the salt so valuable that it built the first road into the county to get the salt out. It was not much of a road, but a road.

Considering the isolation of Clay County and the difficulty of transportation, the salt industry grew fairly rapidly. In 1802 there were two wells in the county, with an output of less than 500 bushels a year. By 1845 there were fifteen deep wells—some drilled to depths of a thousand feet—whose waters yielded a pound and a quarter of salt per gallon. With the accompanying furnaces, they were producing 250,000 bushels a year, and with salt selling for a dollar and a half to two dollars a bushel at the well, or as much as five dollars a bushel downriver, the producers soon became rich, influential men. This was at the time when a daily wage of twenty-five cents was common.

There was also abundant game in the dark-hollowed hills—bears, elk, deer, wolves, foxes, and beavers, as well as rabbits, raccoons, squirrels, and sky-darkening flights of game birds. It was an elk hunt, incidentally, that in 1806 triggered the first burst of bloodshed in the region in what became known as the Cattle Wars.

In that year Clay County was formed. Manchester, a rough vil-

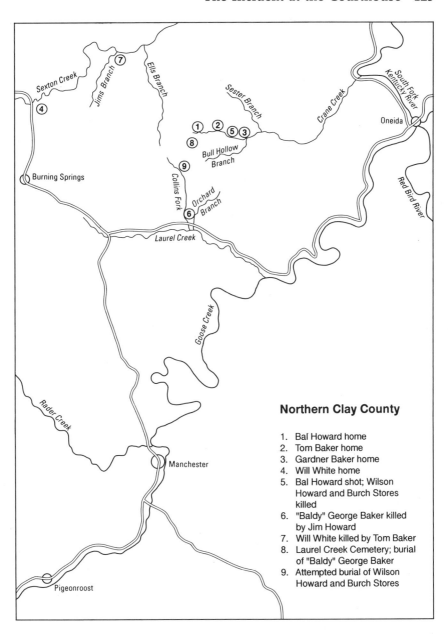

Northern Clay County

1. Bal Howard home
2. Tom Baker home
3. Gardner Baker home
4. Will White home
5. Bal Howard shot; Wilson Howard and Burch Stores killed
6. "Baldy" George Baker killed by Jim Howard
7. Will White killed by Tom Baker
8. Laurel Creek Cemetery; burial of "Baldy" George Baker
9. Attempted burial of Wilson Howard and Burch Stores

Map 3

lage of about a hundred people, was chosen county seat, and plans were made to open roads west to London, south to Barbourville, and toward present-day Leslie, Owsley, and Breathitt Counties to the north. Wealthier settlers such as the Whites, Garrards, Baughs, and Johnsons had claimed or bought large tracts of land containing salt wells and developed a thriving industry employing dozens of white settlers as well as slaves brought in by the well owners.

But hunting was still a popular way to replenish the family larder, and in the early fall of 1806 a group of men living on the South Fork of the Kentucky River (now Clay County) went over to the Middle Fork (now Leslie and Perry Counties) to hunt elk. They found not only elk but, on an upland meadow above the river, a herd of cattle, apparently abandoned or left to graze by Middle or North Forkers. Adopting the convenient view that finders were keepers, they killed and dressed one cow for food and were driving the rest home when North Forkers appeared and took exception to their casual roundup. A gunfight ensued in which one man on each side was killed, several were wounded, and the South Forkers were obliged to retreat. But bitter resentment had been planted, gunfights between the two settlements continued for years, and until the Civil War travel through the area was often a risky business.

It is hard to say how many people fell in the Cattle Wars, since the warriors seldom appealed to the courts, preferring to settle matters the way they began. In eastern Clay County there is a memorial highway named for John Gilbert, who led the South Forkers in the battle of Hanging Rock against North Forkers under the command of two men named Callahan and Strong, names that would later figure prominently in the notorious Breathitt County feuds. The South Forkers were reportedly headed for an ambush when Gilbert spotted the glint of sunlight on a rifle barrel in the brush above Hanging Rock, gave the alarm, and then led a flanking attack that saved the day. Like many of the mountain feudists who in old age repented of their wild ways, Gilbert later became a preacher, as did North Fork leader William Strong.

There is no accurate list of casualties in either the Cattle Wars or the Clay County War, or feud, that reached a climax of violence near the turn of the century. Tom Walters, a Clay County native now a retired school official in Florida, has a list of fifty-five people killed in the northeastern part of the county alone, including some, he believes, killed in the feuds. Walters also has a list, compiled by a friend's uncle, from memory in the early 1950s, of over one hundred people "all of them murdered" in the feuds. Stanley DeZarn, another

Clay County native, now living in Hamilton, Ohio, estimates that "over one hundred" died in the feuds. And James Anderson Burns ("Burns of the Mountains"), who was himself involved in the feuds and who founded Clay's Oneida Institute, declared that the feuds, not counting the Cattle Wars, took more than 150 lives. There were dozens of newspaper and magazine articles written about the feuds at the time, but most of them, especially those in the eastern press, were sensational to the point of being ludicrous, and invariably exaggerated the deaths.

This was a time of great movement and ferment along the western border. Though the Appalachian frontier was still raw and primitive, substantial numbers of settlers were pushing their way into the hills and beginning to establish the institutions of stable society—churches, schools, public offices. The Indian wars were, for the most part, finished east of the Mississippi. Daniel Boone, Simon Kenton, George Rogers Clark, and their heroic kind had cleared the way and moved on. It was time for roads, towns, and the structure of law. But in Clay County, the Cattle Wars had left a poisonous precedent, creating an atmosphere of hatred and bitterness that invited violence, and establishing a pattern of conduct that made violence an accepted way of settling disputes and protecting property.

As the frontier yielded, entrepreneurs were drawn into Clay. Prominent among these were the Garrards and Whites who, around 1809, began shipping salt, a vital mineral on the frontier for flavoring and preserving food, curing hides, and mixing home remedies. Until the great salt domes farther west were discovered, wells such as those in Clay County were veritable gold mines. Both Whites and Garrards made fortunes, built fine homes, sent their children away to college, and helped develop the community.

These were not the one-gallus dullards of mountain stereotype. They were educated, enterprising, interesting people, the kind needed to make a frontier flourish. Daniel Garrard, the son of James Garrard, governor of Kentucky from 1796 to 1804, moved to Clay County around 1805 and in 1808 married Lucinda Toulmin, a New Orleans (and Mobile) belle whose father had been secretary of state under Governor Garrard. Daniel and Lucinda had six children, all of whom attended the grade school built near Manchester through the efforts of Garrard, Hugh White (who had thirteen children, one of whom married Mary Garrard), Thomas Johnson, and Abner Baker Sr., Clay's first court clerk.

Theophilus Toulmin (T.T.) Garrard, who was destined to play a major role in the development of Clay County, was the third child of

Daniel and Lucinda. Born June 7, 1812, he attended the school near Manchester until, when he was twelve, his father bundled all the children off to Danville, where they attended Centre College, which at that time included the equivalent of high school and was considered the finest school in the South. While there, they boarded with the family of Josh Bell, who later became a noted state legislator and for whom Bell County, south of Clay, was named. T.T. was being groomed to take his place among the prominent men of Kentucky.

When he was twenty, T.T. married Nancy Brawner. (A curious note: They were married in the home of Alexander White, implying that relations between the families were not as hostile as they would become, and possibly implying also that the county as yet had no church.) They had two children, one of whom died in infancy before Nancy herself died in 1838.

T.T. was left at loose ends. An outgoing, action-loving man, he found the salt business boring, decided to get into politics, and in 1841 ran for state representative against Daugherty White. Like all of the Garrards, T.T. was a Democrat, just as the Whites were Whigs (Republicans after 1860). T.T. lost, but the loss didn't stop him. In 1843 he ran against Josiah Combs for the state senate and won, and the next election he was elected without opposition.

The 1841 election was the first instance of political rivalry between the Whites and Garrards, though it was not the first time their interests had collided. Beginning around 1815 the Whites started cutting the price of salt five cents on the bushel. The Garrards responded with a similar cut. The Whites cut another five cents, and so on, until the Garrards gave up the business and closed their furnaces. But they soon came back. The salt business was extremely profitable, and it was about the only industry in or around Clay. The family still owned a well when T.T. wrote his memoirs in 1899.

Like the Garrards, the Whites had come to Kentucky shortly after the turn of the century. Patriarch John White, whose family had come over from Scotland and Ireland before the revolution, was given a land grant in Pennsylvania for his part in the war. But he was a slave owner, and when abolitionist pressure built in Pennsylvania, he moved his family to Virginia, where he farmed and made salt near Abingdon. From there he moved west to Tennessee and in 1803 moved north to Kentucky, settling on Yellow Creek in what is now Bell County. After hearing reports of the rich salt deposits on Goose Creek, he moved north again to what is now Clay County.

There John's son Hugh, who had been U.S. senator from Tennessee when the territory became a state, formed a partnership with his

brother-in-law Samuel Baugh, making salt on Collins Fork. His son
Alex went into the same business with Hugh's brother James, and
they made a fortune hauling salt across the mountains to southwest
Virginia and floating it down the Powell River to Huntsville, Alabama, where it brought five dollars a bushel. With some of his prof-
its, James bought a plantation in Arkansas and two more in Alabama,
and at his death he was perhaps the richest man in Kentucky. The salt
business was so attractive that young boys were apprenticed to well
owners to learn the trade. In 1830, for instance, young Bowling Baker
was bound to Daugherty White to learn the trade but got into a fight
with Morgan DeZarn, killed him, and fled the county. A portent of
things to come.

Hugh White also prospered and soon became a rich man, head of a
large, influential clan. His son Hugh II drowned in 1856 while taking a
boatload of salt down the Kentucky River. One of Hugh's sons, John,
was five times elected to Congress and became Speaker of the House.
Hugh's son Beverly was elected circuit judge, and other Whites became powers in local and state politics.

They were not without scandal. Shortly before the Civil War,
Hugh's son William killed a woman with a butcher knife in what was
said to have been a crime of passion in an illicit romance. Nothing
was done about it. And then there was John Edward, who was a little
strange and at times a little dangerous. Benjamin Franklin White,
Hugh's twelfth child, married Alabama Taylor, daughter of John Edward Taylor of Tennessee, and their son John Edward, named for his
maternal grandfather, was born in 1838. He caused the family some
anxious moments.

For instance, on March 1, 1859, Dillon (or Dillion) Hollin was born
to a mulatto woman of that name. Everyone knew, and the principals
did not deny, that John Ed was the father. Their back-door romance
had been going on for some time, and John Ed wanted to marry her,
but the Whites begged, threatened, and raised so much trouble that
John Ed finally gave up the idea, though he admitted paternity and
supported Dillon.

He was not a constant lover, however. Ten days after Dillon was
born, John Ed recovered from his infatuation and married Elizabeth
Garrard Brawner, a niece of T.T. Garrard. The Brawners, who lived in
Owsley County but were preparing to move to Texas, disapproved
hotly, probably because of the illegitimate son, so after a brief court-
ship John Ed and Elizabeth eloped. Dashing off into the night, they
rode 125 miles to Tazewell, Tennessee, stopping only to rest the
horses, were married, and shortly afterward left to join the Brawners

in Texas, the parental objections apparently resolved. But they didn't think much of Texas and within a few months, though Elizabeth was pregnant, they left and walked and rode back to Manchester. They were warmly welcomed, probably because Elizabeth was due to produce another White child.

But it was another White marriage that caused serious trouble.

Drawing the Lines

Because of the burst of bloodletting between the Bakers and Howards in 1898, many people accept that date as the beginning of the Clay County War. Actually, aside from the Cattle Wars of 1806-1850, the trouble started in 1844 when young Abner Baker Jr. married Susan White, James White's daughter.

The Whites objected strenuously, though at first glance it didn't seem such a bad match. Abner Baker Sr. was a respected man, having been asked by a committee of citizens to move from Boyle to Clay County in 1806, when the county was formed, to be the county's first court clerk. He had a reputation for honesty, was an experienced surveyor, and, being an outsider, was considered more likely to be unbiased in disputes over property lines.

Several families or "sets" of Bakers came into Kentucky during the first decades of the nineteenth century. Most of them came through North Carolina, where they had settled after coming over from England and Ireland (though E.B. Allen of Rockcastle County, Kentucky, says that the Clay County Bakers came from New England, where Ethan Allen, of the famed Green Mountain Boys, was half Baker). The Clay County Bakers settled around Boston Gap and on Crane Creek, where they claimed or bought a large tract of land.

The first of the Bakers, Judah Robert, called Juder Bob, came into Clay shortly after the turn of the century. His son Robert (Boston Bob) was born in Lee County, Virginia, in 1800. No one knows where the Boston in Boston Bob originated; it may have been a hint of the New England ancestry mentioned by E.B. Allen. The Bakers originally lived in or near Boston Gap, and many are buried in the Boston Gap cemetery.

Boston Bob gained a measure of local fame by whipping a bulldog. The owner of the bulldog boasted that his dog, a fierce, thick-set beast, could "whip anything that moves." Boston Bob was skeptical. He went to the man's home on Sexton Creek, got down on all fours, and crawled through the front gate of the dog's domain. With a vicious (and probably puzzled) growl, the bulldog charged. Boston Bob charged. Grabbing the dog by the throat, he fastened his teeth on the brute's ear and hung on. The strangling dog twisted and snarled, but he could not get a grip on Boston Bob as long as Bob had a tooth-hold on his ear. At one point, Bob bit through his ear, but he got a fresh bite and lightened his grip on the dog's throat. A cluster of neighbors looked on, shouting encouragement to the growling gladiators. The dog thrashed about. Finally Bob released his grip. The dog fled under the porch, and Boston Bob had established a reputation.

It was Boston Bob's son George W. (Baldy George) and George's son Thomas (Bad Tom) who collided with the Whites and Howards in the climax of the Clay County War. The origins of the nickname Baldy George, like that of Boston Bob, are lost in the fog of history. Even Jess Wilson of Possum Trot in Clay County, a prominent Kentucky genealogist and himself part Baker, is not sure. Neither does he know when Thomas came to be known as Bad Tom. He had a reputation as something of a brawler from boyhood but was referred to as Thomas in the newspapers at the time of his death.

But to get back to the wedding.

Abner Baker Sr. was cousin of Boston Bob, though not as rough in personal habits. Young Abner was not unpopular, but he had a reputation for erratic behavior and a bad temper, and the Whites made plain their disapproval when he began courting Susan. He was known to slam out of a room in a rage when he lost at cards or in an argument and seemed to suffer a strong streak of paranoia. Even his friend and later defender Dan Garrard said of him, "Dr. Baker was always very suspicious in little games of cards. When the witness [Garrard] and Dr. Baker were playing, Baker would always shuffle the cards over again, fearing they might be put up on him."

Born in 1813, Abner Jr. grew into a slender, dark-haired, handsome young man. He attended East Tennessee College in Knoxville for three years but quit and returned home where, with his father's help, he was elected county court clerk. But this bored him. He quit and served a hitch in the navy but resigned after an altercation with his superior officer. He then opened a store in Lancaster, Garrard County, but it failed in less than a year and he enrolled in the new Louisville College of Medicine, from which he received a diploma in 1839. For a few months he practiced in Knoxville, but he quit to return once more to Manchester. At the time, a Knoxville friend advised his brothers that Abner was showing disturbing signs of instability. He was nevertheless able to court and marry Susan White in 1844, though his success may have been due to a scarcity of eligible young men in Manchester.

After the wedding, the couple went to live in the home of Daniel Bates, a prosperous salt maker who had married Abner's sister Mary, though they were separated at the time and were soon divorced. The fact that the newlyweds did not build their own home or move into one of the White or Baker residences suggests that their parents were not supportive.

At any rate, soon after the wedding Abner began to show signs that he was playing with less than a full deck. He began accusing Susan, in public and with increasing vehemence, of adultery with any number of men, including Daniel Bates, her own father, casual visitors, and even household servants. He swore that his mother assisted Susan in these liaisons and described in lurid detail how she sat by approvingly while Susan was boarded by her various lovers—or customers, as he charged.

As can be imagined, the Whites took a dim view of such goings on and tried to persuade Susan to return home. Daniel Bates, as well as Abner's brothers, begged Abner to see a doctor. Instead, he stormed out of the house and moved to Knoxville (without Susan, needless to say). But on September 13, 1844, he rode back into Manchester, went directly to Daniel Bates's salt furnace, crept up behind his friend, and shot him in the back.

Bates fell, turned, and, recognizing Abner, uttered a despairing cry as Abner fled the scene. As he lay dying, Bates dictated a will in which he freed his personal servant, Pompey, and his slaves Joe Nash and Joe's wife Lucy. He directed his son to take revenge on Baker and see that he was prosecuted, and to see that if the courts did not hang him, he was killed. He left $10,000 to make sure this was done.

The murder split the community between those who didn't think a crazy man should be hanged and those who thought he should be strung up with the least fuss possible. But after hiding out in the hills for a few days, Abner surrendered to General Garrard. The Bakers, like the Garrards, were Democrats, and the two families had fought several election campaigns together. The Whites and Bateses, who demanded punishment, were Whigs.

Unsure of the legalities involved, Garrard refused to hand Abner over to the sheriff or to the Bates family and, on September 24, took him before two magistrates, one of whom was a Garrard, to decide whether he was sane and should be bound over to the grand jury for a possible charge of murder. This was obviously not a court, nor could the proceedings be called a trial. It was a competency hearing. Neither the Commonwealth's attorney nor witnesses for the Bates family were called, though witnesses appeared both for and against Abner. The magistrates reasonably ruled that Abner was legally insane and released him to his two brothers, both of them doctors, who promised to place him under a doctor's care.

They tried, but Abner, after spending some time in Knoxville with his brothers, left abruptly and went to Cuba, where someone had told him he would have the best chance of recovering his sanity. The Whites and Bateses were not amused and persuaded the Commonwealth's attorney to indict Abner, in absentia, for murder. Governor William Owsley offered a reward for his arrest, and Bates's estate added $850 to it. It was never paid, however, for Abner suddenly and without explanation returned of his own will. It proved an unwise move.

Abner Sr. was heartbroken. He insisted that his son was not a fugitive, pointing out that he had been found insane by a competency hearing. He announced that he would ask for a change of venue, since the powerful White and Bates families had poisoned public opinion against Abner. But for some reason he failed to tell his sons of his intentions, and they brought Abner Jr. directly back to Manchester, where his reception was not cordial. The brothers too might have obtained a change of venue but concluded that it was not necessary, assuming that any sane jury could see the Abner Jr. was crazy as a loon.

The trial was a sensation that rocked the state and became a minor cause célèbre throughout the courts and medical circles of the country, since Abner's attorneys were pleading him innocent not only by reason of insanity but specifically by reason of monomania, insanity on a single subject. The nature of monomania and its validity as a defense were being hotly debated in judicial circles at the time.

The trial began on July 17, 1845, with a bank of prominent attorneys on both sides and the state's outstanding medical authorities on hand to testify concerning Abner's state of mind. George Robertson, considered the premier attorney in Kentucky, led the corps of defense lawyers, among whom was a Garrard. The Whites and Bateses brought in other prominent men to assist in the prosecution, as was the custom.

Defense attorneys offered testimony from doctors across the nation that monomania did exist. Other doctors affirmed that Abner was indeed suffering from the disorder, insanity on a single subject, in this case Susan's lack of chastity and her desire to dishonor him. The jury was not moved. The Bakers were shocked and outraged when Abner was found guilty and sentenced to be hanged.

The Kentucky statutes at the time contained no provision for appeal of felonies, including murder convictions, and efforts were begun to win a pardon from Governor Owsley. Petitions were circulated in Clay and surrounding counties, and a panel of physicians visited the governor to ask clemency. From the Whites and Bateses came other petitions asking the governor to refuse Abner a pardon and to send in troops to make sure that the convicted man was not taken from the jail and freed. In Manchester there were rumors that an army of Bakers and their friends had plans to storm the jail.

And the Bakers were indeed planning to free Abner by force if pleas for a pardon failed. Freeing him would not have been a great undertaking; the jail was a flimsy shack, and the jailer had placed Abner in an upstairs room behind a thin wooden door. The upper porch had been removed, but a ladder had been left, conveniently, against the wall. Abner's brothers slipped him a pen-knife with which he hoped, in extremis, to cut an artery and bleed to death, thus cheating the gallows, but he cut only a vein before fainting. He lost enough blood, however, to make the brothers conclude that he was too weak to ride should they manage to rescue him.

It was all for naught. Governor Owsley said he had no intention of pardoning Abner, and on the morning of October 3, 1845, he was led to the gallows. Despite the barbarity of the practice, public hangings were popular events in those days. A huge crowd filled the square, and 200 armed men surrounded the gallows to block any attempt at a last-minute rescue. Abner, gazing wildly about him, was led up the steps, struggled briefly with his captors, and then cried, as the noose was drawn about his neck, "Go on! Go ahead! Let a whore's work be done."

The hangman obliged. And a hard wedge had been driven between the powerful families of Clay County.

The Bakers wept with rage against the Whites for helping the Bates family bring Abner to trial when he was so obviously insane. The Whites felt justified in demanding retribution for the ruin of Susan's name and took it as a family affront when the Garrards stepped in to help the Bakers. Because both families considered it their duty to maintain the peace of the community, no further violence resulted. But the lines were clearly drawn, and the resentment bred by competition over salt hardened into hostility.

At the time, however, the case was not seen as a benchmark event. Other matters involved the city fathers. The lack of roads was proving a huge handicap both economically and culturally, and delegations went regularly to Frankfort in hopes of getting help. Merchants had to bring in merchandise over rocky trails from Barbourville or London, while salt, timber, and crops had to be hauled out the same way or floated down the Kentucky River.

Such handicaps were momentarily forgotten when, in 1847, the Mexican War erupted and there was a general exodus of young men as they rushed to join the army. (It would become a grim joke that Eastern Kentuckians flocked to the colors without being drafted when they discovered that they could get pay for what they had been doing for free—killing people.) T.T. Garrard was among the first to enlist, was given a commission, and returned to Manchester a captain. He appears to have enjoyed his military service and his first views of the American West.

But he had been a widower for more than a decade, and the family rejoiced when, a few weeks after his return, he met and married Lucinda Burnam Lees. But then a strange thing happened. Ten days after the wedding, T.T. and his brother William and two slaves became Forty-Niners and set out for the gold fields of California. This did not indicate, as one might suspect, a honeymoon rift; in his memoirs T.T. explained that he simply did not want to miss the excitement of the historic gold rush, a desire his new wife understood.

The brothers joined a wagon train out of St. Louis, had a fine time crossing the country, marveled at the great mountains, the buffalo, the clear rivers, and finally the majestic Pacific, and in California bought a share of a gold mine. For a while T.T. hauled provisions to the mine, but the venture showed little profit, and T.T. showed little enthusiasm for mining. He sold his share and left. His brother William, however, had taken a fancy to the coast, and spent the rest of his life in California and Seattle.

T.T. went down to San Francisco and caught a ship for Panama. But before he left, one of the slaves begged to be allowed to stay and promised, in return for his freedom, to send T.T. $500 as soon as he could earn it. T.T. agreed, indicating considerable generosity of spirit or compassion for a pathetic plea; a male slave was worth many times $500, and T.T. must have suspected that he had scant chance of ever getting that. But he wished the man well, and several years later received a letter with $500 enclosed. The former slave had done well and had developed a business of his own. T.T. was delighted. The other slave, William Tillet, was apparently impressed with neither freedom nor California and chose to return to Clay County.

The two of them caught a ship to Panama, crossed the mountains on foot, and took a dugout canoe down the Chagres River to the Atlantic, where they caught a freighter to New Orleans. There they booked passage on a steamboat to Louisville and rode home to Manchester, arriving on February 5, 1850. T.T. had kept a diary, noting the "Panama cane" that grew eighty feet high and was so strong that people made houses from it (bamboo, obviously). He had had a good time and had, as usual, learned a great deal from the experience. T.T. was marked by a lively curiosity and a wide-ranging intelligence. But he said he was glad to be home, settled down to the salt business, and was soon once more a candidate for public office.

Unfortunately, only days before his return, another incidence of violence had shaken the community and further damaged relations between the leading families. For almost four years relations between the Whites and Garrards had been chilly but peaceful and might have remained those of typical political rivals had not another Baker been accused of murder. In the fall of 1849 William Baker, the first child of Sarah and Boston Bob Baker, was arrested for the murder of Frank Prewitt, an itinerant shoemaker.

There was widespread doubt that William was the guilty party. Some thought that Matilda, his wife, had killed Prewitt when he made advances. Others suspected that Matilda's brother had finished him off after Matilda knocked him out with a shoe last. The sheriff, though, testified that bloodstains led him to believe that William had come home, found Prewitt there, killed him for any of several reasons (they had had a dispute over a piece of land; some hinted that Matilda and Prewitt were more than casually involved), threw the body across an ox, and hauled it to the woods, where he buried it under some brush.

Matilda was arrested along with her husband, but her trial was for some reason transferred to Owsley County, and she was cleared of the charge. William was tried in Manchester, and though the Garrards came to his defense and hired outside legal help, he was found guilty and sentenced to hang. Prewitt was a cousin of the Howard family of Clay County, and now that large family was drawn into the trouble.

On the gallows, on the afternoon of January 15, 1850, Baker was completely serene, though John Gilbert, hangman and sheriff, was in tears, as were many in the huge crowd. Baker repeated his declaration of innocence, spoke kindly of Mrs. Prewitt, but asked his friends not to forgive Job Allen, Adoniram Baker, and Robert Hays for testifying falsely against him. (Hays was so fearful of Baker retribution that he left the county.) Significantly, Baker said, "James White has too much money for a man such as me to live." That didn't improve feelings between the families.

William Baker was buried in Owsley County. Five years later, on her deathbed, Matilda confessed to the murder of Prewitt. (Why she had let her innocent husband go to the gallows poses interesting questions.) Too late. Another wedge had been driven, and this time not only between Whites and Garrards but between Bakers and Howards.

Local politics did nothing to improve matters. In 1856 the Garrards backed John Bowling for jailer. Bowling won, but within six months he was found shot to death. The evidence pointed to John Ed White, and he was arrested, tried, and acquitted for lack of evidence, to the surprise of no one. T.T. Garrard ran for the state senate and was elected but resigned and ran for Congress against Greene Adams of Harlan County. He lost, ran against Carlo Brittain of Harlan for the state senate, won, and served until he again entered the army at the outbreak of the Civil War.

Although a staunch Democrat, T.T. joined the Union army, startling his father, who was a hot Confederate. ("I never had a thought of going against the good old Union," T.T. said.) He was named a colonel by President Lincoln, helped to raise ten thousand men in Eastern Kentucky, fought with distinction throughout the war, and emerged a brigadier general. At one point his father heard that T.T. was going to lead his troops against Confederate General Felix Zollicoffer and snapped, "I hope he gets a good whipping." He didn't. But T.T. later said that he would never have fought for the Union had he known that Lincoln was going to free the slaves. Like many Kentuckians, he was concerned with preserving the Union, not with ending slavery. And he had been told, and believed, that Lincoln's Emancipation Proclamation applied only to those states in rebellion. Since Kentucky had remained loyal to the Union, he considered it a breach of faith when Washington would not reimburse slave owners.

Like the Garrards, the Whites had rushed to the colors, but perhaps the most unusual volunteer was Boston Bob Baker, who, at sixty-three, joined the Union army and was said to be the man who, fighting in the command of T.T. Garrard, shot and killed General Zollicoffer at the Battle of Mill Springs. Alexander White also served with distinction and came home a colonel. What he thought of the proclamation freeing the slaves is not recorded, but it cost both families dearly.

As have returning veterans since Ulysses, they found conditions sharply changed. Union forces had come in during the war and blown up the wells to keep the salt out of Confederate hands. The Union officers assured the owners that they would be reimbursed for the loss, but they never were, though resolutions seeking repayment were several times introduced in Congress. Only four wells were in good enough condition to be restored. Furthermore, the discovery of salt domes farther west and on the Kanawha River sent prices plummeting, and though the last Garrard furnaces were not abandoned until 1908, James and Daugherty White quit making salt in 1885. The foundations of the family wealth were shaken. Gradually, in the years following the war, fewer of the sons of the big families went off to college and came home to build the big homes. And the years between the war and the turn of the century saw more of them leaving the county for the Bluegrass, Ohio, or Indiana. The quality of life, for many members of the leading families and other Clay Countians, seemed to be eroding.

Some hostility remained from the war as Rebels and Yankees came home, but most of the Garrards, Whites, Bakers, and Howards had fought for the Union, reducing the grounds for conflict. Locally, the balance of power seems to have swung toward the Whites, who were taking more active roles in local elections than the Garrards, who more often concentrated on state or national office. Perhaps they concluded that, considering the Republican majority in the county, the Garrards had to concede courthouse supremacy to the Whites and Howards.

In any event, 1866 found Beverly White as county judge, John Ed White as commissioner of schools, and Will White as county court clerk. This was significant. State and federal offices held some prestige, but it was the sheriff, not the senator, who could arrest or fail to arrest a man in trouble. It was the tax assessor who could help a friend by lowering the assessment of his property, or hurt an enemy by levying a heavy tax on him.

In the first postwar years, it seemed for a while that hostilities had cooled, but then violence erupted. An argument broke out in the courthouse doorway between Sheriff John G. White and Jack Hacker. White accused Hacker of plotting the escape of two of his friends from the county jail and threatened him. Dale Lyttle joined Hacker to protest White's bullying. White was quickly joined by his brother Will and his cousin Daugh. The argument became loud and abusive, someone pulled a pistol, and Hacker and Lyttle fell dead in the doorway. The Whites were arrested, tried, and acquitted in short order. The Garrard-Baker clan was furious; Lyttle was a kinsman of the Bakers; Tom Baker had married Emily Lyttle.

John Ed White, now in his fifties, added a bizarre chapter to the county's record for violence when he got into a "difficulty" with George Stivers and threatened to kill him. Stivers was afraid that John Ed, with the protection of his family, would carry out the threat and fled to the home of a friend in Rockcastle County. John Ed, in company with his son Dillon and a man named Chestnut, went looking for him.

On the way to Rockcastle County they met seventy-five-year-old William "Booger" Benge and asked if he had seen Stivers. Benge said he had not and tried to joke about the situation, but John Ed was not in a joking mood and threatened to shoot him. Chestnut intervened, saying that John Ed should be ashamed to threaten an old man who had done him no harm. This so angered John Ed that he shot and killed Chestnut, as Benge looked on, horrified. John Ed later came across Stivers in Anse Baker's saloon in Manchester, and they had a drink and settled their differences, a little late for Chestnut. But some months later the two had another argument, and Stivers shot John Ed in the leg. It crippled him. Many wished it had killed him.

A Legacy of Violence

The years following the end of the Civil War were, not surprisingly, a time of violence in Clay County; it was a bloody time throughout Kentucky. Other states had debated the matter of slavery and had gone either free or slave. Kentucky had fought over the question for fifty years and finally tried to go both ways, tearing itself in two. The division and bitterness outlived the war.

In the end Kentucky stuck with the Union and sent almost three times as many men to the North as to the South. But the postwar conduct of federal military commanders, who tended to treat all Kentuckians as though they had been in rebellion, outraged people. Many who had stayed loyal to the Union now became hotly pro-Southern, leading one historian to declare that Kentucky was the only state in history to join the loser after the loss. So deep was the resentment against federal orders and officers that Democrats became overnight the majority party, and it would be thirty years before a Republican could be elected governor.

Returning Rebel and Yankee soldiers clashed. Duels were fought, homes burned. Freed slaves found themselves at loose ends, with no food, no money, and no place to live unless they were permitted to stay with their former owners, many of whom despised them or hated them for their role in bringing about the ruinous war. Patrollers, Regulators, Night Riders, and vigilantes terrorized the countryside by night, driving blacks across county lines, burning their homes, lynching those who resisted, and threatening to kill any whites who tried to help them. Blacks accused of crimes against whites were routinely hanged, usually without trial. Eighty blacks were reported killed in the Frankfort area in a single year. Near Frankfort a gang held up a train and tried to kidnap the black mail clerk for holding a job that a white man wanted. At one time the U.S. postmaster general refused to send mail into Kentucky unless provisions were made to protect black employees.

The near chaos presented an ideal atmosphere in which to settle old scores, real or imagined, and in Clay County, as in other parts of the state, lawmen were often hard put to keep the peace. Most of the freed slaves attached themselves casually to their former masters, found menial jobs in town, or left for Louisville or Cincinnati. And the fact that most of the feudists had fought for the Union helped to keep the feud fires banked. But not for long.

Some deaths were attributed to the "wars" or feuds, but there is no solid evidence of this except that the fighting usually involved the Philpots, who sided with the Garrard-Baker clan, and the Griffins and Benges, who sided with the Whites and Howards. Some of the Philpots had fought for the South, which may have sparked conflict.

The departure of the slaves at the same time the salt business was declining dealt a heavy blow to the Garrards and Whites. Without the salt wells, they had no means of maintaining their growing families at the level of comfort to which they had grown accustomed. The old order was changing, and with the change a measure of frustration probably developed. The Reverend John Jay Dickey, the circuit-riding Methodist minister who arrived in Clay County in 1887, wrote often in his diaries of the lack of respect for law and the excessive drinking on the part of both families and among their followers.

But as the demand for salt declined, the need for lumber increased as America struggled to rebuild or repair the damages of the war. This was a break for the Howards and Bakers, who owned large tracts of timber on the hills above Crane and Sexton Creeks. Ironically, it was Boston Bob Baker who had sold to the Howards the land adjoining the Baker property from which they were taking a rich timber harvest. And, as in so many cases in Eastern Kentucky, it was the boundary lines between these pieces of property that created trouble.

From the end of the war until the late 1880s, relations between the Bakers and Howards were calm, if chilly. The Bakers had been Democrats from the beginning, supporting the Garrards in elections, and were generally considered allied with them since the Garrards had helped to defend Abner Baker in his murder trial. The Howards were just as closely allied with the Republican Whites. But for a time Tom Baker hauled logs to the mouth of Crane Creek for Israel Howard and was in a loose partnership with Bal Howard rafting logs down the Kentucky to sawmills at Beattyville or Frankfort.

At first this logging was considered mainly a winter sideline, something to do during slack months on the farm, but as demand grew and prices rose it became a main occupation, and a hard one. Usually a crew of three or four men manned a raft, one steering with a long sweep oar in the stern, another fending off obstacles and helping to steer with a smaller sweep on the bow. It took between eight and ten days to float a raft from Crane Creek to Frankfort, and a lot of men lost their rafts or drowned along the way. If the crew tied up to the bank at night to get a hot meal and a dry bed, they often found next morning that timber thieves had taken their raft or broken it up and stolen some of the logs.

Once the loggers sold their raft they could treat themselves to a hot meal at one of the Frankfort boardinghouses or some relaxing whiskey at one of the riverside "blind tigers." But this often led to fights or shootings and the loss of raft money. Most loggers pocketed their money, bought whatever they had promised their families, and began the long walk back home, a trip that took the better part of a week. Later they would ride the L&N (Louisville and Nashville Railway) to London and make the twenty-five-mile walk to Clay County. The roads were still primitive, one more factor in the sour mood that gripped the county as the 1880s began.

There were constant reports of gunfights between the Philpots and Griffins. There had been a fight between some of the younger Bakers and two Hall brothers. John Hensley killed John DeZarn and was himself killed by Sammie Howard; in court, Sammie admitted the killing but explained that he hadn't meant to, and was excused. Accidents will happen.

James Anderson Burns, one of the more colorful mountain characters of the time, returned to Clay County in 1882 after growing up in West Virginia, where his family had moved to get away from the feud violence (or so Burns wrote). A tall, dark-haired, craggy-featured man with the booming drawl of a revival preacher, Burns was something of a self-made legend who skirted around the edges of the feuds until 1899, when he claimed to get a message from God and founded the Oneida Baptist Institute, which still flourishes in the village of Oneida.

According to Burns's memoirs, the feuds had prompted his family's move to West Virginia, but as he grew to manhood he was seized with an urge to return, and upon the death of his father, who had forbidden it, back he went to Clay County. He found that things had not mellowed. The following account of his first days back in Clay County was probably embellished a bit—Burns liked to make a good story better—but there are reasons to believe the basic account:

I shall never forget the first feud battle I witnessed. It was election day. The feud leaders were extremely busy, keeping angry men apart, keeping them from discussing politics or drinking whiskey. Two small crowds of vengeful men were crossing the road in opposite directions, and about thirty feet apart. A lad, about sixteen, in one of the groups suddenly pulled a pistol and fired a shot into the ground. Instantly there was a flash of weapons, a deafening roar, and three men lay lifeless on the ground, while several more were wounded. The lad had caught sight of the man who, years before, had slain his father. He fired the shot into the ground as a challenge to battle. He was seeking an opportunity to fire that other shot for which he had been training all his life. His opportunity came and he fired the shot with deadly precision. An old score was wiped out, but many new scores took its place. A feud was resumed which raged for years and in which a hundred fifty men lost their lives.

The idea that a feudist would warn an opponent with a shot into the ground is unusual. As James Watt Raine wrote, "The mountaineer sees nothing wrong in shooting from ambush, and believes there is no sense in hesitating to ambush a man who will shoot you in the back." But there is reason to believe that this incident did take place. It probably involved young John Baker. The record shows that in 1886, when he was only ten, John saw his father, Garrard Baker, shot and killed by a man named Wilson at the Coldiron store near Collins Fork. At the time, John swore he would avenge his father's death, and this story indicates that he did just that. Not only did he kill Wilson, but the home of Wilson's widow was later burned and she felt obliged to leave the county. Both John and Bad Tom Baker were suspected but not arrested.

John grew to be a violent man. When James Howard was being hunted by the Bakers, he wrote that "every time I made the trip [to see his father, wounded by the Bakers] bullets were poured at me from the woods. Only once did I get a sight of my assailants, when John Baker fired at me from behind a log." Later, John, in turn, was shot and killed.

Shortly after the election-day shooting described by Burns, Anse Baker, who ran a saloon in Manchester, was charged with killing a man named Davis but was not convicted. There was a fight at Pigeon Roost between the Philpots and the Griffins that lasted most of an afternoon and resulted in the death of three men and a horse. Again, there were no arrests.

Yet during these years Burns was establishing schools on Rader Creek and later on Crane, and he was doing it with the help of Thomas (Bad Tom) Baker, who was not only feared as a gunman but respected as a school trustee who was eager to bring better education to Clay County.

Setting up a school on Rader Creek was not just readin', ritin' and 'rithmetic. Burns learned during his first week on the job that he was going to have to show that he could whip any boy in his school as well as some of their parents before he could expect any kind of discipline, and some of his boys were in their twenties and as big as he was. He further found that some of the neighborhood cut-ups liked to ride past the school and fire off a few rounds.

He went to Tom Baker for advice. "You go ahead and teach," said Baker. "I'll see you aren't bothered." He then sent out word that anyone giving Professor Burns trouble would have to answer to Tom Baker. Burns had no more trouble, though he did have to whip some of his larger pupils, just to establish a pecking order.

Tom was obviously a power—possibly *the* power—in county school matters at the time. Letters from him to the governor and to newspapers at the time of his trial for killing the Howards show that he had little formal education. His spelling, grammar, and punctuation were atrocious. The fact that he could not express himself well or defend himself in writing probably made him more aware of the importance of schooling and increased his desire to improve his children's education.

Whatever his true nature, Thomas Baker was not the simple murderer that newspaper accounts painted. It would be interesting to know when and how he acquired the nickname Bad Tom. The *Courier-Journal* and the *Times* of Louisville, as well as the newspapers in Lexington, referred to him as Thomas, as did members of the White family in their letters to Governor W.O. Bradley. It was only after his death that he became commonly known as Bad Tom.

Still, it is hard to escape the fact that he was pretty bad, if no worse than others involved in the Clay war. From the time he was fifteen he was in one kind of scrape or another and proved early on that he was not a man to be trifled with. But he was not an uncomplicated mountain killer, the type sometimes found in other mountain feuds. He was a large man, like his father, with cold gray eyes and a truculent expression. He was not given to small talk. At the time he was involved in the troubles with the Howard family, a young woman who had just returned to Clay County after receiving her teaching certificate applied for a teaching job and was told she would have to get the approval of Thomas Baker. With a young woman friend, she rode up Crane Creek to the Baker home, only to find it ringed by armed men. "I was scared to death," she wrote later, "especially when we were stopped by men demanding to know what we wanted, but I decided that since we had gone that far we might as well go on."

She found Tom standing on the porch of his home, unshaven, red-eyed from lack of sleep, with two armed men sitting on the steps in front of him. She said she was looking for Mr. Thomas Baker.

"I'm him," said Tom.

She made her pitch for the teaching job, explaining her background and qualifications and showing her certificate. Tom stared at her steadily as she talked. When she finished, he nodded.

"All right," he said. That was all. She had the job. One of the armed men motioned toward her horse.

"Thank you," she quavered, smiling. Tom didn't return the smile.

On an earlier occasion, a young man named John Fouts had the same experience. Riding up to the Baker home, he asked, "Are you Mr. Baker?"

"I am," said Tom.

"Well, I'm John Fouts and I'd like to have a job teaching. I'm certified, and I've got good recommendations."

Tom looked at him for a minute. "Hell with the recommendations," he said. "You can have the job. We'll see if you can teach."

Apparently that was enough. No one seemed to care to question Tom's authority to hire, fire, or settle school matters.

Not all of the years following the Civil War were violent. After the election-day shooting described by Burns, things were relatively quiet in Clay County, at least among the principal feudists, until 1893, when the Garrards backed Granville Philpot for the state legislature. The Philpots, who were said to be "thicker in Clay than blackberries in June," lived up to their billing, and Granville won. The Whites and Howards charged irregularities and tried to have the election thrown out, but without success. During the succeeding years, local elections saw both the Garrard-Baker and White-Howard factions score victories, though the Whites and Howards usually held the edge.

Still, the years between 1893 and 1896 were among the calmest Clay was to know for a while. There were reports of a major battle in the western part of the county, and there is still a legend that so many men were killed near a store there that the ground still turns red when it rains. But the battle, if it actually took place, was not reported. And during the time there were no major confrontations between Whites and Garrards, Bakers and Howards.

But this relative peace was not to last, and it was, apparently, very relative. When the Reverend John Jay Dickey arrived in Manchester, he wrote that to be allowed to preach in Clay County was the answer to his prayers. Within a month he was confiding to his diary his dismay at "the poisonous atmosphere of hatred and violence in the air."

The Reverend Dickey was surely one of the most interesting—and most admirable—men involved in the early days of the Kentucky mountains. He had previously preached in Breathitt County, where he founded not only a church but a school, which developed into Lees Junior College, and established and published the *Jackson Hustler*, the county's first newspaper. He also taught and preached in Owsley County, which he found badly in need of salvation. But he had heard that the word was even more badly needed in Clay and could hardly wait to begin God's work there.

It was not to be a totally happy experience. He had difficulty getting enough money from the state church even for his daily needs, and he was never able to persuade Clay Countians to build the church he planned. But for almost ten years he kept detailed diaries of his work in the mountains, and they remain the most reliable—and the most fascinating—history of the period. But he had not counted on the level of violence in Manchester, where he found he often had to hold prayer meetings in the afternoon because people were afraid to go out at night, even to church.

How much of the violence was due to liquor is hard to estimate. Dickey told of seeing Will White, then a deputy sheriff, shoot up Anderson Street while drunk, and he mentions that Anse Baker had been drinking when he "shot up the street and no one did anything." (Actually, Anse was later arrested and tried but acquitted.) It seems to have been a legitimate expression of frustration or high spirits to have a few drinks and walk down Main Street shooting off a few rounds. Few people were hurt, but it kept a lot of county people from coming in to trade. Kentucky historian Thomas D. Clark blames whiskey for much of the Clay trouble and much of the mountain violence in general.

At the height of the troubles, Dickey noted that both Whites and Garrards were "drunk all the time," or "killing themselves drinking." The reverend was inclined to exaggerate when it came to dancing and drinking, though there is no doubt that drunkenness was common. As Tom Walters pointed out, the people did not learn to use liquor socially, in part because the better class of wives would not serve it in their homes. But that didn't keep people from drinking it in great quantities. Manchester was voted dry in 1898, but the vote apparently made little impact on habits. There are hints that Bad Tom Baker made and sold illegal liquor, though in a letter to the newspapers he referred scornfully to a man who testified against him in court as a bootlegger. Tom exchanged gunfire with George Hall, who had been a federal revenue agent, though the shooting may have had other roots. Tom also had a reputation for consuming his share of the local moonshine and had an unpredictable temper when he did. Tall, taciturn "Big Jim" Howard, on the other hand, was known to be a tee-totaler, a devout churchman who would not use even tobacco and enjoyed reading the Bible.

The mountain affection for drink was not surprising. After all, these people were accustomed to making, selling, and drinking the powerful white corn liquor, regardless of sermons. It was an easy and profitable way to dispose of their corn crop; it was far easier to carry ten gallons of moonshine into town than to haul a wagonload of corn, and it brought more money. Like the Pennsylvania farmers whose home manufacture of liquor brought on the Whiskey Rebellion, the Kentucky frontiersman considered his use of his own corn crop none of the government's business, and resented, in principle and in practice, government efforts to interfere with free enterprise. This defense of individual freedom continued long after the frontier had been settled.

The trouble was that the uncut moonshine was powerful—it was usually sold at over 120 proof—and seemed to drive the mountain drinker crazy. Mountain men liked to boast of their ability to hold their liquor, but there is little evidence of this. Theirs was often a lonely, monotonous, hard life, and a few drinks of the local product were usually enough to unleash an explosive rage against the boredom and frustration of their everyday existence, an effort to express their vague longing for a richer life.

Considering the physical difficulties involved, Clay Countians traveled quite a bit—to Knoxville, Lexington, Louisville, and Cincinnati, even to New York. They subscribed to state newspapers and available magazines. National events were of intense interest and generated hot debate. The Reverend Dickey devoted a week's space in his diary to events culminating in the Spanish-American War. His attitude was not one of Christian pacifism. He denounced the brutal Spanish for their oppression of the sweet-mannered Cubans, praised the McKinley administration for its patience in dealing with the Spanish bullies, and applauded when the U.S. reacted to the dastardly sinking of the battleship *Maine* by declaring war. Clay County males added their approval by rushing off to join the colors, though few of them got to see much action before the war faded with the fall of Santiago, and most did not give high marks to Cuba upon their return. Dickey, however, was staunch in his support of the war and declared that the Cubans and Filipinos would "forever be grateful to the U.S. for giving them their freedom," a bit of chauvinism that proved somewhat premature.

Clay Countians were also intensely concerned with state politics.

In 1891 Garrards, Whites, and other prominent citizens traveled frequently to Frankfort to observe and take part in the politicking and to hear the oratory attending creation of the new state constitution. Four years later there was wild jubilation in Clay when the first Republican governor in Kentucky history, William O. Bradley, nicknamed "Billy O.B.," was elected. Having a Republican governor did not help Republican Clay County, though; the roads remained uniformly bad, and for his part the governor, before he left office, was probably sick of Clay Countians, who were forever causing trouble and forcing local judges to write and ask for the protection of state troops.

Encouraged by the election of Granville Philpot to the state legislature and the success of the Philpots in a series of gunfights south and west of Manchester, T.T. Garrard, in the spring of 1897, called a meeting of the Garrards, Bakers, Webbs, McCollums, and Philpots and decided to make a frontal attack on White control of the courthouse by running Gilbert Garrard for sheriff, believing that, with the prestige of the Garrard name, they could get all of the Democratic votes and substantial support from Republicans and independents dissatisfied with the Whites.

The Whites, behind the leadership of Judge B.P. White and his son Beverly, called a meeting of their own. Counting on the support of the Howards, Halls, Benges, and Griffins, they chose Beverly White to run for sheriff and James Howard to run for tax assessor. It was a good ticket. Beverly White was, according to the Reverend Dickey, a hard man but relatively sober, while Jim Howard was a quiet nondrinker and, though not particularly popular, well respected. A member of a large family living near the head of Crane Creek, Howard had gone to school in Manchester, studied law for a while, taught school, and served as county school trustee. He clerked in Hill's drygoods store to supplement his income and help support his wife, the former Mary Reid, and their three children.

It was a tense, bitter race, though election day was relatively free of gunplay. Bev White and Jim Howard won, and, though George Baker was elected county attorney, the courthouse remained under White control.

But there were signs that the old family lines were weakening. Shortly after the election, John G. and Gilbert White moved to Winchester. The old family salt works were no longer very profitable, and both men were interested in developing new businesses. They were also interested in farming on a larger scale than Clay's narrow valleys permitted, and were naturally attracted to the rich, rolling Bluegrass land. John G. was also interested in the mercantile business and soon became a thriving merchant. In making the transfer to Clark County, the Whites were setting a pattern in which, throughout the twentieth century, successful Eastern Kentuckians would migrate to the scenic, more affluent Bluegrass.

But life in Clay was more than violence. Roads remained a main concern. There was recurrent speculation that the railroad was going to run a spur from London to Manchester, but the dream was always deferred. How much difference a rail line would have made is uncertain. A spur built in 1914 to haul coal out of the county for war purposes brought only a spurt of prosperity. The fact is that the economy of Clay County never recovered from the decline of the salt industry caused by the Civil War destruction. There were no other sources of income to maintain the wealthy status of the big families and to furnish well-paying jobs. The relative depression that followed the Civil War undoubtedly contributed to frictions and the feuds.

During the week of August 7, 1897, Dickey noted with approval that groups of Clay Countians made the journey over to London to attend the Laurel County Fair which, he said, was a great success. But the "poisonous atmosphere" of which he frequently complained was not improved when, two weeks before the election, Deputy Sheriff George Hall, a former revenue officer, and Holland Campbell met John and Anse Baker and Charles Wooten on the road near Manchester. The White-Howard faction had scheduled a meeting in the courthouse that day, and Hall, suspecting that the Bakers might be planning to disrupt it, asked them where they were going. The Bakers felt that their destination was their own business and said so. Another version has it that Hall suspected the Bakers were on their way to testify before the grand jury. Someone started shooting. (At the time Anse was under indictment for shooting up the street in Manchester.)

The famed marksmanship of the mountaineers seems to have been on vacation, for though they all emptied their guns, no one was killed, though Anse was wounded and his horse was killed. That night Hall's home and Campbell's store at Pin Hook were burned. Anse and Bad Tom Baker were charged with arson. Tom swore he was miles away at the time, in company with a platoon of friends who could vouch for his whereabouts. T.T. Garrard bailed him out of jail.

The Christmas season passed without major tragedy. On December 8, Sheriff Bev White and ex-Marshal William Treadway exchanged words in Treadway's saloon, stepped outside, and emptied their guns at each other. Again, the mountain marksmanship was dormant. Neither man was hit. They had been drinking, however, which may have affected the outcome. Or perhaps their hearts were not in it; they were reportedly friends, though Treadway was usually allied with the Bakers in political matters.

Three days later a shadow fell over the holidays when Abe Pace returned to Clay. A cousin of Francis Pace, a Harlan County outlaw involved with Devil Jim Turner in the killings that sent Turner to prison in 1874, Abe was considered a dangerous man, and his return was not welcomed by the better element of Clay County. On the same day, Robert Lucas, son of Amanda Lucas, got drunk and shot up the street. Nothing was done about it, chiefly because people knew that Mrs. Lucas, a widow, had trouble enough putting up with her rowdy son, who had no daddy to beat some sense into him.

The Reverend Dickey reported, in some indignation, that saloon-keeper Bill Treadway dipped into his own stock and, perhaps in a show of Yuletide spirit, called to Dickey, "Hey, preacher, come in and have a glass of gin." The reverend declined. He was further upset to learn that Professor Burns was leaving his school on Sexton Creek to teach at Berea. (Burns, however, stayed only a year at Berea and returned to promote the founding of the Oneida Institute.)

But quiet could not long prevail. On Christmas night 1897, Robert Bennett observed the holy season by shooting and killing Robert Gregory, who was drunk. And on December 28 Dickey wrote mournfully that three men had been killed over the weekend, two in a saloon on Horse Creek, one at Red Bird. No arrests were reported. On December 29 a big dance was held at Daugh White's. This seemed to sadden Dickey as much as the random killings; he saw dancing as an invitation to lust and lamented that "even during the holidays they can think of nothing but dance, dance, dance!"

The new year of 1898 got off to a bad start. On February 14 a large group of Bakers rode into Manchester, apparently for the February term of court where Tom and Anse were to be tried for arson. Word that they were in town spread quickly, and various Whites and Howards moved quietly toward the courthouse. When Tom and Anse were acquitted, the verdict was received by their enemies as evidence that true justice could not be entrusted to juries. The courthouse was filled with curses and threats.

Sheriff Beverly White was among the more disappointed onlookers, and soon he and John Baker were exchanging words in the hallway. When several Bakers moved to shove past him, White pulled his pistol. John Baker swung. White hit him over the head with his pistol, and blood streamed down his face. As other Bakers rushed to help John, White supporters rushed from nearby offices, and soon the hall was the scene of a bloody fist fight. Strangely, no shots were fired. The Bakers retreated, fighting, to the courthouse yard, where they mounted their horses and rode toward Crane Creek.

A week later someone shot Deputy Felix Davidson, a relative of the Howards, on the town square, wounding him and killing his horse. Tom Baker was suspected, but no one had seen the shooting and no arrests were made. The same week a group of Ku Kluxers, whose numbers had increased sharply with the growing postwar bitterness, shot and killed a man named Barger near Bullskin. One of the Kluxers told Dickey that this had been an unfortunate case of mistaken identity; they had meant to kill Abe Pace.

On March 6, two men were killed at a dance in the bawdy house belonging to "the Hawkins woman." Only Mr. Dickey seemed upset, blaming it more on the dancing more than on the locale. The next day Dan Woods, son of saloon-keeper Reuben Woods, shot Young Hensley, but not fatally.

Two weeks later a grisly event reportedly took place, creating a legend that many people still believe. Bad Tom and Wiley Baker, a man named Banks from Owsley County, and another man, possibly Jesse Fuller "Spec" Barrett, a cousin of the Bakers, were riding along Sexton Creek when they ran into a man identified only as "a peddler," probably one of the Jewish peddlers who, around the turn of the century, walked through the mountains peddling needles, pins, thread, buttons, and so forth door to door. Tom and his friends had been drinking, and for fun they began "rousting" or "hurrahing" the peddler, pushing him around, making fun of him, probably shooting under his feet to make him dance. Apparently he objected to the fun, so one of the Baker crowd shot and killed him.

"All right," said Banks, "what are you going to do with him now?"

"Hell with him," said Tom. "Throw him over in the creek and let the turtles have him." That they did, but that ended only the first phase of the story.

And on Crane Creek events were building toward a tragedy.

The Fatal Clash on Crane Creek

June 9, 1899. As Tom Baker sat in the Clay County courtroom, listening to the droning of lawyers arguing his fate, he found that he was listening without hearing, though the outcome of the talk could mean home or prison for him. More and more, as the morning ran on, he had found himself thinking back to Crane Creek and his home, how it had been to be a boy there, thinking of his mama and daddy, remembering days when he used to walk down the creek to the river. He remembered turning over the flat rocks in the shallows to catch crawdads, remembered the sungrannies and redeyes around the ends of trees fallen into the river. He remembered standing on the bank, wondering where the river went, thinking he'd follow it down some day. How in hell did he get here?

He couldn't remember too much about the Howards back then except that they lived up the creek a way. Pap had sold them their farm. He remembered James. Never did care much for him as a boy. Sort of a goody type. Never talked much. He'd always had the idea James Howard thought he was better than others, always wanting to move into town while the rest stayed out on the creek. And he found himself thinking about that day—*that* day—when they got the Howards. Damn. Well, he didn't have much choice. They were going to get him, sure as hell. He sort of wished he hadn't let Jim come along. And he wondered again if it couldn't all have been gotten around if somebody had done something. Well, things happen. He turned to listen to the lawyer.

Accounts of what happened around Crane Creek during the month of April 1898 are so confused and contradictory that no one can say with any assurance who the villains were, who the heroes, if such there were. A possible, but just possible, key to the situation lies in an entry from Dickey's diary of April 10: "This written by General

T.T. Garrard: 'My son James Garrard was the Auditor's agent when Bal Howard failed as sheriff. As such, he sold Howard's property and the state bid it in. It was the timber off this land that Tom Baker and the Howards fell out over. I understand that James Howard has threatened to kill my son James since this feud has come up because of his official work.'"

If this was accurate, it was the first time Jim Howard's name was connected with any mention of violence. And if it was so, what did it mean? Apparently, when Garrard said that Bal Howard "failed as sheriff," he meant that Bal (who was called Ballard, though his name, according to court records in Harlan County, where he was born, was Adrion Ballenger), when he was sheriff (before the election of Bev White), came up short in his collection of taxes and fees and was delinquent in forwarding the proper amounts to the state treasurer, who would have sent someone from Frankfort or designated someone in Manchester to act for the state to collect the amount in arrears.

But it is hard to understand why, with a Republican administration in Frankfort, the treasurer would have sent or named a prominent local Democrat such as James Garrard to proceed against a sturdy Republican, especially with a race for governor approaching in which the Republicans had some hope of success. One possible explanation is that Bal's "failure" occurred during the administration of Democratic governor John Brown, who would have appointed a Democrat to impose a lien on Howard's property in order to collect an amount equal to the delinquent fees.

James Garrard, if the appointee, might have tried to collect the delinquent funds by putting a lien on some of Howard's timber and then hiring someone to cut and sell it. He would no doubt have relished the chance to embarrass a prominent opponent, and he seems to have done just that, hiring Tom Baker, bully boy of the Baker clan, to collect a debt from the head of the Howard family. If this is what happened, it was a calculated insult to the Howards, sure to hurt their dignity. Garrard was looking for trouble. He got it.

But is that what happened? Another version is that Bal Howard was in arrears on his fees, borrowed forty dollars from the local bank to make it up, and put up some timber as collateral, and that Tom Baker bought the note, or warrant, from the bank and demanded payment from Howard. If that version is accurate, the affront would have been even more direct. This would not account for Jim Howard's alleged threat to kill James Garrard, however.

Another version of the controversy is worth consideration. The Howards and Baker owned adjoining timberland, and though they were not friendly they cooperated from time to time in cutting and selling the timber. Tom Baker hauled logs out of the hills to the banks of the South Fork for Israel Howard; it is possible that he cut and hauled logs for Ballard and that he cut more Howard logs than he delivered. This is quite possible; property lines were indistinct throughout the mountains and a constant source of trouble, violence, and litigation.

Bal and Tom also occasionally made up log rafts together and floated them downstream to the sawmills at Beattyville or Frankfort. On one trip Bal reportedly stopped at a store in Beattyville for supplies and, having no money on him (or possibly seeing a way to even a debt with Tom), told the clerk to charge it to Tom Baker. The clerk, knowing Tom, agreed. The next time Tom went downriver he was told of the debt, paid it, and later demanded repayment.

Whatever the facts were concerning the debt, it seems that Bal somehow owed Tom Baker some money, either fifteen or forty dollars. During the second week of April 1898, the two families were putting together log rafts at the mouth of Crane Creek. Tom, his son James, his brother Wiley, his cousin Jesse Barrett, and Charlie Wooten were hauling logs down from the hills to the lumber yard where the rafts were being lashed together. It had been raining off and on the previous week, and it was apparent that the South Fork would soon be high enough to float the rafts downriver.

Less than a hundred yards away, on the other side of Crane Creek, the Howards were putting the final touches on a raft of their own. With Bal were his sons Israel and Corbin, his adopted son Burch Stores (whom Bal had "taken in" when Stores's Harlan County parents died), John Lewis, young kinsman of Bal's wife, Mary, and two Shackleford boys. The work stopped when Tom Baker approached and faced Ballard.

"I'd like that fifteen dollars you owe me," he said. This could indicate that the dispute had nothing to do with a shortage in Bal's accounts as sheriff and concerned the debt in Beattyville; or it could indicate not one but two instances in which Bal owed Tom money. This is puzzling. The Howards were not poor. They owned a large farm. They were in the the logging business. Bal had been sheriff, and Jim was tax assessor. How did the head of the clan fail to have fifteen dollars? Or to be forced to borrow forty dollars from the bank?

"I don't owe you fifteen dollars," Ballard replied. "I don't owe you nothing. You owe me. The way I figure it, you took off 300 more trees of mine than that warrant called for. [That would indicate that he did, indeed, borrow from the bank—but only fifteen dollars—and give a note on his timber, a note that Tom apparently bought.] You pay me for the 300 trees, I'll give you fifteen dollars."

As the two sides gathered quietly around their leaders, someone appeared to reach for a weapon. Tom threw an auger at Bal, who ducked and swung a peavy at Tom. Tom hit Bal a glancing blow with a pistol. Israel Howard then fired at Tom, giving him a slight flesh wound, but Corbin Howard and Jesse Barrett jumped in to separate the battlers before anyone was killed. The two groups, eyeing each other nervously, backed off.

There was no more trouble that day, but a fuse had been lit. The next day Tom Baker was standing in his yard, waiting for some of his men to arrive, when Hudge Allen came walking down the road. The two men nodded and exchanged greetings.

"Tell you what," Allen said in a low voice. "I'm not looking to take sides or nothing, but if I was you I wouldn't go down to the yard just now."

"How come?" asked Tom.

"Well," said Allen, "as I heard it, the Howards are hiding in the weeds down there, waiting for you. Now, as I say, I don't know that, it's just as I heard."

Tom nodded and went back to the house, but he decided not to go to the lumber yard just then. But just after dinner (the noon meal), as he was sitting on the porch, a shot was fired from the nearby woods, and a bullet slammed into the doorframe behind him. Bolting into the house, he grabbed his rifle and scanned the road and the surrounding woods but saw no one.

Tom stood there for a while, thinking. Then he went into the house and said to his wife, Emily, "The Howards are after me, that's certain. We're going to have to do something. We can't just sit here and let them pick us off."

Earlier that day Big Jim Howard, sitting in his tax assessor's office in Manchester, had heard about the trouble out on Crane Creek and decided to try to head it off before it became bloody. In a move that his defenders later pointed to as evidence of his peaceful nature, Howard went down the courthouse hall to the office of George W. ("Baldy George") Baker, county attorney and patriarch of the Baker clan, and proposed a truce.

"My father had discovered," Howard wrote later, "that Tom Baker was giving him the worst of a deal by which Baker had contracted to take off some timber on shares [another version of the root of the trouble]. So I went down to George Baker's and proposed that we settle our trouble by means of arbitration, before there was serious trouble. Baker agreed, and we reached an agreement which I thought was favorable to our family."

Regardless of the terms, or who acted as arbiter (some say it was

Judge John Wright), the two men reached an agreement, shook hands, and seemed relieved to have found a peaceful solution to the matter. Unfortunately, neither Howard nor Baker seems to have informed their families out on Crane Creek of the agreement, at least not at once.

Newspaper accounts at the time made Baldy George Baker appear to be something of a mountain saint while James Howard was depicted as a born killer, a feared marksman, and a man of violent temper. Actually, there is no record that either man had previously been involved in any act of violence. On the contrary, Baldy George, while a big, tough man, was the generally well liked father of fifteen sons whose main failing seems to have been a tendency occasionally to drink too much, a very common fault. It was told of him that, shortly after the war, he got drunk at a party, passed out, and was dumped into a coffin recently made by the host who, not knowing he was so ensconced, piled a bunch of harness on top of him. Awakening, George felt of his enclosure, concluded that the worst had happened, and cried in a woeful voice, "Dead! Oh, dear God, dead and in hell! And they're going to hitch me up like a horse!"

"Big Jim" Howard, tall and broad-shouldered, was a quiet, somber thirty-two-year old former schoolteacher whose tight-lipped expression made him seem somewhat forbidding and who seemed to have little levity about him. Governor Bert T. Combs (1959-1963), a Manchester native, recalled in 1991 seeing Jim Howard, years before, walking down the street from his home, carrying a sample case like any other salesman.

"He was a tall, well-built man," Combs recalled, "a handsome man. Wore dark gray suits and usually a bowler hat, and in the winter wore a long black overcoat that made him look even bigger than he was. I don't remember hearing much about him one way or the other, except that he had been in some trouble. As a lot of people had. He had worked in a store in Manchester, and was a shoe salesman. He traveled all around the towns in the region. He'd take orders and send them in to the company to be filled. Polite, friendly man as far as I knew. We surely weren't afraid of him."

But word of the agreement between Jim and Baldy George had not reached Crane Creek when, the next morning, the Howards finished making up a raft and were preparing to shove off for Frankfort on the rising waters of the South Fork of the Kentucky. On the other side of Crane Creek the Bakers were pushing logs into position for a raft of their own. No one had made any move to resume the troubles of the day before, and when noon came the Bakers nodded cordially as they left for dinner.

But they were not concerned with the noon meal. With Tom as he arrived at his home were Charlie Wooten, Jesse Barrett, and Tom's brother Wiley. Tom nodded to his wife and said to James, his eighteen-year old son, "Come on."

"Where we going?" asked James.

"There's something we have to do," said Tom. But James seemed to sense what was afoot and complained that he had been feeling sick all morning. Tom looked at him for a moment, then turned and walked out, the others following. James lay down across the bed, but his mother came and stood over him.

"Get up from there, you sorry thing," she snapped, "and go with your daddy."

James got up. His mother handed him his rifle, and he followed the others, who were walking rapidly and silently up the road.

Back at the lumber yard, the Howards cast off the lines to their raft, and Israel, Corbin, and a man named Davidson waved and shoved off for the dangerous trip downriver.

"You be careful," shouted Bal.

"You all the ones to be careful," called Israel, leaning into the big sweep oar as the current caught the raft. In a minute, as the raft cleared the bend of the river, Bal, his son Wilson, Burch Stores, John Lewis, and the Shackleford boys got on their horses and started up Crane Creek toward the Howard home.

It was a bright, soft April afternoon, the trees in new foliage, the waters of Crane Creek filling the narrow valley with a spring sound. As the group cantered past the home of Gardner and Cythena (called Thena or Theenie) Baker, Thena came out and rang the bell that hung from the top of a tall pole in the front yard, the kind used to call workers in from the fields.

"What's Thena doing ringing the bell now?" Wilson wondered aloud as they rode past. They didn't have long to wait for an answer. As they approached a turn in the road about two hundred yards past the Baker home, from the top of a low, brush-covered ridge a volley of shots suddenly crashed out.

Wilson Howard fell, riddled with bullets. Burch Stores had his head practically blown off. Bal Howard, hit in the upper chest, fell forward across the neck of his horse, which, fortunately for him, reared and bolted back down the trail, as following shots ripped through his clothes. As he fled, the ambushers reportedly ran from hiding and finished off Wilson and Stores, though Wilson, shot six times, lived for almost four hours and, according to the Howards, identified the Bakers as his murderers. The Howards also claimed that the Bakers robbed the bodies of their victims, but this is unlikely; the Bakers were not robbers.

Bal escaped, along with John Lewis and the Shackleford boys, but he was badly wounded, and as he reached Gardner Baker's house he slipped from his horse and fell to the road. Jesse Barrett said later, "If old Bal hadn't been riding that fast horse of his I'd of got him. He was the one I was after." The killing, incidentally, did not seem to shock too deeply the reluctant young James Baker. He later killed his father-in-law, perhaps finding he had a talent for it.

And then a curious thing happened: As Bal lay bleeding in the road, Gard and Thena Baker hitched a mule to a wood-runner sled, went down to the road, and hauled him up to their house, where they bandaged his wounds as best they could and sent word to the Howards. (Years later Ernest Sester of Clay County said that his father, John Sester, coming down Crane Creek, saw Gard and Thena come down to help the wounded Bal Howard. "Thena set down there on the road and took Bal's head in her lap while Gard went to get a sled to take him up to the house," Sester said. "Bal opened his eyes and looked at her and said, 'Thena, tell me why you rang that bell.' And Thena just looked away and said, 'Some day I will.'" She never did.)

Thena and Gard later helped the Howards retrieve the bodies of Wilson and Burch Stores. Why would they do this, after Thena had obviously conspired in the murder by ringing the dinner bell? But then, why did she ring the bell? Gard and Thena Baker were religious, gentle people, fond parents, and trusted neighbors. Gard was a deacon in the Christian Church, and Thena was active in mission work. All four of their sons—Frank, Horace, Lloyd, and Ben—graduated from the University of Louisville law school and established sound law practices. Stanley DeZarn tells of how neighborhood children loved to visit the Baker home to read the *Courier-Journal* and the *Pathfinder* magazine or to hear Thena tell stories of the early days. Perhaps it was a matter of family loyalty.

At any rate, they cared for the wounded Bal until Howards arrived to take him home. The Shacklefords took a roundabout way home to avoid the Bakers. At the time they thought Bal was dead.

Jim Howard was at work in the store when one of the Shacklefords rode into Manchester, leading Bal's blood-stained horse, and told him the bad news. According to later reports, he told Jim that all three had been killed and that their bodies were lying in the road, where the buzzards or hogs might get to them. Jim was furious, not only because of the murder of his father and brothers but because he felt betrayed by Baldy George in a way that almost made him an accomplice to the murder of his own people. He and Baldy had reached an agreement and had shaken hands on it, a gesture not to be taken lightly. And that, Jim thought, had led his kinsmen, when they heard about it, to let down their guard. He did not know which Bakers were involved, but he had no reason to assume that Baldy George, head of the clan, had not taken part or given his consent to the ambush.

Early the next morning Jim rode out toward the family home on Crane Creek. Accounts of what followed were typical of newspaper and magazine stories of the time. According to Harold Wilson Coates: "For two days the bodies of the slain men lay in the roadway, their relatives and friends not daring to visit the scene of the encounter for fear of running into another ambush and sharing a like fate. It was at this time that Jim Howard determined upon action. Grabbing his rifle, he set out for the site of the ambush, his aim to avenge. . . . "

Munsey's Magazine in 1903 offered a more lurid account:

Then Jim Howard, son of the head of the family, started forth to kill. He learned that Tom Baker's father was away from home. The elder Baker was one of the most beloved and esteemed men in that part of the state. It was his boast that he never carried a weapon. Jim Howard knew it was safe to attack him.

They met on the road, and Howard ordered Baker to dismount. Falling to his knees, he pleaded for his life. He begged the young man not to plunge the county into a deadly feud, and solemnly swore that none of his family had killed the two Howards. A shot was the reply, and a bullet pierced Baker's thigh. A second disabled the other leg, making him helpless. Jim Howard, the second best shot in a community famous for its marksmen [the writer didn't say who was first] stood before the white-haired, defenseless old man and shot him again and again, using nice skill to avoid a fatal spot, yet not missing. Twenty-five bullets pierced Baker's body, and he bled to death, living only long enough to tell who had murdered him.

Horace Kephart in his *Our Southern Highlanders*, published in 1913, used much the same version: "Thereupon Jim Howard, son of the clan chief, sought out Tom Baker's father, compelled the unarmed old man to fall on his knees, shot him 25 times with careful aim to avoid a vital spot, and so killed him by inches."

Alvin Harlow, author of *Weep No More, My Lady*, added some dramatic dialogue to his version: "Jim Howard met Tom Baker's father, a stalwart man in his later fifties, in front of a country store and levelled his gun at him. 'Get down on your knees,' he ordered, his handsome face distorted with passion. 'You laid the plot to have my people killed, and I'm going to kill you!' 'Don't, Jim,' cried the old man. 'I didn't have anything to do with it. You know I tried to settle things peaceable.' But the cold glare in Howard's eyes, a professing Christian who didn't drink or even use tobacco, did not waver. 'Down on your knees, I said,' he commanded." And so on.

There is no evidence that any of this has more than a casual acquaintance with the truth. Baldy George Baker, the pathetic old gray-haired saint of legend, was actually only fifty-two years old, stood six feet tall, and weighed around 225 pounds. And he was certainly not known for going unarmed. He was no troublemaker, but he was the strong leader of a tough clan.

What seems to have happened is this:

The morning after the murder of his people, Jim Howard rode out toward Crane Creek to retrieve the bodies of his kin, see to their burial, and visit his family. As the oldest surviving man of the family, that would have been his responsibility. Near the Laurel Gap post office he rode by the home of Wiley and Lushaba (Shabie) Baker. Wiley was a brother of Bad Tom and was suspected of being one of the killers. Shabie was a Howard from Harlan County before her marriage. She was one of three orphans adopted at an early age by John D. Coldiron, who ran a store a few yards from Wiley and Shabie's home. Shabie was on the porch, washing clothes, when she saw Jim riding past but did not consider it reason to warn the Bakers. That could indicate that Howard's reputation was not as violent as described if, indeed, he had any reputation at all. Or it may have been that she sympathized with him. He was, after all, her first cousin, and she is said to have told Wiley a few days later, "If there's any more Howards killed, I'll poison you."

But when Jim reached the Laurel Creek post office and store he found workmen making two, not three, coffins, and learned that his father was still alive, while the bodies of Wilson and Burch were being prepared for burial. So he turned toward his family home on Crane Creek to see his father. But near the Boston Gap cemetery he was fired on from ambush and retreated to the Willow Grove school. He knew he couldn't go up Crane, past the Baker home, so he took another route and, near Collins Fork, was shot at again. Trying to figure out how to get home alive, he went back to the store and stood talking to John Coldiron—"so mad he looked crazy," according to Mrs. Coldiron—when a young girl standing nearby said, "Well, looks like Baldy George is out early," and Jim turned to see the head of the Baker clan, astride a large bay horse, not twenty yards away.

Years later, according to Stanley DeZarn, Coldiron, then living in Indiana, gave Jess Wilson an eye-witness account of the shooting.

Jess told me that he had been wanting to talk to Coldiron because he had witnessed the shooting. He told Coldiron that he would like to come and see him about it, and Coldiron said he'd be glad to talk to him, so when he was in the neighborhood he went by to see him. . . . And from what I got from Jess, what he said was this:

'Jim Howard was standing in the road talking to me and a couple of others when somebody said something like "Wonder what old Baldy George is doing out so early"—something like that, and when Jim looked up the road there was Baldy George, not twenty yards away. Jim was standing by his horse, and he reached up and grabbed his rifle, and about the same time Baldy George saw him and grabbed his rifle and slid off his horse. And Jim shot him. Jim was shooting a .45 x .90, and the shot went right through the horse's neck and hit Baldy George in the stomach, and Baldy went down in the road. Jim didn't say anything but walked over and saw for sure he was down. Some people in the store came out and carried Baldy George into the store and laid him on the counter and sent for a doctor. I read later that Jim said they asked him if he minded if they carried Baldy George in and got a doctor, and Jim said no, he was just trying to protect himself, but I don't recall that. Two doctors came out from Manchester and operated on Baldy, there on the counter of the store. Took out his bowel and sewed it up and put it back again, but he died the next day.'

Coldiron's version follows closely the account written by the Reverend Dickey: "The following morning James Howard, County Assessor, met George Baker on the road at Laurel Creek at Coldiron's store and killed him on sight. Baker lived about 24 hours. The doctors took his bowel out and sewn up the torn parts and put them back in but it was of no avail." No mention was made of any wound other than the shot in the abdomen.

A question here: If Baldy George Baker had no part in the murder of the Howards and thus had no reason to feel guilty or apprehensive when he saw Jim Howard on the road, why did he grab his rifle and slide from his horse when he came upon Howard? Did he have cause to think Jim had incited the killers by firing at Bad Tom the day before? Or was there something to the legend that, on the day the Howards were killed, Baldy said to his son Wiley, "That's going to be a bad one over on Crane Creek, and I'd advise you to stay out of it." If he did say that, was he referring to the conflict at the rafting site or the plan to ambush the Howards? If he was referring to the ambush, then he was, in effect, an accomplice to the murders and could have prevented them, and Jim would have been justified in assuming that Baldy had violated their agreement and might well be planning to kill him, too. After all Baldy was riding from the same region on Crane Creek where Jim had been shot at only minutes before.

And it must be emphasized that Coldiron did not mention that Jim fired more than one shot, though he apparently discussed details of the shooting and its aftermath. He would undoubtedly have mentioned such a bit of savagery had it occurred. So would the Reverend Dickey, who mentioned only the one wound. Where the legend of the twenty-five shots came from is anyone's guess, though it is worth noting that Bad Tom Baker, in a letter to Governor Bradley months later, accused Jim of shooting Baldy twenty-five times.

At any rate, Jim then abandoned plans for reaching home that day and rode up Collins Fork and down Ells Branch, past the spot where men were digging graves for Wilson and Burch, and surrendered to Deputy Sheriff Will White at his home near Burning Springs. White was a personal and political friend. They had supper and talked, and Jim spent the night with Will and his wife Kate. The next morning the two of them rode into Manchester, and White turned Jim over to Judge Brown, who released him on his own recognizance.

Jim promised to return when trial was set but asked the judge to put a guard around his father's house. Brown deputized forty men under Riley Sparks and sent them to the head of Crane Creek to protect the Howard home. (Dickey wrote that Bal Howard swore out warrants for John and Tom Baker and Charles Outen [Wooten] and asked for a guard to protect his life; it is surprising that Bal was physically able to do this at the time.) The wisdom of the guard soon became apparent, as gunmen began shooting into the Howard home from the surrounding woods. Bal remained at home until he was able to travel. Then Jim, accompanied by guards, took him to the Harlan County home of one of Bal's cousins, probably Berry Howard. (Bal's father, and most of the Howards, had come from Harlan.) Bal stayed there, recuperating, until time for the June term of court in Manchester.

Meanwhile, tension in Manchester made it dangerous to go out on the streets. The Garrards were demanding the immediate trial of Jim Howard for the murder of Baldy George; the Whites and Howards were demanding the trial of Tom Baker and his accomplices for the murder of the Howards. "Several times I was ambushed on my way between Manchester and father's," Jim Howard told newsmen later. "Every time I made the trip bullets poured at me from the woods. Only once did I get sight of my assailants, and that was when John Baker fired at me from behind a log. I fell across the neck of my horse and the bullet burned a stripe across my back. As father hovered between life and death, the house was fairly besieged."

That, at least, is the version carried in the New York papers. The language seems rather stilted for Jim Howard, though he was a literate man. Like many news accounts of the time, it should be regarded with caution.

At any rate, the Howards were protected by a forty-man guard until Bal could make the trip to Harlan. Incidentally, the fact that Jim Howard felt it necessary to ask for a guard to protect his father indicates that he didn't regard himself as the greatest gunman in the hills. It also indicates that the Bakers were a more numerous clan than the Howards. After all, Baldy George had fifteen sons and Bad Tom had thirteen. Their families alone would have constituted a formidable force, though not all of the Bakers—or all of the Howards—were eager to take part in the war.

Trouble on the Burying Ground

At noon Judge Cook gaveled a recess, and Bad Tom, along with James, Wiley, and others who had ridden into town with him, filed out of the courtroom. Outside, Tom stood to one side, talking to General Garrard, while the others waited.

"Well," said Garrard, "I guess I'd better be getting back to the house."

Tom nodded. "Again, I've got to thank you," he said.

"Not at all," said the general. "I'd stay, but I think they have things pretty well in hand. This is just going to be drawn out. I doubt you will get through before tomorrow sometime, maybe late. But you'll get your change of venue. Don't worry about it. And don't let your boys get out of hand and start trouble. The sooner they get on back to Crane Creek, the better, I'd say."

"Yeah," said Tom, nodding. "Well, then, I'll see you tomorrow." The two men shook hands, and T.T. went out to where two of his men were standing by his buggy. Tom turned to the men bunched around the courthouse steps.

"Let's go over and get some dinner," he said, and a group of them crossed the street to the Potter House. Tom didn't feel much like eating. Leaving the table, he went out and sat for a while on the long bench on the porch, smoking. The events of the morning had left him feeling down. It seemed to him that he had spent half his time lately in courtrooms listening to some bastard talk. Too damn much talk. He wished he could just go home and sit a while and do nothing, not hear anybody.

And now here he sat, probably going to have to go down to London and sit in that damn jail, face another trial, maybe time in prison. He didn't know that he could stand much time in prison, but it wouldn't be easy finding somebody to believe he didn't kill that son-ofabitch Will White. And Jim and Wiley; he'd gotten them into a fix, all right. Maybe he'd made a mistake going after the Howards, but what else could he have done, sit there and wait for them?

And Pap. He'd probably still be alive instead of lying out there on Laurel Gap. Oughtn't have happened. Remembering the day Pap was buried, he wished now that he and the others had gone. Em had said they ought to, but he'd been all for rooting out the Howards and hadn't gone to the burying. Well, they could hold a real service later, and they'd all go. If he was free to go. He felt bad now, thinking about the burying. But then he straightened up, stood for a minute looking around, and walked back across the street to the courthouse.

He was right about the burial services for his father. He had handled it wrong. The whole thing had been bad—left a lot of hate in the air without doing any good.

A brief shower had added a slight chill to the morning of April 20, 1898, and low, wispy clouds hung over the hills above Laurel Gap as the Reverend Dickey began services for Baldy George Baker in the cemetery between Crane and Laurel Creeks. It was a strange and sad ceremony. Though Baldy George was a well known and well liked man, only twenty people attended his burial. This may have been due in part to mountain custom. Since there was no means of embalming, the bodies always had to be buried soon after death, giving distant relatives little time to travel, so funeral services were often delayed until the crops were laid by and it was convenient for relatives and friends to attend. For these reasons, a funeral, or memorial, service was of more importance than a burial.

In the case of Baldy George's burial, the sparse attendance may also have been due to fears of violence. The Howards were burying Wilson and Burch Stores the same day, and, in the prevailing atmosphere of bitterness and hatred, a clash between the families was not out of the question. Nevertheless, as Dickey noted, it was sad that none of Baldy's fifteen sons was present.

In all probability, their absence had nothing to do with the date or with the possible danger. The Reverend Dickey noted in his diary that while they were lowering Baldy George's body into the ground, the solemnity of the occasion was broken by the sound of gunfire from the adjacent hollow. Dickey thought it came from the home of Bal Howard, where men had been shooting into the yard. More likely it came from the Laurel Creek cemetery, where the Howards were attempting to bury Wilson and Burch. No sooner had the mourners arrived than a blast of gunfire erupted from the woods nearby, and bullets whizzed past the funeral party. The Howards and their friends had not expected violence on such an occasion and were not armed. But with bullets ripping the damp air around them, there was nothing to do but take the coffin and retreat. They finally were obliged to settle on Maxline Baker cemetery, several miles away, near Oneida. Jim Howard stood with his mother, trembling with rage even as tears wet his cheeks. Then they turned and went to his home in Manchester rather than chance an encounter on Crane Creek. The two graves at Laurel Creek remained empty for years.

As the Howards assumed, it seems likely that the gunfire came from the Baker men, who preferred to shoot at Howards rather than attend the funeral of their father. This would indicate a fierceness of the part of the Bakers, just as the fact that the Howards were not armed and were forced to flee from the cemetery would indicate that Jim Howard was less concerned than the Bakers with vengeance.

But now the die was cast. There would be no more truces, for no one on either side showed any inclination toward peace. Relations were not improved when, the day after the burials, Will White, walking down the hallway of the courthouse, saw Baldy George's sign on the county attorney's office and said to the man with him, "Well, I guess old Baldy George is roasting in hell by now." Unfortunately, his remark was overheard by Allen Baker, who was sitting in Baldy's old office going through some papers, and he reported it to other members of his family, Bad Tom among them.

On April 28, charges against Tom, John Baker, and Charlie Wooten for arson were dismissed in local court for lack of evidence. This was not as unexpected or as surprising as it may seem now. There was a great reluctance on the part of early juries to convict on circumstantial evidence. It was customary for a defendant to produce witnesses who would swear that he was miles away from the scene of the crime, and the jurymen, many of whom were probably related in some way to the witnesses, were not inclined to question their honesty.

A story persists, but seems unlikely, that on June 1, Tom and Dee Baker and Jesse Barrett were sitting in the home of Wiley and Lushaba Baker, drinking. They were still in a bitter mood; another of their number had been killed, Baldy George's grave was still raw, and the Howards were walking around armed. Tom was not made happier by the fact that Shabie, his brother's wife, was a Howard. She was a constant reminder of the hated enemy, and sometime during the afternoon Tom quietly slipped poison, probably cyanide, into her drink. Fortunately, at that time Jesse Barrett said he wanted some water to drink with the fiery moonshine, and started to the kitchen.

"I'll get it for you," said Shabie, and she followed Jesse into the kitchen. As she poured him a glass of water, he said in a low voice, "I wouldn't drink that," then turned and went back to the front room. Shabie threw her drink out the back door, filled her glass with some honest whisky from a crock sitting under the table, and went back to join the others. Tom probably spent the afternoon wondering why she didn't fall over dead.

If the story is true, it may have marked a turning point in the career of Jesse Barrett, one of the more curious characters in the Clay War, and one who later appeared to regret his role in the violence. A short man of medium build, Barrett wore a dirty gray hat turned up all around, sported a bushy mustache, and squinted through wire-rimmed spectacles from which he got his nickname of "Spec." They didn't seem to bother his aim much.

Three days later, Tom was more successful. Will White was out in the county trying to collect delinquent taxes when he ran into Tom and Dee Baker and James Helton near the mouth of Jim's Branch. Accounts of what happened differ but there is no dispute about the outcome. They killed Will, Tom supposedly firing the fatal shot. Everyone knew that he hated Will, who had tried to arrest him for burning George Hall's home and Frank Campbell's store and had sheltered Jim Howard after Jim killed Baldy George. Will had also been overheard speaking disparagingly of Baldy George in the courthouse after the Baker patriarch was killed. Tom later claimed that Will had tried to draw on him and that he was forced to kill him. A fair fight.

But the shooting took place in front of the home of George and Lucretia Goforth. The Goforths were another peaceful, church-going, respected family who wanted nothing to do with the feuds. The situation was difficult for them, however, for their daughter, Lizzie, had married Beverly Baker, a son of Wiley and Shabie Baker and thus a nephew of Bad Tom. The Goforths were sitting on their porch when they heard a sudden burst of gunfire, looked down toward the road, and saw a horse rear and its rider fall as several men rode away.

They hurried to the road, found Will White mortally wounded, and carried him to their home, where he died in the family rocking chair. Before he died, he grabbed Mrs. Goforth's hand, and said, "Promise me, Lucy, that you will testify in court that Tom and Dee Baker and Jim Helton killed me." "I promise, Will," she said, knowing the danger her promise held.

Now the Whites as well as the Howards were out for revenge. Will White had not been a popular man. He was known as a good businessman with a fine farm and a good family. He was also a man of violent temper and a hard drinker. But he was a White, feared as well as respected. His kinsmen were not likely to take his murder lightly.

Will was buried on June 4. "The corpse was brought to Daugh White's yesterday and at 9:30 this morning we buried him," wrote Dickey.

Miss Alice Callahan and I sang, "I will sing you a song." I prayed and when they were filling the grave we sang, "Nearer my God to Thee." Just as the grave was made ready to receive the earth John G. and Gilbert White rode up. They live in Winchester. Theo Cundiff went to Winchester for them. Theo accidentally shot himself this morning. A flesh wound in the leg.

This killing is the result of the Howard-Baker feud. On the 19th, just as I was starting to Hyden, I saw Will White jump on Jim Tish Philpot and beat him about. White was drunk. During his term of office he acquired the habit of drink. He has been the most offensive citizen of the county since I have been here. He was often drunk, and at such times he was insulting and disagreeable. He has a fine farm, a wife and several children, was about 35 years old. The Whites will now help the Howards to exterminate the Bakers. If there could be such an upheaval here as the French-Eversole war made in Perry County, we would have a new era in this county. The old White-Garrard feud has been going on for 50 years. But it has never broken out in virulent form. It has kept the county back in every respect, and has really protected crime, as each took sides in nearly every trouble.

For the past week or ten days the Howards and their friends have carried their Winchesters all the time. James Howard and two of his brothers, and Sid Baker, his brother-in-law, do this. The past few days a large number of the Whites and their friends have been under arms. I suppose there were 30 Winchesters in town today. The Bakers were in town last week but kept off the streets. Allen Baker rode into town yesterday in a buggy, Jim Howard saw him and made at him with a Winchester, but was prevented from doing any violence. Sheriff Beverly White, brother of William White, deceased, was present, but took no notice of it.

Yesterday Miss Ibbie Baker, sister of the Baker boys, was at the Lucas Hotel, where I board. She sent for me to accompany her out of town; she was afraid the Howards would kill her. I complied, though I could not believe she was in danger. . . . We met Miss Emma Baker, another sister, as we returned from the burial today. Many people believe Jim Howard would kill any of them if he should meet them on the street. This county is in desperate condition. John G. White is now on the ground and has shown himself a very dangerous man in other days. He has killed his man, and has always shown himself ready for a fight. William White, deceased, was a bright business man and a scion of two of the most prominent families in the county, but his tyrranical nature cost him his life. Tom Baker is doubtless a very bad man . . . cool, calculating, daring. . . . May God lead in the councils of the people and direct everything to the clearing of this foul atmosphere.

The foul atmosphere was not improved when Sid Baker, Jim Howard's brother-in-law, shot and killed Charlie Wooten. As he lay dying, Wooten confessed that he had been with the Bakers and Jesse Barrett when they killed the Howards. Deathbed confessions seemed popular, and most of the people who died during this time, especially those who died of gunshot wounds, seemed to have something to confess.

A few days before the June term of court, Sid Baker came into the courthouse, surrendered for the shooting of Wooten, and was released without bail. The tension in Manchester was so bad that few people would walk the streets at night. Almost everyone went armed. When Bal Howard returned on June 5 for the June term of court, he rode into Manchester and not to the Howard home on Crane Creek.

With both Bakers and Howards in Manchester, gunplay was expected, but the first day of court went off peacefully. Bal Howard asked the court to process the warrant for the arrest of the Bakers for killing Wilson Howard and Burch Stores. The Howards were furious when the Commonwealth's attorney asked for, and was granted, a change of venue for the trial of Jim Howard for the killing of Baldy George. Jim later said that the change of venue was asked because the Commonwealth's attorney knew that no Clay County jury would convict him. He was probably right, and in retrospect it might have been better had he been tried at home and released.

With such bitter currents swirling around the court in Manchester, Judge William Brown decided to seek help and on June 10 caught the train from London to Frankfort and asked the governor for troops. He got them and returned next day with a company led by Captain Mc-Cain, with Colonel Forrester in company, attesting the seriousness with which Governor Bradley viewed the conditions in Clay.

For some reason, Judge Brown and Colonel Forrester did not get along well, adding to the unpleasant atmosphere of the court. Judge Brown thought that Forrester's troops were unnecessarily intrusive and that Forrester himself had no respect for the court or the local people. Forrester complained that Brown had no regard for him or his men. Nevertheless, the term of court went off without trouble. The judge transferred the case of Tom and John Baker and Jesse Barrett to Barbourville, and sent Jim Howard to jail in London. The Howards muttered against the decision but did nothing to interfere with the troops when they left with their prisoners. When Forrester and his men delivered their prisoners, however, they went home to Frankfort, surprising Judge Brown, who had been under the impression that they would come back to Manchester for the remainder of the session.

While court was in session, someone shot a black named Collins on Town Branch, and two days later Jim Tish Philpot, William Philpot, and James Fisher rode into Manchester and surrendered for the killing. No one paid much attention. They paid a lot more attention when, on June 24, John Howard was shot and killed at his home on Sexton Creek. He had been sitting in the front room of his house when a shot came through the window, hitting him in the arm. Grabbing his pistol, he ran outside, saw a man running toward the woods, and dropped him with a single shot, only to be hit again and killed. The body of his victim was retrieved, apparently by John's killer, and no one was ever arrested.

The Reverend Dickey noted in his diary that Judge B.P. White was drinking himself to death. This was an exaggeration.

On July 1, Bad Tom was tried and acquitted for the murder of the Howards after witnesses swore that he was miles away at the time of the killing. Legend has it that Wilson Howard had lived until four in the afternoon and identified his killers. But to whom? Even Thena and Gard Baker, who knew who did it, could not swear to it, even if they were willing, as they surely were not.

Tom's return did nothing to ease the situation in Manchester. On the contrary, it was as though his homecoming had sounded a signal. The tempo of violence at once increased. On July 3 Gilbert Garrard and his wife were shot at on their way to church. One shot cut Garrard's coat, another creased the neck of his horse. "Oh, God!" he cried, "I'm shot!"

"No, you're not," said his wife calmly. "Now, get out of here." A week later he announced his intention of leaving Clay County.

Hardly a day passed now without some new incident that added to the violence. On July 8, T.T. Garrard bailed John Baker out of jail in Barbourville. "I am told by a young man named Brittain," wrote Dickey, "that the Garrards are bringing John Baker back so that he may kill Howards. I am afraid that is the way the Howards and Whites will see it." He was right about that.

The cases of John Baker and Jesse Barrett were heard in Clark Circuit Court in Winchester. The trial proceedings were enlivened when John Hacker, considered a Baker adherent, testified that he had seen the defendants and Tom Baker kill the Howards. He had testified to the contrary at Tom's previous trial and now explained this inconsistency by telling the jury that he had been threatened with death if he didn't lie.

"How can we tell you're not lying now?" asked the defense attorney. "Well, I can't be lying both times, now, can I?" Hacker replied.

The power of his logic didn't seem to sway the jury, who found the Bakers not guilty.

A gruesome note was added to the sour symphony the next night. Tom Baker's wife Emily had sold a fine saddle horse to William Treadway, who stabled him in the livery stable run by Amanda Lucas, who also operated the Lucas Hotel. That night someone broke into the stable, shot and killed the horse, and set the stable on fire, killing several other horses. No one was arrested, and the finger was never pointed very sharply at anyone. John G. White accused Tom Baker, but he couldn't prove it, and few people believed it, since Tom and Bill Treadway had always been on good terms.

The constant feeling of danger was apparently getting on people's nerves, and public drunkenness became more noticeable. On July 10, a drunken Gilbert Garrard told Tom and John Baker, "Kill who you want. We stand with you." Asked about this, T.T. Garrard would say only, "Yes, we stand by the Bakers." His statement indicated the general deterioration of moral standards. The T.T. Garrard of old, of the Gold Rush and the Civil War, would never have condoned murder.

"Tom Baker's second son has been arrested for drawing a pistol on Ballard Howard," wrote Dickey. "He is out on bond. The criminal record of this county is fearful. So many men have killed their man and created so many widows and orphans. It is a small thing here to kill a man. It is so common."

Bad Tom was tried in Barbourville for the murder of Will White, found guilty, and given a life sentence, but he appealed and was released. He didn't seem very upset about his conviction. Later that week Gilbert Garrard and his wife left Manchester, with four bodyguards, for Pineville. Near Red Bird they were fired on. Two of their bodyguards were killed, but the rest of the party escaped. T.T. blamed the Whites, who said nothing.

"We have had heavy rains," wrote the Reverend Dickey. "Time for tides to carry the logs to mill. There are several cases of smallpox in Clay County. Several people have subscribed to the twice-weekly Courier-Journal which is now available for 50 cents a year, but you can get the weekly Courier-Journal and the Clay County Republican for 50 cents."

The murder of John Howard did not go unnoticed. On July 20, John Baker and Frank Clark were on their way from Ibby Baker's to the home of T.T. Garrard, where they had been doing guard duty, when they met Alfred "Nigger" Neal. They had been drinking and were casually shooting when they met Neal, and he protested. They had words, but Neal got away and rode into Manchester, where he reported the incident to the sheriff. Felix Davidson and Daugh White, both deputies, rode down Mud Creek and intercepted Baker and Clark at the mouth of Horse Creek. They surprised the two and informed them that they were arresting them for shooting at Neal. (If this is what really happened, it was an open invitation to violence, for it would have been highly unusual to arrest anyone for shooting to frighten a black man.) As usual, words were exchanged, or so it was reported. Someone reached for a gun. White and Davidson shot first. The coroner said John Baker had thirty-two bullets in him, Clark eleven.

At the time, no one knew who the killers were, and there were no arrests. "After the first fire, the assassins ran on their victims and dispatched them," Dickey reported, though it is not clear how he knew this. "John Baker has been charged with all manner of crimes, though he is a young man, inside 25 years." Baker had been charged with burning the home of the Widow Wilson and with stealing meat from a neighbor's smokehouse but had been acquitted. As Dickey said at the time of his death, "He was one of these men who could always escape punishment. He leaves a wife and one or two children. His father, Garrard, a relative of George Baker, was killed when John was only 10 years old." This was the Wilson shooting.

"Dick McCollum was with them but escaped," wrote Dickey. Again, this is strange. If McCollum saw the shooting, he would have been able to identify the killers, which he did not do. He may have been afraid to. On the other hand, White and Davidson may have killed Baker and Clark from ambush, at which point McCollum fled. But Neal said nothing of seeing McCollum with Baker and Clark.

The killing of Clark, a black, was, as Dickey noted, incidental. He just happened to be present and had to be killed to prevent him from identifying the killers. It was nothing personal.

The Best Men in the County

Early on the morning after John Baker and Frank Clark were killed, Tom Baker and twenty of his men rode into Manchester and, while the good people of the town were finishing breakfast, methodically and unhurriedly shot up the place. Galloping around the courthouse, they shot out practically all of the windows while prisoners in the jail hooted and cheered. Down the hill into the main part of town they rode, shooting as they went. They shot twenty times into the dry-goods store of T.M. Hill, where Jim Howard worked. They shot the windows out of J.B. Marcum's store. The attack apparently caught the Whites and Howards completely off guard. There was no pursuit as the gang rode out of town, and no arrests. No one ever explained what the purpose had been. Fortunately, no one was hurt.

During the first week of August 1898, Sheriff Beverly White moved from the county into Manchester, fearing that he might be killed from ambush. The lines were now drawn. The Bakers did not feel safe (and probably weren't) in Manchester. The Whites and Howards didn't feel safe (and probably weren't) out in the county, especially in the Crane Creek area where both Howards and Bakers had lived almost since the settlement of Clay, and along the Goose Creek region ruled by the Garrards.

And the Garrard family, even with the guidance of the redoubtable T.T., was in a state of crisis. The sons of T.T., unlike the younger Whites, appeared to have no stomach for gunplay, and gunplay appeared to be a prerequisite for survival. "General Garrard," wrote Dickey,

lives in his ancestral home, built of brick in 1835. His grandfather, the governor, was a Baptist preacher, but the General's father was a skeptic, though a moral man. The General is perhaps the same, a good citizen but profane and a good hater. He has hated the Whites for 60 years and has been hated in return. Now the hate has issued into violence. His son James is afraid to stay at home and lives in Middlesboro with his sister. Gilbert has moved to Goldsboro, North Carolina. The old man's life is thought not to be safe. He had an armed guard around the house when I visited, and he says it has been there since Gilbert was shot at.

Things may have eased a bit when Tom Baker, during the first week of August, was tried in Barbourville for the murder of Will White and found guilty. But he was freed on appeal and was soon back home again. The next day James Helton, who was thought to have been with the Bakers when Will White was killed, was shot at in Manchester but was not hit. He was with James Carmack, who had testified for Tom Baker.

When things are going wrong, nothing goes right. The Reverend Dickey couldn't even preach a funeral without trouble erupting. On September 8 he wrote:

Yesterday a dreadful scene occurred at a burial in this neighborhood. A young man named Frank Parker died from chloroform which was given him that the surgeon might operate upon his leg which had the white swelling [gangrene]. His body was being buried, the people were singing, when the dogs began to fight in the midst of the women, who stood in a close group. A man named York picked up a board and began to pound the dogs to part them. One of the dogs proved to be the property of Charles Parker, father of the dead man. Parker rushed to York, jerked the board from his hands and knocked him down with it and struck him several times. The women screamed, especially the relatives. Mrs. Parker, mother of the dead man, fainted. The relatives all rushed together for battle, but no one offered resistance. The Murrays, who are enemies of the Parkers, ran to the homes nearby and got their guns and pistols, but the people dispersed. No further violence was offered. York and Parker are neighbors but not friendly. York says he did not know whose dogs they were. Brother Riggs says he had never seen anything so heathenish in his life.

Frank Parker, the dead man, was a wicked boy. Parker, his father, is a church member but a man of violent temper. He is raising a family of boys who are the dread of society.

While all this was going on, James Baker and Jesse Barrett were indicted for the murder of the Howards, and Judge Wright ordered them transferred to the jail in Stanford. He directed Sheriff Beverly White to take a guard and escort them to the jail, despite the protests of Tom Baker, who swore that White would kill them or pretend to be overpowered by others who would kill them. Everything considered, Tom's fears were not illogical, but the judge ignored him, and the prisoners were in good time delivered to the jailer at Stanford. This set off an interesting exchange of letters between the principals that was published in the *Louisville Courier-Journal*. The first was a letter to the governor, allegedly from James Baker and Barrett, who were in the Stanford jail, warning that they would be killed if they had to return to Manchester for trial and begging the governor to furnish them an escort of troops for the journey and for protection during the trial. The two accused the Whites of an impressive list of crimes, chiefly against the Bakers and other purportedly peace-loving citizens. This brought a prompt reply from John G. White in Winchester, a copy of which was published on September 10, 1898, in the *Courier-Journal*:

Hon. W.O. Bradley, Governor of Kentucky, Frankfort, Ky.
Dear Sir:
   I noticed a letter in yesterday's Courier-Journal addressed to you from Stanford, supposed to be written by Jesse Barrett and James Baker, when in fact it was either written or dictated by one of the worst criminals that Kentucky has ever known, Thomas Baker, the father of James Baker and the man who caused and led James Baker and Jesse Barrett to the bushes within two hundred yards of his house and shot down two of his nearest neighbors and wounded A.B. Howard, a man of sixty-odd years of age. After shooting two of them down in the road, he went down to the road and finished them. They were arrested by my brother's deputies, tried before the county Judge [who] ordered the sheriff, B.P. White, Jr. to deliver them to the Stanford jailer, which he did, unharmed, over the same road that these bushwhackers and midnight assassins are so uneasy now to travel. If they are afraid of anything it is that God will cause the trees and rocks to fall upon them and grind them to pieces when they go back to the scenes of the terrible crimes they have committed.
   I do not write you this to try to induce you or to prevent you from sending soldiers with them to Clay County, but I do write you to remove the slander that they have undertaken to impose upon my brother. They know they are doomed under the law and evidence that is against them, and that they are to die on a scaffold by a jury of their own selection or to remain in the penitentiary the rest of their natural life for the crimes they have committed.
   Governor, Tom Baker, as I have stated above, beyond any doubt is one of the worst criminals that have ever marked Kentucky soil from his boyhood up. His first act in his boyhood was to cut a man who was under the influence of liquor, and if he had not been prevented would have cut him to pieces. His next act was to visit New York city, obtain counterfeit money to take amongst his friends and neighbors of his county and distribute. His next act, as I remember, was to slip up behind a brother mason and strike him in the head with a rock, from which at least the size of a half of a dollar of skull was taken from his head. His next act was to get his cousin to go to the Kentucky River and buy rafts from the raftsmen and dispose of them at a sacrifice and divide the money and run his cousin off to the far West. . . . his

cousin has never been heard of since that time. His next act was to lie in the bushes withing two hundred yards of his house, take his own son, James Baker, and this man Barrett and shoot two of his neighbors to death from ambush and seriously wound another. His next act he made two trips below where my brother lived to meet him and take his life, which he did meet him and shot him to death, and took money from my brother's pocket.

I would be very thankful to you if you would have this letter published.

Your friend, John G. White.

White's effort served to bring a ringing response from Thomas Baker, who on September 13 wrote to the Hon. W.O. Bradley:

Dear Sir:

I see in this morning's Courier-Journal a letter from John G. White pretending to say that Tom Baker was the worst criminal that ever walked Ky soil and pretending to give a history of the Clay co feud between the Baker and Howard and White factions. I will now give you a history and it is correct as every good man in Clay co will wittness to this. When Tom Baker was 15 years old Reuben Woods, a man 23 years old and 50 pounds heavier than Tom Baker and a man Tom Baker did not no [know] walked up to Tom Baker and knocked him down and was on him when Tom Baker cut his clothes several times. Baker was tried and acquitted & Woods was fined $5 as records of Clay co will show. The next act he said I went to N.Y. to buy counterfiet money which is a black lie. The next act he says I slipped up behind a Bro Mason & hit him in the head which is another lie. I did hit a man with a rock. It was in a difficulty & we was face to face when I hit him. the next act he says I drove off a woman & burned their house & burned a store house the same night which is another one of John G. Whites black lies. at the time they claim I burned the houses I was 5 miles away where my Bro was shot by one of these good deputies of B.P. White who is sheriff. They was 21 men stayed with me that night who knows that I could not a burned the house for I was not away that night.

Whites could only get two witnesses to swear that I burned the house. one is a mooneshiner who I arrested 3 years ago & is one of the worst characters in Clay co. The other is a half-witted boy who does not know right from wrong. he says Tom and Jim Baker and Jesse Barrett killed two men and wounded old man 60 years old which is another one of his lies. Tom Baker, John Baker and Charley Wooten was tried and acquitted. John G. White would have you believe that they Dan Hacker and Jim Robinson was afraid of Tom Baker to swear the truth on first trial when Tom Baker & all his bros was under arrest at the time they swore & could not even talk to witnesses & all they pretend to say is that they did not no where Jim Baker and Jesse Barrett was when the men was killed when on first trial they stated that they was with Jim Baker and Jesse Barrett when the killing was done & this is all the proof that was against them when they was refused bail & when the grand jury failed to indict them. When Tom Baker & Will White met White turned his horse before Baker & pulled his pistol & while in the act of shootin Baker Baker raised his gun & shot White & this is proof that Baker was convicted on. He had forgot to tell that 2 weeks before Will White was killed he Will White in Manchester drove an old woman 60 years old up to where my two lonely sisters lived who neither had father or mother to protect them & made this old woman when he had torn her clothes off of her and shot over her head and under her feet go up to my sisters house tell them to send out ans & Tom Baker that he aimed to kill them and all the rest of the Bakers as he came to them for murder was in his heart. It has been a few years ago that John G. White and his bro Will & his cousin Daugh White shot and murdered Jack Hacker and Dale Lyttle in the courthouse door and put all the witnesses in fear & never was indicted for this brutal murder & for the same case John G. White said he had to leave Clay Co and did so leave a short time ago & he John G. made open sport of his old uncle B.P. White and barked at him like a dog to try to get a difficulty out of him . . . his bro who is sheriff of Clay Co., a few years ago abused & shot under his old uncle's feet B.P. White who a few days later was sent to asylum and came back a dead man from the abuse he received from this good man who is sheriff now of Clay Co. & he has forgot to tell you that since James Baker and Jesse Barrett was put in jail that Daw White & Felix Davidson a cousin of John G. White's & a deputy sheriff of B.P. White waylaid and killed John Baker and Frank Clark near Manchester and shot them 36 times each & the people of Clay Co is afraid to have them arrested & never will be unless they is soldiers send to Manchester to give protection to the citizens witness in the case. And he forgot to tell that Gilbert Garrard of Manchester who was a candidate and run for sheriff against B.P. White last Nov. & was a friend of Tom Baker was waylaid and shot while on his way to Sunday school & since has had to leave Clay co. & he did not tell you about James Howard killing old man Geo Baker who was unarmed and never carried a weapon & was a peacemaker & Baker with his hands up begging for his life. I am surprise that John G. White would attack my character when every good man in Clay co know Tom Baker and the Whites too and their characters. But I will look over him for a streak of insanity runs in the White family old Daugh White drowned himself a few years ago & Hugh White hung himself over at Richmond Ky. & B.P. White killed himself in the asylum over the abuse that B.P. White, Jr. gave him & I hope that John G. White will miss this streak of insanity & kill himself when he thinks of the black murder he committed when he killed Jack Hacker and Dale Lyttle in Manchester & I hope he won't have to call for the rocks and mountains to fall on him & hide him from the face of him that sits on high in the judgement day. . . . All I ask is a fair trial & investigation of all cases & I think as John G. White has given you one side of the case that you have here my side & I vouch for every word I have said to be true and refer you to any man in Clay co. who is not interested on either side. . . . Published so that the truth may be known. Yours truly.

Thos. Baker.

In this letter, Baker protests his innocence of White's charge that he, Baker, burned the home of a woman, though no such charge is contained in White's letter. It is possible that White had accused him of the arson in a previous letter, though Bradley's papers contain no such letter. Or the reference to the fire may have been evidence of Baker's feeling of guilt. The incident to which Baker refers was, obviously, the burning of the Hall home and Campbell store after Hall and Campbell stopped Tom and John Baker as they were approaching Manchester and demanded to know where they were going. The Bakers declined to answer, a gunfight ensued, and John Baker was wounded. Tom was arrested and tried for arson but acquitted when he produced witnesses who swore he was miles away on the night of the fires.

A note: When Tom says "the governor rewarded Howard," he means that the governor put out a reward for Howard. I can find no other reference to this. When Judge Eversole had warrants issued for several Bakers and Howards, Jim Howard came into court voluntarily. No Bakers were reported as present when court began.

Commenting on the two letters, the *Courier-Journal* reported that "fifteen men have been killed in Clay County during the past month." The report did not list the victims.

Meanwhile, back in Manchester, life went on as usual. Someone took a shot at William Treadway as he was sitting in the Lucas Hotel, but missed. "He is afraid of the Bakers," said Reverend Dickey, "and is a wicked man," a statement that might be considered the mother of all non sequiturs. It may also indicate that the reverend had his Howards and Bakers confused, since Treadway was a friend of Tom Baker and had had a gunfight with Beverly White.

"A few weeks ago, Sheriff B.P. White, Jr. got drunk and shot into Mrs. Lucas' house and cursed her fearfully," wrote Dickey. "He also shot into the Post Office." And on December 4, Dickey noted that Theo Cundiff, jailer, was so drunk he had to be carried home on a board (which seems, in retrospect, a rather common-sense conveyance for someone in such a state).

But then the reverend put his finger on the deep and tragic effects of the violence. "The two principal business firms of the town have consolidated," he wrote, "leaving but two stores that sell dry goods, a little grocery store and a small Negro store. [Apparently blacks were not allowed to buy in stores that sold to whites.] Manchester is looking very seedy. The devil seems about to destroy the town. In the 21 families making up the town proper, only ten have children between 6 and 20 years, and two of these are leaving. There are only three young ladies and one is leaving in January."

Jim Howard's trial was transferred to Laurel Circuit Court in London because, according to his account, "So great was the sentiment in my favor in Clay County that a change of venue was taken to Laurel County by the Commonwealth. After two trials and several continuances the case was practically abandoned." This is a rather generous interpretation. Howard got a hung jury, then was found guilty but appealed and was awaiting the judgment of the Court of Appeals at home in Manchester when he became involved in the Goebel affair (to be described in a later chapter). He was never retried for the Baker murder. As he said, the case was just abandoned.

So as the last year of the century approached, both Jim Howard and Tom Baker were at liberty. Manchester was a dangerous place—and, in Dickey's eyes, licentious. When Dickey spent the night at the home of Henry Marcum on New Year's eve, he was properly distressed when the family ushered in the new year with that tempter of the flesh, a dance. "Five young men, and as many young women," he wrote, "were drunk, and danced past midnight."

And, on a more ominous note, about this time mention was made that Chad Hall had been seen visiting the Howards. Hall, a shadowy character who seemed often on the scene when violence occurred but was never himself implicated, had been involved in the earlier Howard-Turner feud in Harlan County and had reportedly been with Wilse Howard and his "gang" when, in the fall of 1889, the Cawoods were killed. A tall, slender, leathery man, Hall was an itinerant blacksmith and cattle dehorner. Born April 15, 1859, he was the son of Alford and Sarah Hall of Lee County, Virginia, across the mountain ridge from Harlan. His father had been a fairly prosperous mill owner, but Chad chose to move to Harlan, where he married Susan Nolan and bought a house on Martins Fork. While Susan stayed home, Chad traveled through Harlan, Leslie, Clay, and Bell Counties dehorning cattle, trimming hooves, shoeing horses, and doing general blacksmith work. His sister Jane married Jim Shackleford, who was with the Howards when the Bakers killed Wilson and Burch Stores and wounded Bal. Chad himself was a friend of the Howards in both Clay and Harlan Counties, and a lot of people thought he was something of a hired gun for them. That is unlikely. Mountain gunmen usually worked out of loyalty or for revenge, but in the Clay County trouble most were attached to one side or the other much as cowhands were attached to ranch-owners in the West. General Garrard had as many as a dozen men who acted as guards around his Goose Creek home. Furthermore, though Chad Hall had often been spotted around the scene of trouble, or reported to have been seen riding out after trouble occurred, no one had ever pinned anything on him.

In February 1899, the bitterness pervading Manchester exacted a further price when Allen Baker announced that he was moving to Breathitt County, and put his house up for sale. It was a sad commentary on Clay County when someone had to move to "Bloody Breathitt" to find a more peaceful environment. The next week Anse Baker said he was selling his saloon and moving to Barbourville. This was more understandable, since Manchester had been voted dry in December and the value of his saloon had undoubtedly depreciated. But this marked two Garrards, two Whites, and two Bakers who had left Manchester in eighteen months. The war was draining the town.

The Turtle Calls
for Bad Tom

The morning of June 10, 1899, dawned warm and humid under a gray overcast. Tom and Emily woke and dressed in the unfamiliar confines of the tent on the courthouse lawn. They were joined for breakfast by Wiley, Allen, and James, who had been quartered in an adjacent tent. Afterward, they sat on the hotel porch watching the soldiers going about their duties. After an hour or so the Baker followers who had not spent the night rode in, and after what seemed like an interminable wait Judge Cook rode up and went into the courthouse. He was followed by the lawyers and court officers. After a few minutes a bailiff came out and announced that court was in session. Tom, Wiley, and James walked Emily back to the tent, then went into the courtroom.

To one side of the room, near the table where Colonel Williams sat, two neatly dressed men watched the proceedings intently, writing hurriedly on loose sheets of paper. A.C. Lyttle told Tom that the men were newspaper reporters from Louisville and Cincinnati. Tom was impressed and watched the men closely throughout the proceedings.

Much of the morning was taken up with arguments for and against a change of venue and in hearing witnesses. After dinner there was a sudden flurry of interest when Big John Philpot, all seven feet and 300 pounds of him, took the stand and was asked whether he thought the Bakers could get a fair trial in Manchester. Big John said if it was all the same, he'd rather not say.

"Are you afraid to state your opinion?" the prosecutor asked, Big John looked at him calmly for a long minute.

"I don't guess I'm afeard of no man," he said. "But you could say I've got a feeling for the Bakers." Judge Cook thanked him, and Big John ambled out, nodding and smiling to Tom as he passed.

Five other men were called. Those friendly to the Whites or Howards said that the Bakers could get a fair trial in Manchester. Those siding with the Bakers held that it would be impossible to find an impartial jury in Clay County. A little after four o'clock Judge Cook called the attorneys to the bench and, after conferring briefly, gaveled the court to order. He announced that in his opinion counsel for the defense had made a compelling argument and that in the interest of good order and a fair trial he was granting a change of venue to Knox Circuit Court. He directed Colonel Williams to provide a suitable escort to assure the safety and security of the accused and to deliver them to the jailer in Barbourville as expeditiously as practical. In view of the hour and the distance involved, however, he directed that the transfer be delayed until the next morning.

Outside, Tom talked for a minute with General Garrard, who had once more come in for the trial.

"I want to thank you again, General," he said.

"Don't mention it," said Garrard. "I'm sorry about this, but I'm glad you got the change of venue. You'll have a much better chance of a fair trial down in Barbourville. Try to get some rest and don't let your men get out in town and start trouble. I'd say the sooner they get back to Crane Creek, the better."

"I'll see to that," said Tom.

"Well," said the general, "I guess I'd better be getting back. Try not to worry. I'll be down to Barbourville for the trial. If there's anything you need, I'll see what I can do."

"I appreciate it."

The general drove off. Tom walked over to the tent that some of the soldiers referred to as the guardhouse and sat on a cot, talking with Emily, telling her of the change of venue, making plans for the morrow.

"You might as well go on home," he told her, "and try to get some rest. John and some of the boys will come with you down to Barbourville when it's time. But you might as well go on now."

"I guess I'll stay," she said.

A photographer from Louisville came up to the door of the tent and asked if he could take Tom's picture. He had already taken James's and Wiley's. Tom said he guessed it would be all right, and he walked outside. One of the reporters was standing by, writing, as the photographer prepared to take Tom's picture. Tom looked rumpled and dusty but stared unsmilingly into the camera. The photographer thanked him and asked if he could take a picture of Tom with his son James. Tom said all right, and James joined him. The soldiers looked on with obvious interest. The reporter got on his horse and headed down the hill.

Tom walked back and stood with Emily in the doorway of the

tent. After the hectic day it was fairly quiet around the courthouse. The soldiers were lounging around the tents or sitting on the ground, talking. Small groups of people were leaving, going home. Some of the Baker kinsmen, having retrieved their guns, were mounting their horses for the ride back to Crane Creek. Others had decided to stay until morning to see Tom and the others off.

Suddenly a shot, strangely muffled, shattered the afternoon. Bad Tom Baker, with a soft moan, fell forward across his wife's feet.

For a few seconds no one seemed to grasp what had happened. Then soldiers, responding to Emily's screams, rushed to Tom's side. Tom had landed on his right side and rolled over onto his back. The red stain of blood was spreading around the bullet hole near the center of his chest. Tom Baker was dead.

Everyone began looking frantically around to see where the shot might have come from. Captain Bryan, his face ashen, came running up. There was a great shouting of orders and rushing about, and someone pointed across the street to the home of Sheriff Beverly White, where a small wisp of smoke drifted from a partly opened window.

Making little sense but doing the only thing they knew to do, the soldiers, with fixed bayonets, formed a line of attack, while others wheeled the big Gatling gun around and pointed it toward the sheriff's house. Captain Bryan raced up and stopped them before they could do any damage. "Follow me!" he shouted, and a platoon fell into line and charged across the street. They were stopped by a locked gate and stood for a moment as though wondering how to overcome this obstacle. It was not an eventuality for which their training had prepared them. Then Captain Bryan ordered them to break it down, and they frantically kicked it open. But then they had trouble with the locked front door. When they finally got in, they raced through the house, found no one, but discovered on a bed in the front room a rifle, its barrel still warm. By an open rear window lay a hat with Sheriff White's name in it.

Bryan raced back to the courthouse, where Colonel Williams waited, red-faced with anger. Members of the Baker group raged around the grounds, demanding that the troops get Bev White. Others demanded that they arrest Jim Howard. But when Williams entered the courthouse he encountered Howard coming out of his office. Outside on the sidewalk he met Sheriff White.

"It's very unfortunate that the gun that killed Baker was found in your house," he said sternly.

"Before God," declared White, "I didn't kill him."

"Well, who did then?" demanded Williams.

"Could have been anybody," said White. "Dozens of people have access to my house."

A crowd of people had gathered by this time, gawking at the fallen feudist and speculating on his killer. The *Courier-Journal* reporter, who had been heading out of town when he heard the shot, had returned and was scribbling away. Standing behind him, looking over his shoulder, was Chad Hall, looking down on Tom with a fascinated stare. Big Jim Howard, stone-faced, looking neither right nor left, walked down the sidewalk toward town. The Bakers were too astonished to try to stop him.

The killer of Bad Tom Baker was never found.

The next morning a wagon carrying James, Allen, Wiley, and three troopers pulled up in front of the courthouse. A white-faced, dry-eyed Emily stood beside them a moment and bade them goodbye, as Captain Bryan ordered his men to form up for the trip to Barbourville. He then turned to Emily, who was sitting in a wagon with two of her children.

"Mrs. Baker," he said, "why don't you leave this miserable county and escape from these awful feuds? Move away and teach your children to forget."

Emily turned toward him with a face filled with hate.

"Captain," she said, "I have twelve sons. It will be my chief aim in life to bring them up to avenge their daddy's death. I intend to show them this handkerchief, stained with his blood, every day of their lives and tell them who murdered him."

That, at least, is legend. It is doubtful she said it. If she really did, it was a promise she couldn't carry out. She didn't know who had killed her husband any more than anyone else did. At least anyone willing to talk.

Then the wagon carrying the body of Bad Tom Baker pulled slowly out of Manchester, headed for Crane Creek.

There was a further saddening aspect of Tom Baker's murder. On June 9, when Tom had come into court, George and Lucretia "Lucy" Goforth rode toward Manchester, prepared in spite of the danger involved to keep their promise to the dying Will White and testify to the manner of his murder by the Bakers. They were not called, and they came back the next day, heard that the trial had been shifted to Barbourville, and were on their way home when they heard of Tom's death. They did not have to testify.

But Wiley Baker, Tom's brother, was not one to forget. Or forgive. After his trial in Barbourville, which acquitted him and Allen and

James, he regarded the Goforths as enemies. They had not testified, but they had been willing to. That was enough. Wiley condemned them, even though his son Bev was married to Lizzie Goforth, the daughter of Bud and Lucretia. Bad Tom had liked and respected Bud Goforth. Once, when George Hall sent word to Bad Tom that he was tired of fighting and wanted to meet and talk, Tom replied that he would talk, unarmed, if Bud Goforth talked with Hall and was convinced that he was sincere in wanting peace. Bud acted as intermediary, and a truce was arranged.

But now Wiley refused to speak to any of them, Lizzie and his own grandchildren included. Some years later, when the elder Goforths moved in with Bud and Lizzie and their two children, Wiley would ride by and, if he had had a drink too many, fire a few rounds toward the house, despite the fact that his grandchildren were playing in the yard or on the porch. Like the Howards, the Bakers forgave slowly, if ever.

On the night after Bad Tom's murder, there was a massive wake at the Baldy George Baker home, where Tom's body had been taken, with the usual eating, drinking, mourning, and commiserating. All evening people streamed in and out of the house. Tom lay in his coffin beneath the lamplight. And then, when the casual mourners had gone and only the family members and old friends were left, a strange thing happened. (I do not offer this as truth. You can believe it or ignore it. But when Stanley DeZarn asked Tom Baker's grandson, "Do you believe that?" Baker looked at him in surprise. "Of course I do," he said. "Everybody I know does, everybody that was there or knew somebody that was there." I merely pass it along.)

It was after midnight, well toward morning. Talk had quieted, voices drifting in from the kitchen, people speaking softly, the sound of men sucking on their pipes, sipping whiskey from cups. Suddenly there was a strange scratching at the front door. One of the men got up, went to the door and, seeing no one there, opened it to look around the porch. When he did a huge turtle pushed past him, plodding slowly, resolutely into the room and made straight for the coffin. Those familiar with the incident of the murdered peddler drew back in fright. Then Pleaz Sawyer got up, grabbed the big turtle, hauled it outside, cut off its head, and threw it into the draw behind the house. Tom had said of the peddler, "Let the turtles have him." This time the turtle had come for Tom. Perhaps Pleaz had exorcised the spell.

Thomas Baker was buried in Boston Gap beside his father, George W., Baldy George. An era was over, no doubt of that, though a few days later it was reported that Big John Philpot had announced that he was assuming Bad Tom's leadership role.

The violence had not yet run its course. Tension and hatred still gripped Manchester. Bal and Big Jim Howard still led their clan and vowed to bring to trial every Baker involved in the killing of Wilson and Burch. A few weeks later Dickey lamented to his diary, "Judge B.P. White is drinking himself to death, I fear. General Garrard sits in his great house, alone, surrounded by guards."

Spirits picked up somewhat when surveyors for the Black Diamond Railroad rode into Manchester. They were surveying, they said, for a line from London to a point about three miles east of Manchester. There was great excitement, and plans were made to move the county seat out to the railroad. But nothing came of it. Again the dream collapsed. The line was not built until 1914.

Young Lewis, drunk and dancing, shot and killed Cotton Collins and wounded Dan Collins, both blacks, in the house of the Hawkins woman. He was arrested and fined. This had no relationship to the feud.

But then the war burst out anew. Out on the road toward Red Bird a group of Philpots and Fishers were on their way to a log-rolling when they were stopped by deputy sheriff Wash Thacker, who had a warrant for Bob Philpot. The two of them rode to the side of the road to arrange bail so as not to interfere with the log-rolling, when suddenly a group of Griffins and Morrises rounded the turn in the road and were practically on them before the two groups recognized each other. There had long been bad blood between the two clans, but feelings had intensified since Christmas 1897, when Jim Crow Philpot and Jim Bundy, a friend of the Griffins, shot and killed each other. Now the two sides jumped from their horses, dived down the banks of the road, and began firing. Big John Philpot, who had testified at Tom Baker's hearing, was quickly wounded but got his back to a tree and directed his forces. The shooting lasted only a minute or so, but in that time two Griffins and a Morris were killed and three Philpots were wounded, two of whom later died. Bud Griffin, shot in the stomach, held his bowels in with one hand and ran down the road, shooting with the other, before he collapsed. He recovered but was later shot and killed at a party.

Out of ten combatants, five were killed. No official action was taken, since no one reported the fight and no one could say who had started it. And it seemed to have been a fair fight. In the courthouse the Whites shed no tears. In the previous election George Philpot, despite his numerous kin, had lost the primary race for sheriff to Bev White. Philpot did not take the loss lightly, and in the general election he bolted to support Gilbert Garrard. He lost that one, too, but won the enmity of the Whites.

For a while it seemed that the Philpots and Griffins were determined to take over from the Bakers and Howards. In July, out at Pigeon Roost, the two families held another shoot-out. This time Granville Philpot, a member of the state legislature and thus an officer of the law, led his family's forces. One Philpot, two Griffins, and two horses were reported killed.

Meantime, another fight was tearing Kentucky apart, and Clay County with it. It was to have a strange and tragic impact.

Bloody Time in Frankfort

The last year of the nineteenth century was a time of intense political ferment in Kentucky as the voters prepared to elect a new governor. Four years earlier they had chosen William O. Bradley, a decent, fairly progressive man and the first Republican governor in the state's history. But Bradley's efforts to improve roads and schools had been balked at every turn by the Democratic-controlled legislature, his record was chiefly one of failure and frustration, and the Republicans had faint hopes of electing a successor. When Attorney General W.S. Taylor, a plodding, unimpressive lawyer from Western Kentucky, sought the Republican nomination he won it almost by default, since few thought it was worth having. Then the Democrats nominated state senator William Goebel in a stormy convention that split the party, with former governor John Y. Brown leading the splinter Real Democratic or "Brownies" Party and John G. Blair heading the Populist ticket. Suddenly Republican hopes were rekindled.

Goebel, the son of poor German immigrants who had come to Northern Kentucky after the Civil War, was totally lacking in charm, humor, or social graces. He remained a bachelor throughout his life, was noticeably uncomfortable around women, and viewed most social life as a waste of time. But a keen, tireless mind and ruthless ambition earned him respect and wealth as a lawyer, and enabled him, despite his lackluster personality, to do well in politics and claw his way to the position of president pro tem of the state Senate. There he waged a dogged fight against big business, especially the L&N Railroad, and his battle to expand civil rights for women and blacks. In his campaign against Taylor, he was often called "assassin," a term stemming from the shooting in which he had killed banker John Stanford, whom he had angered by calling him "Gonorrhea John." Goebel was not noted for diplomacy.

Throughout the campaign Republicans warned that they would not permit the Democrats to steal the election with the Goebel election law, which stipulated that the state election board had to certify voting results. The law, rammed through the legislature by Goebel and his supporters, would give heavy advantage to the majority party, which could dominate the election board.

The campaign oratory of both candidates was inflammatory. Taylor called the legislature a "vicious body of deformed Democrats and degenerate Americans" and warned that "the deadly coils of tyranny will crush to death your liberties" if the Democrats should win. He referred to Goebel as a liar, a vampire, and an assassin. Goebel referred to Taylor and other opponents as villains, thieves, helpless liars, and ignorant charlatans. Taylor and Governor Bradley stumped the mountains of Eastern Kentucky calling for a majority so large that the "vote-stealers can't overturn it." The heavily Republican mountains were incensed by the idea that they might be deprived of their rightful victory, and editorials in several papers warned that "we will not let them take through deceit what they cannot win at the polls." Frankfort was swept by rumors that Bradley and the Republicans were hoarding rifles and ammunition in the state arsenal to counter those of the Democrats in the state penitentiary. Actually, the rumors were false, but so many people believed them that at one point Bradley asked President McKinley for a thousand federal troops to keep the peace. McKinley didn't send them.

In the election of November 7, 1899, Taylor appeared to be the winner, with 193,714 votes to Goebel's 191,331. Former governor John Y. Brown, nominee of the Democratic splinter party, picked up 12,040, Blair even fewer. The election had to be certified by the all-Democratic Board of Election Commissioners, and in the two weeks between the election and the convening of the board, between 500 and 1,000 armed mountain men descended on Frankfort, recruited by Caleb Powers, a thirty-one-year-old Knox County school superintendent who had been elected secretary of state with Taylor. They were carried to the capital free of charge by the L&N, whose officials were determined to prevent a Goebel victory. The danger eased, however, when the board, to the surprise of everyone, gave the victory to Taylor by a 2-1 vote.

That, it seemed, was that. On December 12, Taylor was inaugurated. Considering the bitterness of the race, Goebel accepted the outcome with good grace, thanked his supporters, and said he was tired and was going to visit his brother in Arizona. But two days later the Democratic State Central Committee met and urged Goebel and his running mate, J.C.W. Beckham, to contest the election. Goebel showed little interest at first but relented and filed a contest, and the Democratic majority in the legislature announced that it would investigate the results through a select committee. Again the Republicans armed themselves to prevent the Democrats from stealing their victory. Outright civil war seemed a very real threat.

All of this did not go unnoticed in Clay County. During the campaign, Taylor did not speak in Manchester, but more than a hundred Clay Countians went down to London to hear him, and others traveled to Barbourville to hear Caleb Powers. When Powers called for men to go to Frankfort to protect the party victory, a long line of rifle-carrying horsemen rode toward the depot in London. The new century threatened to be as stormy as the one ending.

Jim Howard followed the race and its outcome closely but took no part in it. He was at the time free on appeal of his life sentence for killing Baldy George Baker. When, on January 29, he told Alexander Morgan that he was going to Frankfort the next day, Morgan was surprised.

"What are you going to do that for?" he asked.

"Well, I'm not going to get a striped suit, I'll tell you that," Jim replied. Ever since, it has been assumed that he meant that he was going to Frankfort to do something to keep out of prison—to get a pardon. But how? Did he have reason to believe a pardon was possible? What was he willing to do to receive the pardon? And why was he seeking a pardon when he was out on appeal, one that he might well win?

What happened the next day, January 30, 1900, will always be a source of conjecture. No one knows, and it is likely no one ever will know who performed the lethal deed, but at 11:15 A.M. William Goebel was shot as he approached the state Capitol with two companions. Witnesses said the shot (or shots; some say four shots were heard) was fired from a window in the office of Secretary of State Caleb Powers. Mortally wounded, Goebel was carried to the Capital Hotel, where he died four days later, on February 3, 1900, after being declared the winner of the contest for governor by the legislative committee of ten Democrats and one Republican, and sworn in on his deathbed—sworn in twice, in fact, since some questioned whether he was alive, or if he was conscious enough to take the oath the first time. (He was conscious enough to drink some wine and to ask for some oysters, a favorite food.)

According to historians, Goebel's last words were: "Tell my friends to be brave and fearless and loyal to the great common people." But according to Allan Trout of the *Courier-Journal*, what he actually said was, "Doc, those oysters were no damn good."

Whatever the details, the essential facts are that William Goebel

died of his gunshot wounds, and that moments later J.C.W. Beckham, who had been elected lieutenant governor with him, was sworn
in as governor. The courts eventually upheld the Democrats' claim to
the governorship, and Taylor fled to Indiana.

The role of Jim Howard in the affair has been debated ever since.
The generally accepted theory is that he received a message from Caleb
Powers, who was in Frankfort, offering him a pardon for killing Baldy
George Baker if he would come to Frankfort and "do a job for us." Both
Howard and Powers denied this to their deaths.

Whatever the truth, Jim Howard went to Frankfort on the day
Goebel was murdered, and he had some reason to believe he was
going to get a pardon. He arrived on the L&N from London at about
10:30 A.M., went to a hotel across the railroad tracks and about a block
west of the depot, and rented a room. He then left the hotel and
started toward the Capitol, supposedly to pursue the matter of a pardon. According to his Democratic prosecutors, he went to the Capitol, met with Powers and others, and shot Goebel as he came up the
walk toward the Capitol. According to his own version, he had just
stepped out of the hotel when he heard the news that Goebel had
been shot. At any rate, he remained in Frankfort three days but failed
to receive his pardon and returned to Manchester. But the trials of Jim
Howard were by no means over.

The Democrats were almost hysterical in their rage at the murder
of Goebel. In a haphazard catch-all, police arrested sixteen men and
charged each with being in one way or another involved in the assassination. There was, for example, Holland Whittaker, who was jailed
for no apparent reason except that he was a Republican with a pistol.
Joe Adkins, a known killer and a figure in the French-Eversole war in
Perry County, was reportedly seen in the capital on the day of the
assassination but was never apprehended. This may have reflected
the fact that he was thought to be a Democrat or to have worked for
Democrats in the Perry County feud.

Caleb Powers was arrested at once, as was Henry Youtsey, an employee in the state auditor's office. Berry Howard of Bell County and
a cousin of Jim Howard, Garret Ripley, a minor Republican official,
and eleven others were indicted over the next two weeks. Jim Howard was indicted much later. Little evidence led to his arrest, except
that a witness later said he saw Jim running from the executive office
building shortly after Goebel was shot. (Another witness testified
that, at the same time, he saw Jim or someone who looked like Jim,
standing near the doorway of the building.) When Jim was informed,
on April 3—three months after he returned to Manchester—that he

was being sought in the case, he sent word that he would come to Frankfort and surrender as soon as he was served the proper papers. He later told reporters that he had seen several Bakers in Frankfort during his brief stay and assumed that they had implicated him.

Eventually, three of those accused turned state's evidence, two under suspicious circumstances. Five were tried, of which two (Berry Howard and Garret Ripley) were acquitted and three (Powers, Jim Howard, and Youtsey) were found guilty and sentenced to life in prison.

The trial was little short of a kangaroo court. Judge James Cantrill, who presided over Jim Howard's trial, had been a Democratic legislator and a strong Goebel supporter and had sworn in Goebel as he lay dying. His instructions to the jury were tantamount to a demand for a guilty verdict, and his conduct was so flagrantly biased that all three of the verdicts were later reversed at the appeals level. Jim was tried three times, and only once was there a single Republican on the jury. In the jury pool of 368 men, 360 were Democrats. Three former aides to Powers swore that Powers had instructed them to bring gunmen to Frankfort to kill Goebel and Democratic legislators, but they admitted that they had been offered immunity from prosecution for their testimony. Another witness admitted that Goebel's brothers had warned him that he would go to prison if he did not testify for the prosecution. Youtsey, an excitable, obviously unbalanced man, testified that Powers had sent for Howard and that Howard had appeared at the office of the secretary of state, where Youtsey, acting under orders from Caleb Powers, opened the door. Youtsey admitted that he had never seen Jim Howard before and had not heard his voice, but said that the man at the door when he opened it said, "I am Jim Howard." (He usually identified himself as James.)

Howard allegedly did not ask who Youtsey was or ask to see Powers, who had allegedly sent for him to "do a job." Instead, according to Youtsey, Howard walked into an anteroom next to Powers's office and was shown into an adjoining room on the southwest corner of the building, given a Marlin rifle and some special bullets, and left alone to kill Goebel. During the trial, Youtsey screamed, fell in a fake faint, and remained inert and supposedly unconscious for the remainder of the trial. It was apparent from the beginning that the court was more interested in hanging a Republican than in finding the killer.

The prosecution charged that Powers had become familiar with Howard through Howard's trial in Barbourville for the killing of George Baker (Powers swore that he had never seen Howard) and that he had seen in Howard a cold, ruthless killer and had determined that Howard wanted a pardon badly enough to risk a high-level crime.

According to the prosecution scenario, Jim left his hotel, walked across the railroad tracks and up the sidewalk to the executive building (today the old Capitol Annex), where he located the office of the secretary of state and told Henry Youtsey, who answered his knock, "I am Jim Howard." Youtsey then took him into an empty outer office of Caleb Powers by a roundabout route so that no one would see them, handed him a rifle, showed him to a corner window from which the walkway approaching the Capitol could be easily viewed, and left him alone. Shortly afterward Howard saw three men coming up the walk, identified one of them as Goebel, and shot him. Seeing that Goebel was properly wounded, he placed the rifle on a table, put on his coat, and left the building by a rear door.

Powers was tried four times, in July 1900, October 1901, August 1903, and November 1907. Convictions in the first three trials were overturned on appeal; his final trial ended in deadlock, and he was in jail awaiting appeal when he was pardoned. Youtsey turned state's evidence after his first trial, was also given a life sentence, and was not pardoned until 1919.

Jim Howard's trials were in September 1900, January 1902, and April 1903, the last three years after he was indicted. His third trial lasted thirty-four days; the jury was out half an hour. When Judge Cantrill asked him if he had any words to say before sentence was passed, Jim Howard stood "ramrod straight and without a trace of emotion on his face," according to newspaper accounts, and said: "I do. I want to say that I will be back breathing the free ozone of the mountains when you and all of you here who have framed me are in hell."

It is hard to escape the feeling that Jim was, as he said, framed. It takes a considerable exercise of the imagination to believe that Jim Howard, who was neither reckless nor stupid, would present himself to a stranger—Youtsey—of whom he had never heard and whom he had no reason to trust, without either presenting or asking identification. If Powers had sent him word to come to Frankfort and "do a job for us," wouldn't he at least have asked to speak to Powers (who, incidentally, was not in Frankfort at the time but on a train to Louisville)? Would he not have asked the nature of the job? Would he not have mentioned the promise of a pardon or asked for proof that the pardon existed or would be presented within a reasonable time?

If Powers was indeed the instigator of the plot, why would he have chosen Youtsey, a near-deranged man who was not even a Powers employee or the employee of a friend, for such a delicate mission? Assuming that Jim was stupid enough to follow the directions of a man he had never seen and who might well have been leading him into a trap, how did he and/or Youtsey know that Goebel was coming to the Capitol on this particular day and at this particular hour? Did they have someone watching the doors to the Capitol? If not, how did they know that Goebel had not already arrived and entered the building? If Jim was left alone in the room, how did he know, when three men approached, that one of them was Goebel? And how did he know *which* was Goebel? He had never seen the man. It was a cold, blustery day, and all of the three men had their heads bent against the cold.

If Jim Howard did indeed kill Goebel, he must have been the fastest killer on record, to arrive in Frankfort at or around 10:30, walk down the street and across the railroad tracks to the hotel, obtain and check into a room, leave the hotel, walk down the street and again across the tracks, walk up the walkway to the Capitol Annex or office building, find the office of Caleb Powers, locate Youtsey, whom he had never seen, identify himself, receive the key to the empty office, enter and lock the office so that no one could interfere with the killing, find and load the rifle with the special bullets, select the best window from which to fire—the one offering the best view of the approach to the Capitol next door—pick Goebel from the three men approaching on the sidewalk, and shoot him at 11:15—all this in forty-five minutes.

Furthermore, assuming that Jim spotted Goebel correctly and shot him and left the office, why did he not get his pardon and leave for Manchester as quickly as possible? Why did he stay in Frankfort for three days while all hell broke loose around him and police arrested anyone with any remote connection to the case? And why, if he did the job and waited three days for payment, did he never get his pardon? All the time he was in Frankfort, Republicans were in power, and Taylor, Powers, and others who were supposed to have conspired with him were in office, in a position to grant him his pardon. Why didn't they?

And if he and Powers were guilty—indeed, if the Democrats in control of the trials did not know that they were innocent—why was it necessary to rig the trials so blatantly? Why did they feel it necessary to threaten witnesses, to give such prejudicial instructions to the jury that appeals were granted in five trials? Why did Cantrill refuse to step down from the bench when he was so obviously biased?

On the other hand, there is one question that was never adequately answered, though it did not concern Jim Howard directly: Caleb Powers, on his way to Louisville by train, allegedly got off the train in Shelbyville and asked the stationmaster, "Have you heard about anything happening in Frankfort this morning?" or words to that effect. What was he expecting, if not the assassination? And why was he on a train to Louisville at such a critical time unless it was to remove himself from an incident he had helped to plan?

In 1906 Jim Howard joined Youtsey and began serving his sentence. Two years later, after Republican Augustus Willson had been elected governor, Jim and Caleb Powers were pardoned. Willson announced that he considered both men innocent and stated his belief that Youtsey was the real killer. The process, however, had cost Howard and Powers eight years of their lives.

Powers returned to Knox County as something of a hero and was soon a candidate for Congress. During the campaign, a man in Middlesboro came up to him and asked, "Caleb, tell the me truth: Did you kill Goebel?"

"No, I did not," Powers replied.

"I'm sorry to hear that," said the man. "I was going to vote for you."

Powers won and served five terms in Washington. It was his boast that he served longer in Congress than he had served in prison. In his book, *My Story*, he denied, as he denied to his death, any implication in the assassination. But the question remains: If he did not send for Jim Howard, who did?

Jim Howard returned to Manchester, resumed his job as a clerk in Hill's store, and later became a shoe salesman, then a salesman of trees, traveling in the six counties around Clay. Gradually public memories of the murders of 1898 dimmed.

Questions about Howard's role in the Goebel affair and in the feud must always remain. I have never been satisfied that Jim Howard killed anyone except Baldy George Baker, and then possibly in self-defense as well as revenge.

On the other hand (there is always an "on the other hand" in this matter) there is one alleged fact that is hard to rationalize. In June 1992, Ernest Sester told me in a telephone conversation from Manchester that he had talked to Jim Howard when he was "an old man, not long before he died." Howard, said Sester, asked him where he lived.

"I live in the old Tom Baker house," Sester told him. Jim Howard looked at him, he said, and smiled.

"Did you ever see that bullet hole there on the porch where old Bad Tom was almost shot?" he asked. Sester said he had.

Jim laughed. "I almost shot the pipe out of old Tom's mouth," he said.

That requires second thoughts. Tom was shot the day after the Baker-Howard fight at the rafting site, the same day Jim Howard and George Baker met and reached their peace agreement. The Howards later concluded that Baldy George had violated his trust when he told his son Wiley, "That's going to be a bad one over on Crane Creek. I'd advise you to stay out of it," indicating that he knew about the murder plans and did nothing to stop them. (But was he referring to the coming ambush of the Howards or further disagreement over Bal's debt and logs? And who heard him say this?)

Furthermore, if Jim fired at Bad Tom on the day before the ambush (it is possible that when he spoke to Sester he was referring to another occasion) he also violated his word. And if that was the case, both he and Baldy George had reason to feel guilty and defensive when they met and Baker was killed.

One more question: How did Jim Howard have time to get out to Crane Creek and shoot at Tom? The initial fight on the rafting site had occurred the day before. Jim, by his own account, did not hear about it until the following day, which sounds logical. That same day he made his agreement with Baldy George Baker. Yet it was on this day, the day following the altercation at the rafting site, that Hudge Allen warned Tom that the Howards were "lying in the weeds" to ambush him. And it was on the same day, shortly after noon, when someone shot at Tom as he sat on his porch. How could Jim Howard have found Baldy George, gotten an arbiter, reached an agreement, mounted his horse, gotten a rifle, ridden all the way out to Crane Creek (a distance of ten miles or more), hidden in the woods, and shot at Tom, all in apparently little more than an hour? If it was a Howard who shot at Tom, would it not more likely have been one of the Howards only a mile or so away, at the mouth of Crane Creek where, according to Hudge Allen, they were waiting to kill him? That is another question about Big Jim Howard to which we are not likely to learn the answer.

Big Jim Howard is buried in the cemetery on Anderson Street in Manchester. The stone reads simply: James Ballenger Howard, 1866-1954.

The Feuds Wind Down

While Jim Howard was facing his tormentors in Frankfort, trouble continued at home. During the first week of September 1900, Chad Hall and Abe Gilbert were shot from ambush. Abe was killed; Chad was fatally wounded but lingered long enough for a remarkable deathbed confession.

A note here. In 1984 James Pope Jr., editor of the Sunday Magazine of the *Louisville Courier-Journal*, received a letter from Colonel E.B. Allen of Totz, Harlan County, referring to the mountain feuds. It was an interesting, literate letter, and the man seemed to know what he was talking about. When the magazine was discontinued, Pope turned the letter over to me, and after several years I discovered it in my files and went looking for Allen. I finally found him building a home near Pine Hill, in Rockcastle County, where he had retired. In his letter, Allen had stated: "An Eastern Kentucky historian wrote that two mysteries would never be solved—the killing of Colin Campbell in Scotland in 1745, and the killing of Bad Tom Baker in Clay County in 1899. I discovered Tom Baker's killer last fall while talking to his killer's grandson."

"Do you really know who killed Bad Tom?" I asked Allen.

"I do," he said. "I was talking to this fellow, and he said to me, 'You know, my mother was Chad Hall's daughter, and she told me that just before grandaddy died, he told her, "There is something I want to tell you. I was the one that killed those five Cawood boys over in Harlan County. And I killed Bad Tom Baker. Wanted to tell you."' And he told her how he did it. He went into Bev White's house by the back window, and there was a rifle in the front room, loaded, on the bed by the window looking across at the courthouse, and he propped the blind partly open with a chair so he could have a view without being seen, zeroed his rifle in on the door of the tent where Tom was lodged, and waited. When Tom came out and stood there, all he had to do was pull the trigger. Then he said he slipped out the back window, went down the bank to the creek, walked along the creek a few yards, then up the bank to the road, and waited till some people passed, walking out of town, and fell in behind them. But when they heard there had been a shot, they decided to go back to the court-house to see what it was, and he just went with them. And when they got to the courthouse they heard about Bad Tom and tried to go over and see him, but it took him some time because there was a crowd of soldiers and people around.'"

As far as I can discover, Reb Allen was the only man who knew this, although Hall was suspected of several killings, including that of Goebel. His words fit the pattern of deathbed confessions of gunmen at the time, as though by getting the killing off his chest the killer would get it off his record in heaven as well. Incidentally, Hall was wrong about the Cawoods. Only two were killed on that occasion; the other Cawood was not hit, and the man killed with John Cawood was, ironically, a Hall.

But this raises other question. First, who paid or persuaded Chad Hall to shoot Bad Tom? And what motivated him, not only in the murder of Bad Tom but in the Cawood shootings?

The way in which Chad purportedly shot Bad Tom raises specula-tion as to whether he was the killer of Goebel, who was killed just as he passed a large tree along the sidewalk leading to the Capitol, as though someone had zeroed in on the tree and waited for Goebel to walk in front of it, at which time the killer would need only to pull the trigger. The bullet that went through Goebel's chest was later dug out of the tree.

At the same time, details of the shooting bring to mind a conver-sation that former governor Bert Combs had with Big Jim Howard when Combs was a boy in Manchester. "Howard said if you wanted to shoot a man you didn't aim at the man himself," said Combs. "That way your gun would be moving when you pulled the trigger and it could throw your aim off. What you wanted to do was to pick a spot he would have to pass and zero in on the spot. Then when he passed in front of the spot, all you had to do was pull the trigger." That, too, would fit the pattern of the shot that killed Goebel and the one that felled Bad Tom, though Jim Howard was seen in his office when Tom Baker was shot. Was Chad Hall the killer in both in-stances? No one knows. And how did Jim Howard know that method for killing a man?

At any rate, Jule Webb and Dennis McCollum were charged with the murder of Chad Hall. They were put in the Manchester jail, which was under control of the White-Howard faction and probably not too safe a haven for Webb and McCollum, who were pro-Baker. Sure enough, the next night, before their bail could be arranged, someone placed a ladder against the jail wall, climbed to the window of Jule's cell, and, spotting him lying on his cot, shot him. The shooter's aim was good; the bullet entered under Jule's right ear and came out under the left. Miraculously, Jule was able two weeks later to appear in court. As historian J.W. Raine put it, "Either he had brains to spare or not enough to hit." After that, however, he was hard of hearing in one ear.

At the next session of court, Webb and McCollum were transferred to London for trial in Laurel Circuit Court. They were acquitted and apparently left the county.

On March 8, 1901, with Judge J.H. Tinsley presiding over court, T.T. Garrard, with his son Edward and seventeen supporters, rode into Manchester and tied their horses in front of the courthouse. T.T. and two others went into the law offices of County Attorney Sam Kash and were conferring with Kash concerning bail for Webb and McCollum when a shot was fired from inside the courthouse, apparently at the Garrards sitting out front. The Garrards rushed from the courthouse and began firing from behind trees. At least a hundred shots were reported, but no one was killed. Ed Garrard was shot through the ear. Steve Spurlock was shot in the arm.

Judge Tinsley was furious. Storming into the office of Sheriff Beverly White, he demanded to know who had started the firing and why. White explained that someone had discharged a rifle into the ceiling accidentally, and that when the Garrards started shooting outside, the people inside returned the fire in self-defense. Tinsley refused to accept that. He ordered White to disarm everyone in the courthouse except himself. Then, with the help of D.L. Walker, a young attorney allied with neither side of the feud, Tinsley called a conference of the Whites and Garrards. Into his courtroom strode the aging T.T. Garrard and a dozen of his relatives, and Beverly White and the leading members of his family. The participants seemed to be less hostile than weary.

John G. White had come from Winchester to represent his family in drawing up the formal terms. C.B. Lyttle and Dr. J.R. Burchell represented the Garrards. (No one represented the Howards or Bakers. Apparently it was assumed that when the generals stopped, the war stopped.) With surprisingly little difficulty, and with few objections from those present, Judge Tinsley arranged a truce. Both sides promised to go about unarmed. The Garrards and Bakers could safely come and go from Manchester, and the Whites and Howards would be able to move safely around the county, especially the Crane Creek and Goose Creek areas.

Apparently the hostility had worn thin with everyone concerned. To the amazement of most people in Clay County, Bev White announced that he was tired of the job and resigned as sheriff. Maybe he was just tired of the danger. Maybe the last skirmish with the Garrards had been one too many. In any event, he quit. D.L. Walker took over as sheriff. And the Clay County War, as far as the Whites and Garrards were concerned, was over.

The fighting sputtered on, but without any real leadership on either side. After Bad Tom was killed, John Philpot was assumed to have taken over as leader of the Baker-Philpot clan, but the post didn't seem to amount to much. If there was a recognized leader of the Howard-Griffin clan, no one seemed to know exactly who it was. Jim Howard was never mentioned in connection with violence, nor were Israel or Corbin. Though the Howards were feared by some for the next thirty years, there is no hard evidence that they were part of any of the subsequent killings.

Gradually the Griffins and Philpots settled their differences and came to an unspoken agreement to quit the shooting. But the emotions that had fueled the feuds—pride, hatred, revenge—had not disappeared. In 1904 someone, supposedly Jim Philpot, although some held Pete responsible, shot and killed Bud Griffin. (It was either Bud or Hugh Griffin who had had his stomach shot open in the Red Bird fight. Hugh was sometimes called Bud.) It happened at a party, and the mere fact that Philpots and Griffins were at a party together indicates that the old bitterness was subsiding, though the old fondness for liquor survived. Sometime during the evening, a group of men gathered in the kitchen of the home where the party was being held, and for some reason Pete Philpot hit Bud Griffin with a beer glass. A fistfight broke out, and in the melee someone pulled a pistol and shot Bud. Killed him. Then Sam Griffin shot and killed Jim Philpot. But the incident was attributed to high spirits, human and alcoholic, and did not incite a renewal of hostilities.

In the years following, Clay County was relatively quiet. The Eversoles and McCollums were in conflict from time to time, but this only indirectly represented a continuation of the Baker-Howard trouble. The McCollums were usually allied with the Bakers, but the Eversoles were not directly tied to the Howards. Bud Eversole lived in Boston Gap; Joe McCollum lived two miles away. Bud Eversole got into an argument with Joe McCollum when one of McCollum's mules got out of his pasture and into Eversole's cornfield. Eversole chased it out, but in fleeing, the mule fell over a cliff and was killed. Joe McCollum accused Eversole of killing the mule and promised to get even.

Joe was a frequent source of trouble. He was married to Lily Hensley, to the anguish of her family. The Hensleys were good people, and Lily's father, Bob, and her brother, Vernon, were often hard put to get Joe out of trouble. It is likely that Joe was a little unbalanced. When he was in his twenties, he would go down to the schoolhouse and play with the children, bullying them and sometimes starting fights when things did not suit him. One time he even cut a teen-age girl across her back. All this was very trying for Vernon, his brother-in-law, who was the teacher.

A week after the mule incident, Joe McCollum got Pleaz Walker, and the two of them hid on the bank of Elderlick. When Bud Eversole rode by they shot him in the chest. Bud managed to stay on his horse until it reached the home of Bobby Baker, where he staggered to the door and knocked. Mrs. Baker came to the door. "I hate to bother you," Bud said, "but I've been shot," and he fell into the doorway.

Mrs. Baker sent the children to get Gard and Thena Baker, who lived up the road. Gard and Thena took Bud home where, Thena said, "He suffered awful." But he survived and two weeks later went out West to recuperate. Gard and Thena met John Eversole, Bud's brother, on their way to church a few weeks later, and asked about Bud.

"He's out in New Mexico," said John, "trying to get well. But let me tell you this: The day he passes this life, Joe McCollum's doom is sealed."

Bud died soon afterward. And early on the morning of July 2, 1916, Joe McCollum came out of his house and went around to his corn crib. He had just opened the crib door when there were two shots, and Joe fell, shot in the back. He got to his feet and staggered down to the road, where he collapsed. His son, Dennis, who had followed him to the crib, ran to the house crying that daddy was hurt, and Lily, sick with tuberculosis, ran to the road, took Joe's head in her lap, and stroked his face, weeping and telling him how she loved him.

Dennis ran and got Gard and Thena Baker, who seemed always to be on hand to help when trouble arose, and they came and carried Joe into the house. He was shot shortly after six o'clock and lived until ten, when he died, shrieking in agony, blood frothing from his mouth.

Bob Hensley, Joe's father-in-law, got bloodhounds and tracked the Eversoles into the hills above Crane Creek, where they were arrested and taken to Manchester for trial. They were acquitted, however, the jury deciding that no one had seen them do it.

The Eversoles now swore they would kill Bob Hensley, who had outraged their dignity by running them down with dogs. Bob, as the saying went, "worked away from home," that is, was a traveling salesman. Upon returning from a selling trip in the late summer of 1919, he and his wife went to see his brother Bill, who ran a store on Crane Creek. That evening the Hensleys were returning and fording the creek at the mouth of Elderlick when there was a shot from the nearby woods, and Bob fell from his horse, shot in the side. He died while his wife held his head out of the water. She saw two men running away, and thought they were John Eversole and George Alex Bush, but she could not be certain, and they were never arrested. John Sester, a neighbor, came by, ran to Gard Baker's (again) and shouted, "Somebody's shot Bob Hensley!" Gard got a wagon and took Bob's body home.

Tragedy wasn't through with the Hensleys. Vernon, a thoughtful, book-loving teacher, finally decided to leave Clay County and moved to Cincinnati. He might have lived happily there had not his daughter Ellen met "Little Steve" Bowling, who also had come up from Clay County. Vernon warned Ellen of Steve's violent reputation and warned Bowling to stay away from his daughter. Bowling laughed at him. That night he waited around the corner until Ellen slipped out of the house and came to meet him. But Vernon had followed her. He confronted Bowling. Both drew their guns. Bowling was faster. Vernon was killed.

Nor was violence done with the McCollums. Jim Baker, Bad Tom's son who had taken part in the Howard killings, had married Rose McCollum, and they lived near her father, Dick. Two years earlier Dick had been indicted but acquitted in the killing of John Hacker, who had allegedly come to the McCollum home drunk and looking for trouble. Hacker had begun singing, shooting under McCollum's feet, and demanding that he dance. McCollum danced. Hacker ran out of bullets. McCollum went into the house, got his own gun, and came back and killed Hacker. The jury felt he had been justified.

Jim Baker had a young son, Oakley, who was fond of visiting his grandparents, Dick and Rose McCollum, who always petted and played with him. One day Jim sent Oakley up to his grandparents' to borrow a meal sack, and when he was through with it he sent Oakley to return it. For some reason Dick McCollum, who seemed to adore his grandson, spoke harshly to the boy, saying that he should be ashamed to bring back a sack so filthy. Hurt and confused at being scolded by his beloved Papaw, Oakley went home crying and told his father what had happened. Jim washed the sack carefully, took it back to McCollum, and told him in no uncertain terms what he thought of someone who would hurt the little boy's feelings. An argument ensued, and Jim shot and killed his father-in-law. Not long afterward, Jim was shot and killed in a gunfight at the schoolhouse.

One final act of violence remained to be played out. Bakers were once more involved. Some Bakers charged that Howards were, too, but there is no proof of it.

It started when John Baker got into money trouble and allegedly hired or persuaded Dewey Hensley, Little Tom Baker, and Frank McDaniel to burn his wholesale house so he could collect the insurance. (This is not the same John Baker who was shot with Frank Clark. There were several John Bakers.) McDaniel was another of the shadowy figures who often seemed to be around when trouble occurred. His seemingly peaceful occupation—selling Hoover vacuum cleaners—kept him safely on the move, but he had served time at least once in the state penitentiary for murder and was said to be on the run after escaping from prison at the time Baker wanted his warehouse torched. Doc Hornsby, a friend of the Bakers, was said to be involved in the matter but not in the arson.

According to Tom Walters, who was told the story by his father, Jan Walters, Police Judge Pitt Stivers caught John Baker and some other men gambling in Baker's warehouse in 1926 and threatened to arrest them. Baker told Stivers that he would "regret this as long as you live." One night sometime later, Walters said, Baker's warehouse caught fire.

"My grandfather, Rev. F.R. Walters, who lived close by, became aware of the fire and hurried to see," Walters recounted. "Just as he arrived a black man, Alfred Neal, also came up and apparently saw some suspicious activity from Baker and some of his friends that would lead to the suspicion that the fire had been purposely set. My grandfather returned home, but Alf Neal was shot and killed." Apparently the arsonists had seen Neal and realized that he had seen them setting the fire. It was an unfortunate end for poor Neal, who seemed often to witness acts of violence. It had been Neal who saw John Baker and Frank Clark shooting up the countryside and reported it to the sheriff, leading to the shooting deaths of Baker and Clark.

"There was some fear for Grandpa's life, since he had apparently seen the same thing as Neal," said Tom Walters. "Dad said that John Baker liked Grandpa and that his being a minister gave him additional protection."

But Pitman Stivers had seen the killing of Neal and testified to it when McDaniel, Dewey Baker, Hornsby, and Bobby Baker were arrested. The Reverend Walters, exercising more discretion, did not come forward to testify. A few days later, after McDaniel and the Bakers were indicted but before their trial, Pitt Stivers was killed.

"Pitt lived across the road from Grandpa, and they would walk to town together each weekday as Grandpa would go for his mail," Walters recounted. "On the morning Stivers was killed, he stopped for Grandpa, but Grandpa said he was not feeling well and would come on shortly. Stivers walked up the hill and turned down toward town and was between the old First National Bank and Dr. Anderson's house when a car with darkened windows pulled up and blasted Pitt with shotguns. Dad said he heard the rapid reports of the guns. Floyd Hatton, later Dad's brother-in-law, was at the foot of the courthouse hill in town and also heard the shots. He looked up the hill, saw the body on the sidewalk, and thought it was possibly a dog gone mad that someone was shooting. When he arrived on the scene he said that Stivers' shoe soles were literally shot off his feet. The car sped away, and it was later found that the telephone lines into Manchester had been cut to aid in the escape."

This incident led to one of the strangest chapters in the Baker saga. McDaniels, Dewey Baker, and Bobby Baker were indicted for the killing of Alf Neal, but when the indictments were handed down, Frank Baker, commonwealth's attorney and son of Gard and Thena Baker, simply stuck them in a drawer of his desk and refused to process them. It was the second occasion on which Frank, a man with an otherwise spotless reputation, failed to perform his duties properly, apparently because of family connections.

The first case concerned his cousin, George Barrett. Even considering family ties, Frank's loyalty to George was puzzling, for George, once called by the FBI's J. Edgar Hoover "the meanest man I ever knew," was not just a killer. He was a crook, a thief, and a swindler. As a boy he got into a fight with a cousin who shot out his left eye, and afterward he wore glasses with one dark lens. A notorious philanderer, he deserted his first wife and married a high school sweetheart, but this time she deserted him, leaving him with an infant son.

George made his living selling stolen watches and diamonds, working most of the time north of the Ohio River or west of the Mississippi. He would buy a diamond ring from a jewelry store, substitute a fake for the real gem, return the ring to the store, get his money back, and sell the real diamond. He also sold stolen guns and cars and at one time boasted of importing stolen diamonds from Mexico. George also bootlegged whiskey when business was slow and boasted that no revenue agent would ever take him. That proved wrong. In 1929 one did. George was wounded, taken to Louisville, fined a hundred dollars, and sent to prison for a year, the usual sentence for a first-time bootlegger.

When away from home on business, George left his small son with his mother, who lived with her daughter between Manchester and McKee. Returning from a trip to Ohio in 1931, he went by to see the boy. While he was there his mother reprimanded the boy, who was showing off for his daddy, and slapped him across his bottom. This infuriated George, who shouted that no one on earth should touch his son.

"You ain't doin' right by him," he screamed. "You're supposed to be taking care of him. Well, dammit, do it!"

"I been treating him like I would any grandbaby," said his mother. "I don't know how to do any better."

"Ma's been good to the boy, George," said his sister Rachel. "You oughtn't pick on your own mama."

This criticism was more than George's tender ego could bear. Pulling his pistol, he shot his mother dead. Rachel rushed to help her mother and George hit her across the head with the gun, laying her scalp open. Blood streaming down her face, Rachel ran for the door, but George shot her before she could make it. But she got to her feet and staggered across the porch and down to the road, where she flagged down a passing rural mail carrier. He took her to a doctor in town.

George rushed into town, reported the incident to Frank, his cousin and commonwealth's attorney, claiming that he had killed his mother and sister in self-defense. Eventually George was arrested and tried. In fact, he was tried twice and twice got a hung jury, partly because Rachel had died in the meantime and could not testify against him, partly because Frank failed to prosecute him energetically. Indeed, the judge, commenting on the case, denounced the manner in which Frank had conducted the case for the prosecution, declaring that the commonwealth's attorney had "sounded as though he was defending the accused."

Only family loyalty can explain Frank's conduct. Or perhaps it was just that George Barrett poisoned everything he touched. He surely seemed to lead a charmed life. He not only escaped punishment for the murder of his mother and sister, but five months later escaped a hail of bullets from the courthouse at Manchester. Five years later, however, he killed a federal agent and was wounded in both legs during the gunfight. Sentenced to hang, he wept that prison authorities couldn't hang a man who couldn't walk to the gallows. They could. They carried him.

After George's trial, Frank was under a great deal of pressure. A grand jury had handed down indictments against Dewey Hensley, Little Tom Baker, and Frank McDaniel for burning the warehouse and murdering Alf Neal, but Frank refused to process them, as he was legally obliged to do. Judge Cap Stivers, Pitt's father, and some of the Howards were demanding that he prosecute these cases. The Bakers were demanding that he revive some of the old cases against the Howards and Whites for the killing of Bakers. The strain was beginning to tell, and Frank confided to his mother that he had a premonition that he was about to die. When his brother Ben, the county attorney, became suddenly ill and died that summer, Frank stood by his grave and said, "I'll be with you before long, brother."

Such was the situation when the September 1932 term of court opened. The Bakers were in town in force for the occasion, staying at what had been the Potter Hotel but now seemed to be the home of Wiley Baker; or he may have been operating it. The Webb Hotel down the street was said to be full of Howards, though it was never clear which ones or why they were there. Were the Howards worried because Frank might prosecute cases in which Howards were involved? If so, which ones? Or were the Howards harboring lingering hatred of the Bakers because of the deaths of Wilson and Burch Stores and the wounding of Bal?

Or was this gathering the work of Big Jim Howard? After all, he had lost almost eight years out of his life and been forced to endure the ignominy of prison, and there is no doubt that he blamed the Bakers, who were in Frankfort at the time of Goebel's killing, for implicating him in the assassination.

The only outstanding Baker death that remained unsolved was that of Bad Tom, and that was not the work of the Howards.

With Frank around the breakfast table on September 18, 1932, the morning court was scheduled to open, were his wife, his parents (Gard and Thena), Wiley and Shabie, Doc Hornsby, Bill Hensley, George Barrett, Frank Young, and Frank Brockman, a nephew of Frank Young who was originally from Breathitt County and was visiting from Cincinnati.

Bill Hensley had argued with Frank the night before, contending that he was making a bad mistake in not acting on the indictments handed down by the grand jury for the murder of Pitt Stivers. He insisted that if the killers were not imprisoned they would kill Frank to keep the indictments out of court. Now Hensley as well as his parents begged Frank not to go to the courthouse. "I swear there are forty-five men in there waiting to kill you," he said. "And a bunch of Howards among them."

"I can't help that," said Frank. "I was elected commonwealth's attorney. I've got no choice."

So, after he finished breakfast, Frank Baker, accompanied by Brockman and George Barrett (some accounts say it was Jesse Barrett, but most specify George) left the hotel and started across the street to the courthouse. They had hardly reached the sidewalk when a hail of bullets cut down Frank and Brockman. Barrett somehow escaped. Shabie raised the window to call to Frank, and bullets smashed the glass around her head. Thena made one desperate effort to reach her fallen son, but bullets kicked sidewalk splinters into her face and thudded into the building behind her, and she retreated. Wiley ran from the back door and was shot, for some reason, by Dr. Porter, a pharmacist. Frank Young ran with him and was shot in the leg, a minor wound.

Who killed Frank Baker? Again, no one knows. His body lay on the sidewalk for several hours because everyone in the hotel, his mother included, was afraid to retrieve it. By the time his family reached the body, the killers had, of course, left the courthouse. Some people, including Baker descendants, think the fatal bullets came for the rifle of Big Jim Howard, still trying to erase the memory of what happened that fateful day on Crane Creek. As his grandson said, it was not his style.

Four years later, Bobby Baker, Bad Tom's youngest son, who lived in Hamilton, Ohio, came to Manchester on business. He was staying at a hotel at Burning Springs and was having a beer with Lloyd Baker and Ed Manning. Two men at the bar heard Bobby say he was going into Manchester, and they asked for a ride. Bobby agreed, and the three of them started toward town. As they drove into Manchester there was a shot. Bobby slumped over and, as his white-faced passengers tried to grab the wheel, the car slammed into the curb. Bobby Baker was dead. No one was arrested for the killing. One of his passengers was a Garrard.

The Baker-Howard feud was finally over.

But bitter memories refused to die. One day in 1936 Thena Baker ran into Jim Howard on the Town Square in Manchester. Did she suspect Howard of the murder of her son Frank? Had she found the will to forgive him? Jim very studiously ignored her, but Thena blocked his way, looked at him steadily, and said, "Jim, we are getting old. I've found my peace with God, and I'd like to find my peace with you. Can't we all forget the past and forgive?"

Big Jim Howard looked at her coldly. "Get out of my way, you bell-ringing old bitch," he said.

The feud had produced several outstanding characters, among them General T.T. Garrard, Bad Tom Baker, and Big Jim Howard. And Gard and Thena Baker, those kind people who always seemed to be on hand when they were needed.

Thomas Baker lay beside his father, George Baker, in the family plot on Boston Gap. T.T. Garrard was buried not far from where he had spent so many tumultuous years of his interesting, active, valuable life. A village in Clay County bears his name.

And what had happened to James Ballenger Howard? Well, not much really, nothing sensational at any rate. After his release from prison, he returned to his home, his wife Mary, and their three children—James Jr., Earl, and Edna, who soon married and left home. For a while James Howard thought of returning to the family farm at the head of Crane Creek, but he had never been and was not a farmer. He became a salesman of shoes and trees—fruit and ornamental—traveling through the counties around Clay.

"You could see him coming down the hill carrying a big sample case," former governor Bert Combs recalled. "He was an impressive looking man, the impression of size emphasized by the long, black overcoat he wore." Stanley DeZarn says that Howard was reputed to carry a "big, black .45" in that sample case, but Combs doubted that. For one thing, he said, Howard was never known to use a pistol, only a rifle. This was not entirely true, either. According to his grandson Jim Burchell:

Grandaddy carried a .45 pistol, but not in his sample case. He carried it in a shoulder holster. Funny thing: One day in Manchester he bent over and that pistol fell out on the street. It took a strange bounce and went off, shooting him in the back or fleshy part under the shoulder. They took him up to the hospital and called Dr. Anderson, who patched him up and said, "Jim, we've got a nice bed here for you until that wound gets better," and when Grandaddy heard that he jumped out of bed and did a jig, right there in the hospital room. And he told Doc Anderson, "Doctor, I'll see you in a week. Maybe." He believed that if he lay in bed, his blood wouldn't circulate to the wound and heal it. He was a great believer in exercise, getting the blood circulating. He did what they call now aerobic exercises, four hundred a day. And he drank great amounts of water, kept a tall glass full by his bed, and would drink it if he awoke in the night. He walked a lot. Sure enough, he went back a week later and Dr. Anderson said he couldn't believe it, said the would was hardly blue, completely healed.

Ironically, Jim was in Georgetown, Kentucky, the day his old nemesis, Judge Cantrill, was buried, and was asked if he would like to attend. "No, thank you," he said, "but I am willing for it to be known that his funeral has my hearty endorsement." To the day he died, he denied guilt in the Goebel affair.

"He never talked about it," Jim Burchell told me, "but he did say he didn't do it. He said the Democrats raised $100,000 to hang him; wasted their money."

"Grandpa wasn't a violent man," Jim continued. "I loved him. He was a quiet man, read a lot. Liked to read the Bible. That story of him shooting Baker twenty-five times was crazy. That just wasn't his style." But he added, interestingly, that Jim said, "I was going to Frankfort to do the job, and was looking for a partner, but when I got there somebody had beat me to it." That would support the legend, still popular, that Powers offered him a pardon if he would kill Goebel.

We will never know. Dr. Thomas D. Clark, Kentucky's eminent historian, said in 1992, "I doubt if even Jim Howard knew by the time he died. He had lived with the thing for so long, been accused of it, asked about it; I doubt that he could say for sure whether he did it or not."

Just before he died in 1954, Jim was visited by Allan Trout, the famed reporter for the *Courier-Journal*, who begged Jim to tell him the facts so that history could be kept straight, promising to sequester his remarks as long as Jim stipulated.

"We were sitting on the porch," said Trout, "and when I asked him that, Jim looked at me for a few seconds, and then looked away for a long time, as if he was pondering an answer. And finally he said, 'I said all I have to say at that trial.' No one ever got more out of him. But I will say that I wasn't nervous about asking him. He was a very dignified man, very self-contained. But he wasn't intimidating. I didn't sense any violence in him."

Jim's later years seemed placid. He and his wife usually attended church on Sunday. After she died in 1948, he lived for a while in Marcum's boardinghouse. But people said he seemed lonely, often sitting on the porch or walking around the town alone, and he finally went to live with his daughter Mary, who had married Toulmin Burchell. (Note that a man named Toulmin had married a Howard woman, as though symbolic of, or perhaps in memory of, the long-dead feud.) He lived there until 1954, when he died and was buried, without fanfare, in the small cemetery not far from the Clay County Courthouse in Manchester.

Surcease

For a moment after Bobby Baker slumped, dead, over the steering wheel and his car slammed into the curb at the foot of the hill, there was a strange silence around the town square in Manchester, as though a century of violence and death, and the bitterness, hatred, grief, sorrow, fear, and pain that had torn at the hills of Eastern Kentucky and left behind a bloody trail of blasted lives and ruined reputations of both men and towns, had sent up one final cry of misery and then collapsed with a sigh that was itself a recognition of man's futility.

In that final act of what may be called the last and longest of the great feuds, there were echoes from other feuds: the plea of Sarah McCoy, battered to earth by a Hatfield pistol but still reaching out to touch her dead daughter; the screams of the Logan boys, gunned down and trampled by Craig Tolliver's men; the dying cry of J.B. Marcum in the hallway of the Breathitt County courthouse as Curtis Jett's bullets cut him down; the plea of Bad Tom Smith for one more hymn on the scaffold, the sound of his neck breaking as he fell through the trap. There were the pride and defiance of Mrs. George Turner of Harlan demanding that her son stop screaming and die like a man, as his brother had; the sobs of Alice Howard as her beloved son Wilse was led away to the gallows; the dignity of Susan Eversole as she took the fatherless children of Bad Tom Smith, the man who had killed her father and her husband, back to her own home to rear; the bravery of Sue Martin as she ran for help against the Tolliver gang burning her home; the surviving goodness of Thena Baker, imploring Jim Howard to let the dead past bury its dead; the struggles and piety of John Jay Dickey, praying, singing, preaching through the hills torn by bullets, drenched in blood.

And with the dying echoes of gunfire, the questions keep echoing across the years: Why here? Why in those years? There can be, are, people who are simply, inherently bad, but what malign spirits brought so many, in such a short time, into this small cup of mountains? Men who are not bad are taken in an evil time, by forces beyond their grasp, and led to do evil things. Those who resort to violence are not always violent men.

Was there something in the times, something in the circumstances and the stage of development of the nation that led it to internecine war, as adolescence must go through anguish to achieve maturity, a process that was echoed in the feuds? Was there a pioneer, immigrant dichotomy that at once longed for a new, beneficent order while recoiling instinctively from inherited memories of official oppression and cruelty in other places, other times, to which the new place, the new age, bore hope and promise of paradise? Was political freedom, the gift of political participation, wine too heady for people whose forebears had for centuries been denied such self-dominion?

Trouble did not end with the feuds. For another half century Eastern Kentucky remained the victim of violence. Strife tore the mining towns, just as worsening floods tore the valleys. For many years the region's homicide rates remained among the worst in the nation. But roads and colleges and parks have come to mark the mountains. The reputation for violence left by the feuds is now like old scars from some long-past, seldom-remembered accident of youth. Gradually, even the scars are forgotten.

Yet there must be moments even now when in the mists of twilight the ghost of Wilse Howard rides once more the roads of Harlan; when Bad Tom Baker stands, defiant and doomed on the courhouse lawn; when Big Jim Howard strides the streets of Manchester with his sample case, remembering; or when little Cal Tolliver, in his fourteenth year, stands before the America Hotel of Morehead, a little boy facing death, in each hand a blazing .44.

Sources

As far as I know, this book represents the only attempt to compile a brief history of all, or at least the most important, of the feuds of Eastern Kentucky, and having attempted it I can see why. Writing the history of one feud is difficult; writing about all of them is almost impossible.

When I began this I thought I would be able to get most of my information from previously published works on individual feuds. I was wrong. I found almost nothing published on the Turner-Howard feud of Harlan County, the French-Eversole War of Perry County, or, most important, the Clay County War that lasted almost a century and involved at least a dozen families.

Of state newspapers, I found the *Louisville Courier-Journal* and the *Hazel Green Herald* the most extensive journalistic sources, but even these left a lot to be desired. For example, in publishing the account of the jailing of Bad Tom Baker, the *Courier-Journal* stated casually that "a dozen men have been killed the last month." It fails to say who they were, where they were killed, or why, and I could find no record in the courthouse or in regional papers.

In the Hatfield-McCoy feud, the *Courier-Journal* saw the fight as a case of Kentucky against West Virginia and took the side of Kentucky without apology (and often without great accuracy). The *Cincinnati Enquirer* frequently referred to the feud in Breathitt County as the Marcum-Hargis-Callahan-French feud, although there was no French in the Breathitt feud. Fulton French was involved in the French-Eversole War in Perry County.

I probably got more information from interviews and correspondence than from books or newspapers, especially in the Clay County War, about which relatively little has been written. The late governor Bert Combs introduced me to Stanley DeZarn, of Hamilton, Ohio, who introduced me to descendants of the Bakers of the Baker-Howard feud in Clay County. Florence Baker, court clerk of Clay County, also helped me with county records, such as they are. The Clay courthouse fire of 1932 destroyed many of the previous records. Stanley also introduced me to James Burchell, grandson of James Howard, who was extremely generous and helpful. Bert Combs introduced me to John G. White, who confirmed some of what I had heard. All of these people were from Manchester.

I am especially grateful, too, to Jess Wilson, an author from Possum Trot, in Clay County, who gave me access to his maps, excerpts from the Dickey diaries, and copies of his books *When They Hanged the Fiddler* and *The Sugar Pond and the Fritter Tree*, both of which deal with the feuds. Jess, who is himself a Baker, gave me valuable genealogies of the Baker family. I have not been

able to get more (Clay County) Howard genealogy than that furnished me by
Harlan genealogist Holly Fee, who gave me some Turner-Howard genealogy.
But perhaps the best reference work on Clay County I found was the diaries
of the Reverend John Jay Dickey. They were valuable for the Breathitt County
wars as well. I talked briefly to Richard Golden of Pineville, whose grandfather, Captain Ben Golden, was an attorney in feud trials in both Breathitt
and Clay.

Along with Stanley DeZarn and Jess Wilson, perhaps my best source of
information was Tom Walters of Leesburg, Florida, who not only gave me the
records of his grandfather, who was involved in the shooting of Pitt Stivers,
in Clay County, but drew me a map of Manchester at the time of the feuds.
He and his wife, Gail, were most hospitable and helpful.

There are several short works that mention the Clay war. Alvin F. Harlow's *Weep No More, My Lady* (New York: Whittlesey House, 1942) contains a
treatise on "the hundred-year feud," which is interesting but contains errors.
Stories of Kentucky Feuds and *The Great Truce of Clay*, by Harold Wilson Coates
(Knoxville, Tenn.: Darst Coal Company, 1923), contain much that is folklore.
The *Autobiography of Old Claib Jones*, as written by J.W. Hall (Hazard Ky.: Hazard Press, 1915), is entertaining. Robert Ireland's "Judicial Murder of Dr. Abner Baker, Jr." (*Register of the Kentucky Historical Society*, Winter 1990) contends
that Baker was tried twice for the same murder. I tend to believe that the first
trial was no more than a competency hearing and could not have cleared him,
but Ireland is an authority on the trial, and his treatise is certainly worth
reading.

Incidentally, the *Courier-Journal* for September 16, 25, and 26, December
5, 22, and 27, 1932, and January 9 and February 2, 1933, gives good accounts
of the trials involved in the killing of Frank Baker. Curiously, the *Courier-
Journal* of December 2, 1943, tells of the conviction of one of the Benges for
barn-burning and states that fifty people had been killed recently in a continuation of the Clay feud. It did not say who the dead were or how far back that
phase of the feud went.

As far as the Hatfield-McCoy feud is concerned, you can take your pick.
There are dozens of books and articles on the feud, all saying pretty much the
same thing. Altina Waller's *Feud: Hatfields and McCoys and Social Change in
Appalachia, 1860-1960* (Chapel Hill: University of North Carolina Press, 1988)
is the most thorough study of the feud available (the title gives you an idea)
but is more concerned with the times than with the feud. Waller also published a shorter but interesting view of the feud in the *Register of the Kentucky
Historical Society* (Summer 1991), "Feuding and Modernization in Appalachia." The best book on the feud itself is probably Otis Rice's *The Hatfields and
the McCoys* (Lexington: University Press of Kentucky, 1982). The *Courier-
Journal* files in the Louisville Free Public Library offer detailed accounts of the
trials of the Hatfields in Louisville and the court battles between Kentucky
and West Virginia over jurisdiction of prisoners taken in the feud. The *Hazel
Green Herald* of April 26, 1894, had an account of the death of Frank Phillips,
the Pike County deputy and general wild man. The *Register of the Kentucky
Historical Society* for 1982 carried James Klotter's "A Hatfield-McCoy Feudist
Pleads for Mercy," and the summer 1988 issue of the *Appalachian Journal* published Klotter's "Hatfields and McCoys Revised."

John Kleber of Morehead State University not only opened his own files but introduced me to archivists in the MSU library, who found for me voluminous accounts of the Martin-Tolliver feud. Fred Brown of Morehead let me read *Days of Anger, Days of Rage*, which he wrote with Juanita Blair (Morehead, Ky.: Pioneer Press, 1989). Pauline Asher Logan of Pineville let me see articles on the Rowan County feud and photographs of her late husband's father, D.B. Logan, who played such a critical role in the Rowan war. The *Pineville Sun* of March 23, 1954, carried a detailed obituary of Logan.

I had trouble with Harlan. Murphy Howard, an old friend and county attorney at the time, warned me not to ask too many questions about the Turner-Howard feud or I'd risk trouble. I think Murphy was pulling my leg. No one in Harlan seemed reluctant to talk to me, but few knew much about the feud. Ed Cawood of the Bank of Harlan showed me some of the Turner graves, two of which were practically covered with trash in a weedy corner of a building beside a parking lot. He said they had been there almost a century and some of the Turners did not want them moved. They seemed terribly neglected, considering the prominence of the Turners. Cawood said he had heard that the feud had something to do with a dispute over a dog; where these dog stories come from I don't know. I talked with John Egerton, whose *Generations* (Lexington: University Press of Kentucky, 1983) is an account of the Ledford family that came to Harlan early in the nineteenth century but moved out because of feud violence, but he knew few particulars. The Ledfords tended to blame the Howards but left no details. The most interesting item I found was the manuscript "A Cumberland Vendetta" by C.A. Ballou at the Kentucky Historical Society Library in Frankfort. Ballou gives a one-sided view and makes no bones about putting the blame for the Turner-Howard feud squarely on the Turners. That is quite different from the version by Jamie Howard III of Harlan, who wrote the feud entry for the *Kentucky Encyclopedia* (Lexington: Univ. Press of Kentucky, 1992), and who tends to regard the Howards as the outlaws at fault. He was most helpful. Holly Fee, owner of the genealogical library Footprints, in Harlan, was my best source for courthouse records and family genealogies. The *Courier-Journal* of September 23, 1889, gives Wilson Lewis's version of the feud, which is self-serving.

The *Kentucky Explorer*, published by Charles Hays of Quicksand, Kentucky, is probably the best source I found for data on the Breathitt County wars. The issues of April, May, and June 1989 give pretty full accounts. One of the best eye-witness accounts of the feud is a long feature by the late Tom Wallace in the *Louisville Times* of May 22, 1959, in which Wallace recalls the Hargis-Marcum fight and a hilarious interview with James Hargis. The *Hazel Green Herald* also carries a long story on the hanging of Bad Tom Smith at the Breathitt County Courthouse, and in the July 15, 1885, issue, a long defense of Breathitt County by the Reverend Dickey. The issue of March 25, 1885, has an article about Dickey and the schools.

My best source for data on the Perry County French-Eversole war has been Allen Watts of Cincinnati, formerly of Letcher County, who is currently writing a history of the French-Eversole clash that will be far more extensive than my condensed version. Mr. Watts furnished me copies of the *Hazel Green Herald*, and his letters gave me valuable insights into the personalities of Fult French, Susan Eversole and her son Harry. The *Herald* was a major source of regional news stories and other news of the time.

Otherwise, dependable accounts of the French-Eversole War are hard to find. Perhaps the best are: the *Kentucky Explorer*, June 1988; the *Hazel Green Herald* for November 13, 1888 (the letter from Judge Lilly refusing to hold court in Perry unless he was given troops for protection); the November 14, 1888, issue for its account of the fight on Hazard Courthouse Square, and related stories on September 1, 15, 22, and November 24, 1886; June 1, July 6, August 12, and October 7, 1887; November 2, 1889; September 3 and 10, 1890; May 15 and November 21, 1891; April 22, 1892; September 27, 1894; January 3, April 25, May 2, 9, and 23, August 22 and 29, September 26, and December 19, 1895; the *Boone County Recorder* for February 11, 1891; the Dickey Diaries for April 26, 1898; notes from the *Record of the D.A.R. Perry County History*, 1910; the *Cincinnati Enquirer*, June 27, 1895; and the *Louisville Commercial*, May 30, 1895, April 21, 1896, and November 16, 1899. All carry accounts of the Perry County or Breathitt County troubles. Nearly all of the Hazel Green stories were furnished by Allen Watts. Clippings from the *Cincinnati Enquirer* were given to me by Stanley DeZarn. Dr. Samuel Thompson of Louisville helped me with the Filson Club files.

On January 2, 1902, *Frank Leslie's Popular Monthly* published Edwin Carlisle Litsey's "Kentucky Feuds and Their Causes." It is of questionable value. J.S. Johnson's "Romance and Tragedy of Kentucky Feuds," *Leslie's Monthly*, September 1899, isn't much better. I might also mention Charles G. Mutzenberg's *Kentucky's Famous Feuds and Tragedies* (New York: Fenno Company, 1901), J.A. Burns's *Mountain Crucible* (privately printed, 1928), and Darrell Richardson's *Mountain Rising* (Oneida, Ky.: Oneida Mountaineer Press, 1986). Mutzenberg at least tries to stick to facts and does not ridicule the mountain people. Richardson's book, an account of the founding of the Oneida Institute, offers a better description of Clay County and its people than any other work I found.

Also to be included in any list of literature on the feuds are: Hambleton Tapp and James C. Klotter, *Decades of Discord, 1865-1900* (Frankfort: Kentucky Historical Society, 1981); Ross A. Webb, *Kentucky in the Reconstruction Era* (Lexington: University Press of Kentucky, 1979); Lloyd G. Lee, *A Brief History of Kentucky* (Berea: Kentucky Imprints, 1989); and Caleb Powers's *My Own Story* (Indianapolis: Bobbs Merrill, 1905). Powers's account of his trial strengthens the impression that he and Jim Howard were railroaded for the murder of William Goebel.

James Klotter's "The Tolliver-Martin Feud, 1884-87" (*Filson Club History Quarterly*, January 1968), and his "Feuds in Appalachia: An Overview" (*Filson Club History Quarterly*, July 1982), are helpful. Klotter is very even-handed, and tries to stick to facts.

Generally speaking, however, I found interviews preferable to the books and articles available.

Index

Eversole family (Perry County), 76
Eversole-French feud (Perry County), 1, 5, 6, 75-95
Ewen, Benjamin, 49-50, 51, 52

Farmers, Ky., 96, 99, 106, 109
Federal Hill ("My Old Kentucky Home"), 96
Fee, Holly, 20, 28
Feltner, Mose, 49, 50, 51
Ferguson, Lee, 71
Feud: Hatfields, McCoys and Economic Change in Appalachia, 1860-1900 (Waller), 57
Fields, Bob, 90
Fields, Jess, 78, 84, 85, 87, 93
Fields, Mr. (Harlan County), 18-19
Finley, John, 31
Fisher, James, 169
Fisher family, 185
Fleming County, 96
Flinchum, David, 34
Floyd, John, 71
Floyd County, 76, 121
Forrester, Colonel, 168
Forty-Niners, 134
Foster, Stephen Collins, 96
Fouts, John, 144
Frankfort, Ky., 36, 66, 71, 147, 188-94 passim
Frazier, Boone, 87
Freeman, Daniel, 37, 38
Freeman, William, 37, 38
French, Benjamin Fulton. *See* French, Fulton
French, Fulton, 75-76, 87; as attorney, 5, 77; social class, 5-6; as villain, 8, 93; attorney for Jett and White in Breathitt County, 51, 86; as merchant of Hazard, 76, 77; recruitment of Bad Tom Smith, 81; ruling Perry County, 84; brought to trial, 85; empty victory, 86; shooting of, 93-94
French, Susan Lewis (Mrs. Fulton), 77
French-Eversole feud (Perry County), 1, 5, 6, 75-94, 167, 190
Fusionist Party (Breathitt County), 45

Gaither, Capt., 25, 85
Gamble, Alfred, 39
Gambrell, Bill, 80
Garrard, Daniel, 125, 130
Garrard, Edward, 198
Garrard, Gilbert, 147, 169, 170, 176, 185
Garrard, James, 125, 152

Garrard, Lucinda Burnam Lees (second Mrs. T.T.), 134
Garrard, Lucinda Toulmin (Mrs. Daniel), 125
Garrard, Mary (married to son of Hugh White), 125
Garrard, Nancy Brawner (first Mrs. T.T.), 126
Garrard, T.T., 147, 148, 169, 185, 207; as hero, 8; at last Bad Tom Baker trial, 118, 119-21, 163, 181; son of Daniel and Lucinda, 125-26; memoirs, 126; in politics, 126; and surrender of Abner Baker, Jr., 131; marriage to Lucinda Burnam Lees, 134; service in Mexican War, 134; travels, 134-35; joins Union army, 136; political involvement, 136; and events leading to Crane Creek clash, 152; backs Bakers, 170; family in state of crisis, 172-73, 178; and truce with Whites, 198
Garrard, William, 134
Garrard family, 5, 7, 124, 125, 126, 198, 140
Gault House (Morehead), 98, 100, 109, 110
Gayheart, Silas, 78
Generations (Egerton), 15
Gerty (steamboat), 97
Gibson, Eustace, 71-72
Gilbert, Abe, 196
Gilbert, Bill, 14
Gilbert, John, 124, 135
Gilbert family, 13-14
Gill, Alvin, 101
Gillespie, Charles, 67, 72-73
Gist, Christopher, 31
Goebel, Gov. William, 45-46, 178, 187-94, 197, 205, 208
Goforth, George, 8, 166, 183-84
Goforth, Lizzie: married Beverly Baker, 166, 184
Goforth, Lucy (Mrs. George), 8, 166, 183-84
Golden, Ben, 51
Goodin, Sam, 97, 104, 109
Goodin, Tom, 104
Goodin family, 99
Goose Creek (Clay County), 119, 122, 126
Grace, Frank, 83
Graveyard Hill (Hazard), 84-85
Green Mountain Boys, 129
Greenup, Ky., 100, 101, 104
Gregory, Robert, 149
Griffin, Bud, 185, 199

Rayburn, Lewis, 106
"Real" Democratic Party, 187
Red Bird, Ky., 149
Redwine, David, 45, 48, 53
Regulators, 41, 46, 104, 139
Reid, Mary. *See* Howard, Mary Reid
Republican Party, 187-93; in Breathitt
  County, 45; and James Marcum, 52; in
  Rowan County, 96, 97, 99, 101, 110-11;
  in Clay County, 126, 131, 137, 139,
  140, 147
Rice, John, 73
Rice, Otis, 58, 61, 65, 109; *The Hatfields
  and the McCoys*, 57
Ricketts boys, 74
Riggs, Mr. (Clay County), 173
Ripley, Garret, 190, 191
Robards, A.J., 4
Roberts, Breck, 91
Robertson, George, 132
Rockcastle County, 20, 129, 137
Rogers, John, 109
Rogersville, Tenn., 26
Rowan, John, 96
Rowan County, 5, 6, 7, 41, 95-112

St. Claire Medical Center, 96
Sawyer, Pleaz, 184
Scott, Henderson, 64
Scott, John, 64
Sester, Ernest, 157, 194-95
Sester, John, 157, 201
Sewell, George, 39
Sexton Creek (Clay County), 122, 129,
  140
Shackleford, Jane Hall (Mrs. Jim), 178
Shackleford, Jim, 178
Shackleford boys, 153, 156, 157
Sizemore, Adam, 98
Skidmore, John, 12
Smith, Bad Tom, 78, 83-84, 85-86; as epi-
  leptic, 80; joining French forces, 81;
  killing of Joseph Eversole, 82; in
  Breathitt County, 87-88; confession at
  hanging, 87, 90; hanging of, 88-93, 209
Smith, Bill, 86-87, 89, 92
Smith, John, 50, 51, 53
Smith, Mary, 89, 91, 92, 93
Smith, Tim, 8
Smith-Howard Building (Harlan), 28
Smith's Branch of Quicksand Creek
  (Breathitt County), 87
Sohan, Capt., 83
South Fork of Kentucky River, 79, 115,
  124
Southwood, Louise, 90

Spaniards in Clay County, 122
Spanish-American War, 146
Sparks, Riley, 161
Spurlock, Bird, 21, 24
Spurlock, Bud, 17, 19, 23, 26
Spurlock, Steve, 198
Stafford, Mary, 61
Stanford, John, 187
State University of New York, 57
Staton, Bill, 60
Stewart, Cora Wilson, 112
Stewart, County Judge, 98, 99
Stivers, Cap, 205
Stivers, George, 137-38
Stivers, Pitt, 202, 203, 205
Stores, Burch, 153, 156, 157, 159, 161,
  164, 168, 185
Stringtown, Ky., 60, 61
Strong, Capt. William, 39; as villain, 8;
  as feud leader, 33-34; taking over
  courthouse, 34-35; showdown at court-
  house, 37-38; as "Uncle Bill," 41, 44;
  and Deatons, 42; and James B. Mar-
  cum, 43, 52; feuds growing out of Civ-
  il War, 44; last ride, 44
Strong, E.C., 36
Strong, "Nigger Dick," 37
Strong, William, 124
Strong-Amis feud (Breathitt County),
  33, 40
Strong-Callahan feud (Breathitt County),
  41, 44
Strong family: and Cattle Wars, 124
Strong-Little feud (Breathitt County), 7
Strong-Noble feud (Breathitt County),
  40
Supreme Court of the United States:
  and Hatfield-McCoy feud, 72
Sutton, Allen, 98

Tallant, Wick, 91
Taylor, Alabama, (Mrs. Benjamin Frank-
  lin White), 127
Taylor, John Edward, 127
Taylor, W.S., 187, 188, 190, 193
Thacker, Wash, 185
Tharp, William, 43
Thomas, George, 97
Thompson, J.R., 70
Thompson, Lieutenant, 39
Thucydides, 95
Tillet, William, 134
Tinsley, J.H., 198
Tolliver, Andy, 99, 109, 110
Tolliver, Bud, 99, 106, 107, 109
Tolliver, Cal, 107, 109, 110, 210